ALSO BY AMERICA'S TEST KITCHEN

The Cook's Illustrated All-Time Best Series

Cook's Country Titles

For a Full Listing of All Our Books

CooksIllustrated.com

AmericasTestKitchen.com

PRAISE FOR AMERICA'S TEST KITCHEN TITLES

"It's all about technique and timing, and the ATK crew delivers their usual clear instructions to ensure success. . . . The thoughtful balance of practicality and imagination will inspire readers of all tastes and skill levels."
PUBLISHERS WEEKLY ON *HOW TO ROAST EVERYTHING*

Selected as one of the 10 Best New Cookbooks of 2017
THE LA TIMES ON *THE PERFECT COOKIE*

"If you're a home cook who loves long introductions that tell you why a dish works followed by lots of step-by-step hand holding, then you'll love *Vegetables Illustrated*."
THE WALL STREET JOURNAL ON *VEGETABLES ILLUSTRATED*

Selected as the Cookbook Award Winner of 2019 in the Health and Special Diet Category
INTERNATIONAL ASSOCIATION OF CULINARY PROFESSIONALS (IACP) ON *THE COMPLETE DIABETES COOKBOOK*

"A terrifically accessible and useful guide to grilling in all its forms that sets a new bar for its competitors on the bookshelf. . . . The book is packed with practical advice, simple tips, and approachable recipes."
PUBLISHERS WEEKLY (STARRED REVIEW) ON *MASTER OF THE GRILL*

"This encyclopedia of meat cookery would feel completely overwhelming if it weren't so meticulously organized and artfully designed. This is *Cook's Illustrated* at its finest."
THE KITCHN ON *THE COOK'S ILLUSTRATED MEAT BOOK*

"This book is a comprehensive, no-nonsense guide . . . a well-thought-out, clearly explained primer for every aspect of home baking."
THE WALL STREET JOURNAL ON *THE COOK'S ILLUSTRATED BAKING BOOK*

"The sum total of exhaustive experimentation . . . anyone interested in gluten-free cookery simply shouldn't be without it."
NIGELLA LAWSON ON *THE HOW CAN IT BE GLUTEN-FREE COOKBOOK*

"A one-volume kitchen seminar, addressing in one smart chapter after another the sometimes surprising whys behind a cook's best practices. . . .You get the myth, the theory, the science, and the proof, all rigorously interrogated as only America's Test Kitchen can do."
NPR ON *THE SCIENCE OF GOOD COOKING*

"If there's room in the budget for one multicooker/Instant Pot cookbook, make it this one."
BOOKLIST ON *MULTICOOKER PERFECTION*

"Some books impress by the sheer audacity of their ambition. Backed up by the magazine's famed mission to test every recipe relentlessly until it is the best it can be, this nearly 900-page volume lands with an authoritative wallop."
CHICAGO TRIBUNE ON *THE COOK'S ILLUSTRATED COOKBOOK*

"The 21st-century *Fannie Farmer Cookbook* or *The Joy of Cooking*. If you had to have one cookbook and that's all you could have, this one would do it."
CBS SAN FRANCISCO ON *THE NEW FAMILY COOKBOOK*

"The go-to gift book for newlyweds, small families, or empty nesters."
ORLANDO SENTINEL ON *THE COMPLETE COOKING FOR TWO COOKBOOK*

"This book upgrades slow cooking for discriminating, 21st-century palates—that is indeed revolutionary."
THE DALLAS MORNING NEWS ON *SLOW COOKER REVOLUTION*

"Some 2,500 photos walk readers through 600 painstakingly tested recipes, leaving little room for error."
ASSOCIATED PRESS ON *THE AMERICA'S TEST KITCHEN COOKING SCHOOL COOKBOOK*

"This impressive installment from America's Test Kitchen equips readers with dozens of repertoire-worthy recipes. . . . This is a must-have for beginner cooks and more experienced ones who wish to sharpen their skills."
PUBLISHERS WEEKLY (STARRED REVIEW) ON *THE NEW ESSENTIALS COOKBOOK*

FOOLPROOF FISH

modern recipes for everyone, everywhere

AMERICA'S TEST KITCHEN

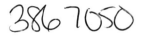

Library of Congress Cataloging-in-Publication Data

Names: America's Test Kitchen (Firm), author.
Title: Foolproof fish : modern recipes for everyone, everywhere / America's Test Kitchen.
Description: 1st edition. | Boston, MA : America's Test Kitchen, [2020] | Includes index.
Identifiers: LCCN 2020002583 (print) | LCCN 2020002584 (ebook) | ISBN 9781948703109 (hardcover) | ISBN 9781948703116 (ebook)
Subjects: LCSH: Cooking (Fish) | Cooking (Seafood) | LCGFT: Cookbooks.
Classification: LCC TX747 .F59 2020 (print) | LCC TX747 (ebook) | DDC 641.6/92--dc23
LC record available at https://lccn.loc.gov/2020002583
LC ebook record available at https://lccn.loc.gov/2020002584

America's Test Kitchen
21 Drydock Avenue, Boston, MA 02210

Manufactured in the United States of America
10 9 8 7 6 5 4 3 2 1

Distributed by Penguin Random House Publisher Services
Tel: 800.733.3000

Pictured on front cover **Roasted Salmon and Broccoli Rabe with Pistachio Gremolata (page 95)**

Pictured on back cover **Crispy Fish Sandwiches (page 208), Spanish-Style Brothy Rice with Clams and Salsa Verde (page 159), Grilled Lobsters (page 285), Butter-Basted Fish Fillets with Garlic and Thyme (page 46), Salmon Tacos (page 227), Broiled Bluefish (page 81), Thai Curry Rice with Mahi-Mahi (page 119), Whole Roast Mackerel (page 305)**

Editorial Director, Books **Adam Kowit**

Executive Food Editor **Dan Zuccarello**

Executive Managing Editor **Debra Hudak**

Deputy Food Editor **Stephanie Pixley**

Senior Editors **Nicole Konstantinakos and Sacha Madadian**

Associate Editor **Camila Chaparro**

Assistant Editor **Brenna Donovan**

Editorial Assistant **Emily Rahravan**

Art Director, Books **Lindsey Timko Chandler**

Deputy Art Directors **Allison Boales and Janet Taylor**

Photography Director **Julie Bozzo Cote**

Photography Producer **Meredith Mulcahy**

Senior Staff Photographers **Steve Klise and Daniel J. van Ackere**

Staff Photographer **Kevin White**

Additional Photography **Keller + Keller and Carl Tremblay**

Food Styling **Catrine Kelty, Chantal Lambeth, Ashley Moore, Marie Piraino, Elle Simone Scott, Kendra Smith, and Sally Staub**

Photoshoot Kitchen Team

Photo Team Manager **Timothy McQuinn**

Lead Test Cook **Eric Haessler**

Assistant Test Cooks **Hannah Fenton and Jacqueline Gochenouer**

Senior Manager, Publishing Operations **Taylor Argenzio**

Imaging Manager **Lauren Robbins**

Production and Imaging Specialists **Tricia Neumyer, Dennis Noble, and Amanda Yong**

Copy Editor **Karen Wise**

Proofreader **Christine Corcoran Cox**

Indexer **Elizabeth Parson**

Chief Creative Officer **Jack Bishop**

Executive Editorial Directors **Julia Collin Davison and Bridget Lancaster**

CONTENTS

WELCOME TO AMERICA'S TEST KITCHEN

facebook.com/
AmericasTestKitchen

twitter.com/TestKitchen

youtube.com/
AmericasTestKitchen

instagram.com/TestKitchen

pinterest.com/TestKitchen

AmericasTestKitchen.com

CooksIllustrated.com

CooksCountry.com

OnlineCookingSchool.com

AmericasTestKitchen.com/kids

This book has been tested, written, and edited by the folks at America's Test Kitchen. Located in Boston's Seaport District in the historic Innovation and Design Building, it features 15,000 square feet of kitchen space, including multiple photography and video studios. It is the home of Cook's Illustrated magazine and Cook's Country magazine and is the workday destination for more than 60 test cooks, editors, and cookware specialists. Our mission is to test recipes over and over again until we understand how and why they work and until we arrive at the best version.

We start the process of testing a recipe with a complete lack of preconceptions, which means that we accept no claim, no technique, and no recipe at face value. We simply assemble as many variations as possible, test a half-dozen of the most promising, and taste the results blind. We then construct our own recipe and continue to test it, varying ingredients, techniques, and cooking times until we reach a consensus. As we like to say in the test kitchen, "We make the mistakes so you don't have to." The result, we hope, is the best version of a particular recipe, but we realize that only you can be the final judge of our success (or failure). We use the same rigorous approach when we test equipment and taste ingredients.

All of this would not be possible without a belief that good cooking, much like good music, is based on a foundation of objective technique. Some people like spicy foods and others don't, but there is a right way to sauté, there is a best way to cook a pot roast, and there are measurable scientific principles involved in producing perfectly beaten, stable egg whites. Our ultimate goal is to investigate the fundamental principles of cooking to give you the techniques, tools, and ingredients you need to become a better cook. It is as simple as that.

To see what goes on behind the scenes at America's Test Kitchen, check out our social media channels for kitchen snapshots, exclusive content, video tips, and much more. You can watch us work (in our actual test kitchen) by tuning in to America's Test Kitchen or Cook's Country on public television or on our websites. Download our award-winning podcast Proof, which goes beyond recipes to solve food mysteries (AmericasTestKitchen.com/proof), or listen in to test kitchen experts on public radio (SplendidTable.org) to hear insights that illuminate the truth about real home cooking. Want to hone your cooking skills or finally learn how to bake—with an America's Test Kitchen test cook? Enroll in one of our online cooking classes. And you can engage the next generation of home cooks with kid-tested recipes from America's Test Kitchen Kids.

However you choose to visit us, we welcome you into our kitchen, where you can stand by our side as we test our way to the best recipes in America.

getting started

There are many fish in the sea (and rivers and lakes and streams): A common cliché, which we'd normally vociferously avoid, in fact aptly sums up the challenges and delights of taking on a fish cookbook. An encyclopedia of fish varieties would be umpteen pages long, but how would it help the cook? This book, as the title suggests, makes fish foolproof by streamlining the encyclopedia to what's commonly available (that's still a lot!), no matter where you live, and utterly appealing. By featuring 23 fish, plus shellfish, we're able to focus on how to easily buy fish, how to cook fish, and how to enjoy fish more often, because fish is the perfect protein for the modern cook—it's healthful, it's quick cooking, it's delicious.

The test kitchen is in New England, in an area of Boston called the Seaport District. Yes, we can smell the salty sea from our building and we're located where some of the freshest local fish is caught, processed, and/or distributed. Fish, therefore, isn't a luxury for us, but we understand that's not the perception for all. We've learned it should be: In creating this cookbook, we tested our way through widely available fish varieties (this includes frozen), using recipe testing results (and not scientific classification of fish) to group fish according to their attributes once cooked. That means if an appealing-to-you recipe calls for one flaky white fish like hake, but you can only find cod (Pacific or Atlantic), you'll be able to substitute it in our hake recipe. In addition to explanations for our fish groupings, you'll see that every recipe features a substitution box so you can immediately identify your options.

Besides breaking down the fish of the sea, how else do we make seafood accessible? With simple, kitchen-tested recipes, of course. Fish shouldn't be scary: We've streamlined our recipes so that one for baking fish like Nut-Crusted Cod Fillets is just as easy to follow as one for roasting a whole fish like Whole Roast Snapper with Citrus Vinaigrette or even frying fish like for Fish and Chips. No sticking, falling apart, or overcooking—we know exactly how to treat a pan or grill surface for cooking fish, how to divide portions so they don't break during flipping, and what internal temperature to cook what fish to.

A chapter of Everyday Essentials helps you build confidence in these skills, putting them to work in straightforward, simple, and fast cooking techniques: Learn to pan-sear, roast, poach, broil, bake, steam, and butter-baste almost every fish we present in the book, from farmed salmon (substitute wild salmon or arctic char as desired, but check for doneness sooner), to catfish (slice fillets down their natural seam so thick and thin sides cook evenly), tuna (try a sesame crust on your classic pan-seared steaks), bluefish (you have to try it), mussels (roast them rather than steam them for even cooking), and scallops (achieve a nutty brown sear every time). Pair these with your favorite side and a number of sauces, relishes, and chutneys that we provide.

Fish is delicious, but it's also the busy (or tired or even lazy) cook's best friend, so a chapter of Easy Weeknight Dinners is the largest in the book, with composed dishes, many made in one pan, that are a breeze to cook while also impressing on a Tuesday. Explore modern flavors and unique seafood pairings in dishes like Pomegranate Roasted Salmon with Lentils and Chard (an appealing pomegranate molasses glaze ties the salmon fillets to the accompanying pomegranate seed–dotted side), Thai Curry Rice with Mahi-Mahi (a deceptively simple skillet supper with a crispy rice bottom and a luxurious sauce), Moroccan Fish and Couscous Packets (fragrant chermoula-slathered tilapia fillets—or another thin fish you have—steam to moist, flaky perfection atop a bed of fluffy lemony couscous within an individual foil parcel in the oven), and Lemony Linguine with Shrimp and Spinach (briefly cooking the shrimp shells with wine creates a deeply flavored seafood sauce).

Recall fish's versatility in the chapters and pages that follow. Soups, stews, and chowders bring out fish's comforting side. Creamy New England Clam Chowder is a must-know classic, while Korean Spicy Fish Stew (*Maeuntang*) is a winter warmer that's also light and bright. Go to the fish shack with Crispy Fish Sandwiches (slathered with tartar sauce and topped with slaw) or New England Lobster Rolls or the taco stand with California Fish Tacos or cheesy Shrimp Tacos. See fish in satisfying salads like Fennel and Apple Salad with Smoked Mackerel. Grill shellfish-filled paella for company or present small plates from casual apps like Baked Crab Dip to crudo like Peruvian Ceviche with Radishes and Orange and even homemade Gravlax. Be inspired with every page to cook from the sea.

CHARTED WATERS

We set out to create a user-friendly guide to cooking fish—no matter where the user lives. There are more species of fish than pages in this book, so we pared down the list to what is widely available fresh to those on both coasts, and frozen to those far from the sea. How did we do this? Objectivity was at first difficult given our New England location, so we turned to you: We surveyed readers across the country to discover what they've cooked, what they've seen in stores, and what they wanted to know more about. This chart delivers the important information about the fish in this book, at a glance. Read the pages that follow for a deeper dive into the fish varieties.

	TEXTURE	FLAVOR	COMMON AVAILABILITY	HOW YOU MIGHT FIND IT	COOKING METHODS	SUBSTITUTIONS
Arctic Char	• moist • fine • moderately firm	• rich • milder than salmon	• frozen • previously frozen • fresh	• whole fish • whole and portioned skin-on fillets	• grilled • pan-seared • poached • roasted	• salmon • wild salmon
Black Sea Bass	• thick • flaky	• sweet • clean-tasting • mild	• fresh	• whole fish • whole and portioned skin-on and skinned fillets	• baked • pan-roasted • pan-seared • poached • steamed	• cod • haddock • hake • pollock
Bluefish	• medium-firm • dark-fleshed	• oily • pronounced flavor	• fresh	• whole and portioned skin-on fillets	• broiled • pan-seared	• mackerel
Catfish	• flaky • thin	• mild	• frozen • previously frozen • fresh	• fillets	• fried • sautéed • steamed	• flounder • sole • tilapia
Clams	• pleasantly chewy	• briny	• fresh • canned	• sold in netting or by piece/weight • canned • usually littleneck or cherrystone	• braised • grilled • steamed	none
Cod	• large, delicate flakes	• mild • delicate	• frozen • previously frozen • fresh	• whole and portioned skinned fillets	• baked • pan-roasted • pan-seared • poached • steamed	• black sea bass • haddock • hake • pollock

	TEXTURE	FLAVOR	COMMON AVAILABILITY	HOW YOU MIGHT FIND IT	COOKING METHODS	SUBSTITUTIONS
Crab	• tender but firm	• sweet • more pronounced flavor than lobster	• fresh	• whole crab (regionally) • king crab legs • fresh lump or jumbo lump crabmeat at the seafood counter • pasteurized	• use meat for crab cakes and salads	none
Flounder	• flaky • delicate • thin	• mild • sweet	• frozen • previously frozen • fresh	• fillets	• fried • sautéed • steamed	• catfish • sole • tilapia
Haddock	• flaky	• very mild • delicate	• frozen • previously frozen • fresh	• whole and portioned skin-on fillets	• baked • pan-roasted • pan-seared • poached • steamed	• black sea bass • cod • hake • pollock
Hake	• thick • flaky	• mild • sweet shellfish-like flavor	• fresh	• whole and portioned skin-on and skinned fillets	• baked • pan-roasted • pan-seared • poached • steamed	• black sea bass • cod • haddock • pollock
Halibut	• meaty • hearty	• mild but rich	• frozen • previously frozen • fresh	• whole steaks • belly steaks • whole and portioned skin-on and skinned fillets	• braised • grilled • pan-seared • poached • steamed	• mahi-mahi • red snapper • striped bass • swordfish
Lobster	• firm • meaty • tender but can be chewy in places	• sweet • delicate	• fresh • frozen tails	• whole lobsters • lobster tails • shelled meat	• boiled • grilled	none
Mackerel	• medium-firm • somewhat flaky • dark flesh	• oily • rich, full, pronounced flavor	• fresh	• whole fish • skin-on steaks • skin-on fillets	• broiled • grilled • roasted	• bluefish
Mahi-Mahi	• medium-firm • meaty • flaky	• sweet • somewhat robust flavor	• fresh	• skinless steaks • fillets	• braised • grilled • pan-seared • poached • steamed	• halibut • red snapper • striped bass • swordfish

	TEXTURE	FLAVOR	COMMON AVAILABILITY	HOW YOU MIGHT FIND IT	COOKING METHODS	SUBSTITUTIONS
Monkfish	• firm	• hearty, rich, sweet • slightly muskier than lobster	• fresh	• skinless, boneless loin-shaped pieces cut from tail	• braised • pan-seared	none
Mussels	• tender	• sweet • lightly briny	• fresh • canned	• sold in netting or by piece/weight • canned	• braised • grilled • roasted • steamed	none
Octopus	• firm • pleasantly chewy	• mild • ocean-y	• frozen • previously frozen • fresh	• whole octopus	• braised	none
Oysters	• delicate	• briny • sweet • complex • ocean-y	• fresh • canned	• sold in netting or by piece/weight • canned	• grilled • raw	none
Pollock	• very delicate and flaky	• mild	• frozen • previously frozen • fresh	• portioned fillets	• baked • pan-roasted • pan-seared • poached • steamed	• black sea bass • cod • haddock • hake
Red Snapper	• medium-firm and flaky	• mild but rich	• frozen • previously frozen • fresh	• whole fish • skin-on and skinless fillets • steaks (occasionally)	• braised • grilled • pan-seared • poached • roasted • steamed	• halibut • mahi-mahi • striped bass • swordfish
Salmon	• moist • moderately firm • large flakes	• rich • meaty	• frozen • previously frozen • fresh	• whole and portioned skin-on fillets	• pan-seared • poached • roasted	• arctic char • wild salmon
Scallops	• tender • firm	• sweet • pristine	• frozen • previously frozen • fresh	• by piece/weight	• baked • broiled • pan-seared	none
Shrimp	• tender • juicy • firm	• sweet	• frozen (preferred) • previously frozen • fresh	• by piece/weight	• grilled • pan-seared • poached	none

	TEXTURE	FLAVOR	COMMON AVAILABILITY	HOW YOU MIGHT FIND IT	COOKING METHODS	SUBSTITUTIONS
Sole	• flaky • delicate • thin	• mild • sweet • pristine	• previously frozen • fresh	• fillets	• fried • sautéed • steamed	• catfish • flounder • tilapia
Squid	• tender with a firm chew	• mild • sweet	• fresh	• whole bodies • separated into bodies and tentacles	• braised • fried • marinated	none
Striped Bass	• medium-firm with large, hearty flakes	• sweet • meaty • rich	• fresh	• whole and portioned skin-on fillets	• braised • grilled • pan-seared • poached • roasted • steamed	• halibut • mahi-mahi • red snapper • swordfish
Swordfish	• very firm	• meaty • somewhat robust	• frozen • previously frozen • fresh	• steaks	• braised • grilled • pan-seared • poached • steamed	• halibut • mahi-mahi • red snapper • striped bass
Tilapia	• firm • flaky • thin	• mild	• frozen • previously frozen • fresh	• fillets	• fried • sautéed • steamed	• catfish • flounder • sole
Trout	• medium-firm • flaky	• rich and flavorful • less fishy than salmon	• previously frozen • fresh	• whole fish • butterflied fillets • portioned fillets	• grilled • pan-seared • roasted • steamed	none
Tuna	• very firm • meaty • richly colored	• mild • meaty flavor	• frozen • previously frozen • fresh	• steaks	• grilled • pan-seared	none

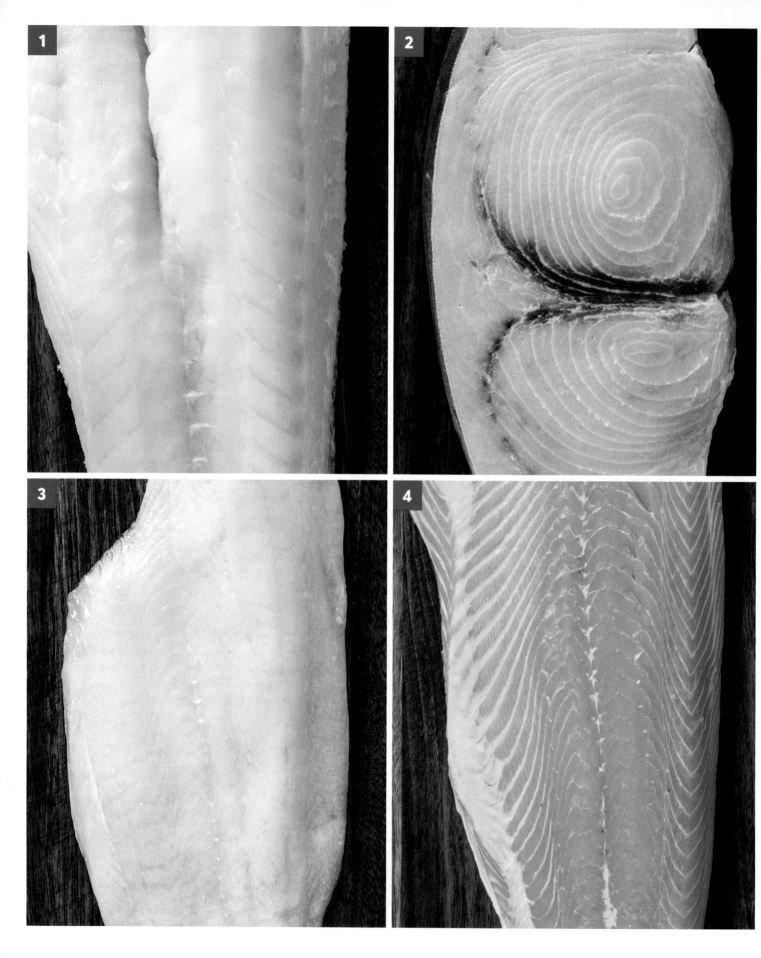

FISH COOKING CATEGORIES

There's no perfect way to categorize fish. Sure, scientific classifications and taxonomy exist. Some fish are available only during certain seasons. Some fish come from fresh water and others come from salt water. But marine biology doesn't help us much as cooks. That's why we put on our chef's coats to categorize fish, grouping them according to how we perceive their texture, flavor, and, sometimes, exchangeability in cooking. The groups we created determine what fish might be substituted for others in our recipes and broaden the scope of cooking possibilities when the fish called for in a recipe isn't available. These options are listed on each recipe page. (Note that shellfish are too distinctive for substitutions.)

1 FLAKY WHITE FISH

BASS NOTES

You see bass in two different cooking categories because, well, bass isn't bass isn't bass. There are a number of different bass, including black sea bass (thick, delicate, and flaky); European sea bass, or branzino (fine-textured, sweet, usually served whole); striped bass, or striper (firm, meaty, slightly higher oil content); and Chilean sea bass, which isn't bass at all but a Patagonian toothfish (we do not cook this fish because its price tag is misleadingly high). Cook the bass in this book according to the categories we've assigned them.

BLACK SEA BASS • COD (pictured, left) • HADDOCK • HAKE • POLLOCK

White fish are very lean because their fat is mostly concentrated in their liver; this particular bunch of white fish dwells near the ocean bottom along continental shelves and does very little swimming, so they require very little enzyme activity (the coagulation of enzymes in the spaces between muscles is what causes them to stick together, resisting flaking) and therefore easily fall into flakes under your fork after cooking. Their relatively lazy lives also give them a clean, mild flavor.

The lack of natural oils and fats makes it important to handle these fish with care: Rather than give them a hard pan-sear over high heat on both sides, we often like to quickly sear them on one side to achieve color and then finish cooking them gently in the oven (see pages 22 and 44). Sometimes we coat them in nuts and bake them on a wire rack at a not-too-high temperature (see page 52). We steam (see page 26), braise (see page 27), and poach (see page 26) them; these moist environments cook the fish evenly and gently, increasing the perception of juiciness. We don't grill these fish (they scorch and stick), and we don't often roast or broil them (they can dry out).

2 FIRM, MEATY WHITE FISH

HALIBUT • MAHI-MAHI • RED SNAPPER • STRIPED BASS SWORDFISH (pictured, left)

Also white fish, this group is mostly lean, but their texture is meatier, breaking off in moist chunks under your fork rather than in flakes. With the exception of halibut, these fish swim a lot more than the flaky white fish, so their intermuscular structure is stronger, holding the fish together. (And halibut is higher in slow-melting collagen.)

We love these fish for their substantial texture and treat them differently than flakier fish. If we're pan-searing them, we flip them frequently, keeping them over a hot flame the whole time; quickly getting the fish up to temperature with this method of radiating heat prevents the fish's dense flesh from turning mushy (for more information, see page 77). While flaky white fish should be cooked to 135 degrees, we cook these meatier fish to 130 degrees and then let them rise in temperature during a rest to prevent moisture loss during high-heat cooking. They take well to the gentle cooking of braising or steaming (in a pan or *en papillote*), can stand up ably to being flipped on a hot grill, and, like most fish, can be poached with success.

Separating Swordfish

It's important to note that while we cook swordfish *steaks*, we cook fillets of the other fish in this category. Swordfish, then, requires slightly different preparation before cooking. First, swordfish steaks typically have a bloodline—a dark muscle rich in myoglobin—running through them. Since that bloodline can have an unpleasant mineral taste, we recommend looking for steaks with as minimal a bloodline as possible. And ditch the skin; thick, rubbery swordfish skin tightens up more than the flesh during cooking and can cause the steak to buckle. You can either ask your fishmonger to remove it for you or **trim it off yourself using a sharp knife.**

3 THIN WHITE FISH

CATFISH • FLOUNDER (pictured, page 6) • SOLE • TILAPIA

This category contains a mix of fresh- and saltwater fish. What brings them together: the shape and structure of their fillets. While an inch-thick fillet of fish is a nice plate centerpiece, thin fish have their own appeal—versatile, impressively flaky, always tender, easy to brown. Usually a fillet comprises one side of the fish's body. But the belly portion of the fillet is thinner than the top portion, a disparity that leads to uneven cooking. Our solution: **Use the seam running down the center of each fillet as a guide to cut the thin and thick portions apart and cook them separately.**

The shape of these fish makes them good candidates for slipping into hot oil to deep-fry or sauté. Flip carefully when sautéing, as the delicate fish can flake apart in the pan. **Work quickly and confidently and use two spatulas to flip the fish, one to do the action of turning and one to hold the fillet steady.**

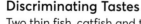

Discriminating Tastes

Two thin fish, catfish and tilapia, have an unnecessarily bad taste reputation that we want to debunk. Most catfish sold in the United States is farmed in the Mississippi Delta and has a clean, mild taste from its grain feeding. The off-tasting stuff? Wild imports from Asia, which are very hard to come by. Fillets should be white to off-white; avoid fish that is yellow. As for tilapia, there's a resounding conception that it's a second-rate, predominantly farm-raised fish with a muddy taste. But tilapia is now the fourth-most-consumed seafood in the United States (after shrimp, tuna, and salmon). Modern freshwater farming practices produce meaty tilapia with a clean, mild flavor, sort of a cross between trout and flounder.

Of the thin fish, one is known to be superior, pearly white, and pristine, with the cleanest flavor: sole. But buyer beware: It's highly unlikely that you are actually purchasing sole at your local market but rather a type of flounder. That's fine—we love flounder! But we don't love unnecessarily high price tags. Dover sole is a European fish—we do not have true sole along our shorelines. (That said, sole is delicious if you can source it.)

4   SALMON AND CHAR

FARMED SALMON (pictured, page 6) • WILD SALMON • ARCTIC CHAR

Salmon is so recognizable its name is a standard color—vibrant and orangey pink. But salmon is actually a type of white fish (gray, really), its flesh turned pink only by the crustaceans it eats. The compound responsible for this coloring, astaxanthin, is stored in the skin or ovaries of other fish, but these fish store it in their muscles. This compound also gives salmon its unique flavor: When heated, it forms volatile aromas.

Beyond color, of course, salmon is a unique fish for a number of reasons. Salmon are anadromous—that is, they're born in fresh water and then travel to the sea. When mature, they typically return to freshwater streams to spawn. To help fuel their upriver swim in cold waters, salmon are relatively high in fat (and also high in good-for-you omega-3 fatty acids) and have stronger muscles than white fish. Unlike the fat that does exist in white fish, which is generally stored mostly in the liver, the fat in salmon is spread throughout the flesh.

Salmon—whether fillets, steaks, or even a whole side—can be cooked nearly any way: poached (bonus: it boasts richer flavor than other poached fish) (page 55); pan-seared (see page 57); roasted, for a hands-off approach (see page 37); glazed and broiled (see page 38); grilled (see page 257); and it even stands up to deep grill-smoked flavor (see page 269) or to curing for DIY gravlax (see page 335). Just don't fry this oily fish.

Farmed versus Wild Salmon

Farmed salmon is available all year round, raised on confined farms in the waters of the Atlantic, primarily in Norway, Scotland, and Canada. Wild salmon is available from spring to early fall and caught in open waters, usually in the Pacific Ocean. They're easy to tell apart. Farmed salmon is thicker and has a lighter color that derives mainly from synthetic astaxanthin and carotenoid pigment in their feed. And they taste different. Once cooked, farmed salmon is richer and more buttery, while wild salmon is firmer and meatier. The size and number of muscle fibers are virtually the same for wild salmon and farmed Atlantic salmon, however. The difference comes down to the structure of the collagen protein that makes up about 90 percent of the connective tissue in salmon. Wild salmon has a higher amount of collagen (and thus connective tissue) and, more importantly, a significantly greater number of chemical cross-links between collagen molecules. The flesh of wild salmon therefore turns noticeably firmer when cooked than farmed salmon does. Farmed salmon also contains more fat, as much as twice the amount in wild salmon. The higher fat content contributes not only to greater lubricity, but also to richer flavor.

MUSCLE MATTERS

Even novice fish cooks know that fish cook faster than land mammals and require more delicate treatment. Fish are built differently because life under the sea is nothing like life on land. Fish muscles, unlike mammalian muscles, are short—allowing for the fish's rapid movements back and forth—and layered in sheets called myomeres (or myotomes) rather than bundled, as in mammals. These sheets allow for the "fast twitching" that fish exhibit on movement (have you ever held a fish after catching it?). In raw fillets of fish, these sheets of muscle are usually very visible bands that stretch from the center of the fillet, often ½ inch thick or less. What does that mean for cooking? They're responsible for fish flaking. Those muscles coagulate and turn opaque when the fish is cooked to doneness, and the connective tissue holding them together disintegrates, allowing the muscles to flake under the fork.

We love the taste of wild salmon, but because it doesn't have the cushion of as much lubricating fat, we like it cooked to 120 degrees (for medium-rare) rather than 125 degrees for farmed salmon. At 120 degrees, the muscles of farmed salmon contract less and therefore expel less moisture. Wild salmon is also thinner, so you need to check for doneness earlier than you would for recipes calling for farmed salmon.

Wild salmon varieties include Chinook (or king), chum (or dog or silverbrite), coho (or silver), masu (or cherry), pink (or humpy or humpback), and sockeye (or red). Farmed salmon will generally just be labeled "Atlantic salmon."

What's Arctic Char?
While a member of both the trout and salmon families, arctic char more closely resembles salmon. Also anadromous, they swim from lakes to salt water. Like wild salmon, arctic char has moderately firm flesh, although it does contain more lubricating fat. Its flavor is milder than that of salmon. Its thin profile and fine flake make it best when cooked like wild salmon, to 120 degrees.

Key Salmon Steps
Unlike fillets of white fish, universally popular salmon usually requires a bit of preparation when you get it home before it hits the pan. You can ask a fishmonger to perform many of these steps, but they're simple and easy to control at home.

◀ Preparing Salmon Steaks
Salmon steaks are hearty, single-serving, uniformly thick pieces that are cut perpendicular to the spine, so they include skin and bones. Here are the steps to removing what you don't want to eat and ensuring the steaks stay together during cooking.

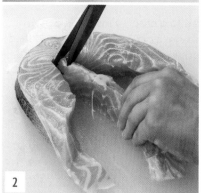

1 *Locate the white line at the top of the salmon steak. Cut around the white line, one side at a time, to separate the meat from the cartilage.*

2 *Use kitchen shears to cut out the spine and membrane.*

3 *Cut along the skin and membrane to separate the bottom 1½ inches of meat, then cut off the skin. Tuck the skinned portion into the center of the steak.*

4 *After wrapping the other flap around the steak, tie the circumference of the steak with kitchen twine.*

Cutting Fillets
When making any salmon recipe that calls for fillets, it's important to use fillets of similar thickness so that they cook at the same rate. We find that the best way to ensure uniformity is to buy a large center-cut fillet (1½ to 2 pounds if serving four) and cut it into four equal pieces.

Removing Pin Bones

Filleted fish has had the backbone and ribs removed, but the thin, needle-like pin bones must be removed separately. They are difficult to see, and while some fishmongers remove them (inevitably missing some), many do not. Here's how to look for pin bones and remove them without damaging the flesh.

Drape the whole fillet over an inverted mixing bowl to help any pin bones protrude. Then, working from head end to tail end, locate pin bones by running your fingers along the length of the fillet. Use tweezers to grasp the tip of the bone. To avoid tearing the flesh, pull slowly but firmly at a slight angle in the direction the bone is naturally pointing rather than straight up. Repeat until all pin bones are removed.

To Skin (or Not)

When seasoned, well rendered, and seared to a crisp, salmon skin can rival great roasted or fried chicken skin (try salmon in our recipe for crisp-skinned pan-seared fish to achieve this, page 57). But when you want skinless fillets, you can easily remove the skin before or after cooking (when a method doesn't deliver crispy skin). *To remove the skin from raw fillets, use the tip of a boning knife or a sharp chef's knife to cut the skin away from the flesh at the corner of the fillet. When sufficient skin is exposed, grasp the skin firmly with a paper towel, hold it taut, and slice the remaining skin off the flesh.*

You can also remove the skin after cooking when achieving browning on both sides is unnecessary. For example, in our recipe for Roasted Salmon Fillets (page 37), *you can simply slip a thin metal spatula between the flesh and skin and slide the fillet right off, leaving the skin behind.*

Saving Salmon

There are countless ways to cure fish—salting, brining, and fermenting among them. Salmon is one of the most commonly cured fish and for good reason. We love lox (seasoned with salt and often sugar and flavorings to remove moisture from the fish), dill-enhanced gravlax (learn to make your own on page 335); and nova, which is cold-smoked and, to be specific, from Nova Scotia; our favorite smoked salmon is **Spence & Co. Traditional Scottish Style Smoked Salmon,** and we love it on our twist on a niçoise salad (page 239).

---

5   OILY OCEAN FISH

BLUEFISH (pictured, page 12) • MACKEREL

Anadromous salmon aren't the only oily fish; we love to cook saltwater bluefish and mackerel, which, if filleted, are interchangeable in recipes. And while their oiliness makes them highly perishable, it also makes them highly delicious. Their dark color comes from being fast and fierce hunters of their prey—they need more oxygen to reach their muscles to make this action happen. Myoglobin is a dark-pigmented protein that stores oxygen in the muscles. The more active the fish, the more myoglobin and the darker the fish. Bluefish can be very large, up to 30 pounds; mackerel range from 1½ to 2 pounds. Given their oiliness, high heat works well (pan-searing, grilling, broiling); avoid them in stews. And their skin is tasty, with mackerel being a good choice for roasting whole. Mackerel is also sold smoked—a seafood lover's treat.

6 TROUT

Trout is a freshwater fish that's exclusively farmed (unless you catch your own)—in fact, the farming of trout is the oldest fish-farming industry in North America. Trout is oily but much milder in flavor than its anadromous cousins, salmon and arctic char, tasting almost nutty (enhance that flavor by trying a pecan crust; see page 65). The flesh has a soft texture with delicate flakes.

Trout is often prepared whole (it usually comes gutted, butterflied, and boned—convenient and perfectly portioned) but is also available in fillets. Or you can simply cut between the fillets yourself. We love to crisp its skin when preparing butterflied portions (see page 129), and the process is quick and easy if you preheat the baking sheet for roasting.

Common types of trout include rainbow, lake, brown, and brook trout, and the flesh can be white, pink, or orange. The freshest trout has clear, bright eyes. It's also available smoked, with flavorful flakes of it great in a grain or green salad.

7 MONKFISH

Compared with other fish, monkfish is a bit peculiar looking, with a large, wide head and fright-inducing mouth and teeth. That's why fishermen typically just save the tail when at sea, and that is the part that's sold for consumption. While the flesh of monkfish is white, the flavor and texture is much closer to shellfish than of white fish, and their sweet taste and firm bite give them the title of "lobster of the sea." Monkfish doesn't flake, so in addition to being pan-seared, it braises beautifully, holding up to any stewing condition (see page 198).

Monkfish fillets require a bit of prep at home before cooking; *you must remove its membrane by slipping a knife underneath it; angle the knife slightly upward and use a back-and-forth motion to cut it away from the fish*. A boning knife (see page 28) makes this easy.

8 TUNA

Tuna is a fast-swimming predator. In fact, tuna swims nonstop, so its muscles need a lot of oxygen, hence the high myoglobin content and dark red color. These dark muscle fibers have more collagen than paler-flesh fish, so they feel moister—pleasantly gelatinous, in fact—when cooked. Tuna, however, is not very high in fat, so it's best when cooked to rare or medium-rare; well-done tuna turns gray and loses its moisture. That requires cooking it fast and hot—it takes well to pan-searing and grilling and can form an appealing crust.

While bluefin tuna is prized and used primarily for sushi, yellowfin (or ahi) tuna is the type you're likely to find in your local fish market, usually cut into steaks.

CLAMS • MUSSELS • OYSTERS (pictured, page 17) • SCALLOPS

Bivalves are interactive seafood, their delicious meat living within shells you pry (in the case of raw seafood) or cook open. They are mollusks with two-part hinged shells. Clams, oysters, and mussels are generally sold within their shells, while scallops are sold shucked. Never buy bivalves with open or gaping shells (with the exception of steamers and razor clams; see below); the shellfish might be dead or dying. *And be sure to scrub before cooking to remove sand and grit.* (Mussels, however, need only a quick rinse under the tap.)

Clams

Clams are sold as hard-shell or soft-shell. Because hard-shell clams stay shut, they're less sandy, good for carefree cooking. We cook largely available little-neck or cherrystone clams. By contrast, soft-shell clams (steamers and razor clams) gape when they are alive, so they contain a lot of sand—we don't cook with these as they're harder to find.

Mussels

The two main varieties of mussels you'll see at the store are the Atlantic blue mussel and the Pacific green-lipped (also called New Zealand) mussel. These mussels are interchangeable when it comes to cooking, although some think the green-lipped mussels are slightly chewier. Most mussels sold are farmed or rope-cultured, which is good because these are minimally gritty.

There can be a small, weedy beard protruding from the side of the mussel that needs to be removed before cooking. *Holding the mussel in your hand, pull the beard firmly out of the shell, using your thumb and the side of a paring knife to grip it firmly.* Don't debeard mussels until you are ready to cook them, since debearding can cause them to die.

You can refrigerate mussels for one day in a colander covered with a damp kitchen towel. If the mussels won't close when tapped, discard them.

Oysters

East or West? Raw bar lovers on each coast have their allegiance. As a rule, Atlantic oysters are crisp and briny, with an intense hit of fresh, cold sea salt. (All Atlantic oysters are the same species: *Crassostrea virginica*.) They range from 2 inches long to nearly 6 inches long (Gulf Coasters call these "tennis shoes" for their size). Pacific oysters are rarely as salty and often taste complex and fruity.

You've likely heard a "rule" that you should eat oysters only in months that have the letter "r" at the end of them. While this made sense when oysters were harvested in the wild (oysters don't taste very good when they're reproducing, and they do so in the summer), oysters are now farmed in hatcheries, so the rule no longer applies.

Scallops

Scallops are available in a range of sizes: A pound of the large sea variety contains eight to 10 scallops, while a pound of the petite bay variety may have as many as 100 pencil eraser–size scallops. Sea scallops are in markets year-round. In addition to being easier to find, these are the scallops we use in our cooking, as they have a larger surface area for searing and remain succulent on the interior. They're shucked at sea (what you're buying is the large adductor muscle that opens and closes its shell), so before cooking, simply *remove the crescent-shaped muscle that attaches the scallop to the shell.*

When purchasing scallops, we strongly discourage purchasing "wet" scallops (ask at the store), which are treated with a solution of water and sodium tripolyphosphate (STPP) to increase shelf life and retain moisture. Unfortunately, STPP lends a soapy off-flavor to the scallops, and the extra water inhibits browning. If wet is all you can find, soak them in a mixture of 1 quart of cold water, ¼ cup of lemon juice, and 2 tablespoons of kosher salt for 30 minutes to mask any chemical flavors.

Scallops are mostly pearly white but sometimes they're pink. Does that mean they're treated? Not at all. The scallop takes its color from the reproductive gland that lies next to it inside the shell. In male scallops, the gland is grayish-white, hence the muscle remains white. Female scallops turn pink only when they're spawning; during this period, their glands fill with orange roe and turn bright coral, giving the adductor muscle a rosy hue. To see if there's any differences besides color, we pan-seared and tasted white male scallops alongside peachy female scallops. They cooked in the same amount of time and had identical textures, although tasters did note that the pink scallops—which retained their tint even after cooking—had a somewhat sweeter, richer flavor. Both colors, however, are absolutely normal and do not indicate anything about the freshness, doneness, or edibility of a scallop.

10 CRUSTACEANS

CRAB • LOBSTER (pictured, page 17) • SHRIMP

The composition of crab, lobster, and shrimp muscles is different than that of fish fillets. The muscle fibers are long, as in mammals, and connective tissue surrounds the individual muscle fibers and bundles of muscle fibers. This is why lobster meat, unlike white fish, does not flake when cooked. Sometimes thought of as delicacies, crustaceans are sweet and firm-textured—and take a bit of work to get into. All good things require a little effort, right? Here we'll crack the shells on crustaceans.

Crab

Since fresh crab isn't accessible in many parts of the country, our crab recipes call for crabmeat. The best crabmeat comes from crab you've caught yourself, but what are the chances of that? And crabmeat at the seafood counter is hard to come by (though sometimes you can find king crab legs). So the appeal of packaged crabmeat isn't price (a common misconception); often it doesn't cost much less than freshly shucked meat, and even the cheapest products are expensive when compared with canned tuna or salmon. The advantage is that, unlike fresh crabmeat, the packaged kind (which comes both refrigerated and canned) is readily available.

To find a worthy substitute for fresh crabmeat, we sampled nationally available lump (typically light in color, with a delicate flavor) and jumbo lump (the largest, most expensive chunks), our preferred grades (we ruled out finer, flakier backfin meat from the start), both straight from the package and in our recipe for Best Crab Cakes (page 216).

We strongly preferred the refrigerated products to canned crab—and for good reason. To be shelf-stable, canned crabmeat is typically pressure-heated at high temperatures (220 to 250 degrees), but the trade-off is drier, chewier meat. Some manufacturers add citric acid, presumably to offset the moisture loss, but we found those products mealy and spongy. Refrigerated crabmeat is typically processed at lower temperatures (182 to 190 degrees) and is considerably juicier—and pricier—than shelf-stable crabmeat, so it more closely resembles fresh crabmeat.

If you can find fresh crabmeat at your seafood counter, try the prized richer meat from the claws or that from precooked king crab legs. And of course, avoid imitation crab. Made by grinding pollock or other white fish and adding seasonings (including sugar), food coloring, small amounts of real crabmeat or crab flavoring, and binders such as starch or egg whites, the meat is sold shredded, in chunks, or as sticks. In most applications, it has an offensively sweet, overly seafood-y flavor.

Since you're most likely to find and use pasteurized crabmeat (our favorite, highly recommended crabmeat, is **Phillips Premium Crab Jumbo** with an affordable option being smaller-lump Blue Star Blue Swimming Crabmeat Lump Meat), we've outlined how to treat it before using. And if the meat tastes or smells a little fishy—this can happen with even top-quality crabmeat—we take an extra step. The smell is due to a compound called trimethylamine oxide, or TMAO, which is found in nearly all seafood, and simply submerging the meat in milk and then draining it does the trick. The casein in milk binds to the TMAO; when drained away, it takes with it the culprit that causes the fishy odor.

◀ Preparing Crabmeat

1 *Pick over the crabmeat for shells.*

2 *Place the crabmeat and 1 cup of milk in a bowl, making sure the crab is totally submerged.*

3 *Strain the soaked crabmeat through a fine-mesh strainer, pressing firmly to remove the milk but being careful not to break up the lumps of crabmeat.*

When cleaning out a lobster, you'll find a soft green mass; that's the digestive gland known to marine biologists as the hepatopancreas and to lobster fans as the tomalley. The latter group prizes the tomalley for its creamy texture and intensely concentrated lobster flavor. Tomalley of cooked lobster is eaten as is, whisked into sauces, or mixed into a compound butter for toast.

There is some concern that eating tomalley can lead to the contraction of paralytic shellfish poisoning (PSP), the illness caused by red tide. Lobsters do not filter-feed, but they consume infected clams and scallops. The PSP could accumulate in its tomalley. It's fine to eat lobster meat, but it's a good idea to forgo the tomalley when there's a shellfish ban. Otherwise, indulge.

Lobster

Lobster's the filet mignon of seafood. But not all lobsters are created equal. The quality of lobster meat depends to a large extent on where the crustacean is in its molting cycle, during which the hard, old shell is replaced with a soft, new one. Hard-shell lobsters taste better and are meatier. To determine the stage of your lobster, just squeeze. A soft-shell lobster will yield to pressure. Like the roe? Look for a female lobster. Her soft "swimmerets" (appendages under the lowest legs) give her away.

The most distinctive thing about lobsters isn't their texture or sweetness, however; it's that they are the only animals we regularly kill ourselves in the kitchen. Lobsters are cooked alive for two reasons, related to both flavor and health: First, the instant a lobster dies, enzymes within its body begin to break down the flesh and cause it to turn mushy. Second, like other shellfish, deceased lobsters are vulnerable to bacterial contamination that can cause food poisoning.

The most common method of cooking lobsters is plunging them into boiling water, where they will continue to move about for a short time. Though there's no way to know the extent to which the lobster suffers during this time, most scientists agree that the lobster's primitive nervous system, more like that of an insect than a human, prevents it from processing pain the way we do. Still, many cooks find putting live lobsters into a pot unpleasant. We tried to figure out a way to sedate the lobster before cooking, and therefore minimize the time it spent moving in the pot. We worked through a number of techniques, including cutting through its head, a soak in clove-scented water, and hypnotization, but landed upon a simple approach: a 30-minute stay in the freezer, which rendered the lobster motionless before it went into the pot.

If we're not boiling lobster (see page 307) and are perhaps grilling it (see page 285) or using it in a chowder (see page 204), we do cut through the head of the lobster. If the thought of splitting a live lobster makes you squeamish, know that this is humane and, of course, the most efficient way to dispatch a lobster. You can still freeze the lobster before doing so to lessen its activity. Don't be surprised if the lobster continues to move after being split; this is the result of twitching nerve fibers. Here are the steps to cutting and cleaning a whole lobster with care.

◀ Preparing Lobster

1 *With the blade of a chef's knife facing the head, plunge the knife into the body at the point where the shell forms a T. Move the blade straight down through the head. Positioning the knife blade so that it faces the tail end, continue to cut through the body toward the tail, making sure to cut all the way through the shell.*

2 *Using a spoon, discard the stomach, digestive track, and tomalley (see left for more information). Using a meat pounder, lightly pound each claw to crack it open slightly for cooking.*

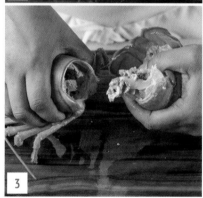

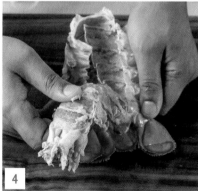

The other lobster puzzle? It's a bit more fun: Cracking a cooked one's thick shell to eat it! Arm yourself with some lobster crackers (and maybe a bib) and get the drawn butter ready. Here are the steps to extracting the meat from a whole lobster to eat or to cut up for a lobster roll.

◀ Extracting Lobster Meat

1 *Twist to remove the claws from the body. Separate the claw pieces and knuckles.*

2 *Crack the shells. Dig out the meat.*

3 *Twist the tail to separate it from the body. Pull off the small flippers from the body.*

4 *Use shears to cut through the underside of the shell, or use your fingers to push the meat out through the larger (body side) opening.*

Shrimp

If lobster is the filet mignon of seafood, shrimp may be the chicken thanks to its ubiquity, appeal, and ease of cooking. Sweet shrimp are great sautéed for a quick dinner with rice and a sauce (see pages 68–73 for options) or tucked into a taco. They add plump texture and sweetness to soups and stews. And they can be roasted in their shells. We use their shells to make quick seafood stocks (see page 186, for example), and we puree their flesh to serve as a binder for seafood cakes (see page 216).

Virtually all shrimp sold in supermarkets today were frozen at some point. Because it's hard to know how long "fresh" (defrosted) shrimp have been sitting, we recommend buying bags of IQF shrimp and defrosting them at home. IQF stands for "individually quick-frozen"; shrimp (or any other seafood labeled IQF) are spread on a conveyor belt and frozen at sea, locking in quality and freshness. Shrimp are also sometimes frozen at sea with water in 5-pound blocks and packed in boxes. We prefer bagged IQF shrimp, as you can thaw exactly what you need.

Make sure your shrimp are preservative-free. Shrimp should be the only thing on the ingredient list. Avoid salt-treated and STPP-enhanced shrimp; the texture of both is unpleasant, and the latter also has a chemical taste. Increasingly, seafood markets and gourmet shops sell a range of different shrimp species. We compared the three commonly available types (pink, white, and black tiger) and found that white shrimp had the firmest flesh and the sweetest taste. And wild shrimp are ideal; they have a sweeter flavor and firmer texture than farm-raised, making their higher price worth it. Shrimp are sold both by size and by number needed to make a pound. Choosing shrimp by the numerical rating is more accurate, because the size labels vary from store to store. See the chart for how the sizing systems generally compare.

Small	51 to 60 per pound
Medium	41 to 50 per pound
Medium-Large	31 to 40 per pound
Large	26 to 30 per pound
Extra-Large	21 to 25 per pound
Jumbo	16 to 20 per pound

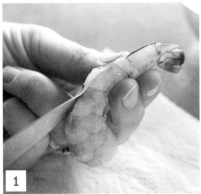

◀ Peeling and Deveining Shrimp

Shell-on shrimp tend to be sweeter, but they require some prep. For most recipes, you'll want to peel and devein the shrimp before cooking. A sharp paring knife makes the task easy.

1 Break the shell on the underside, under the swimming legs, which will come off as the shell is removed. Leave the tail intact, if desired, or tug the tail to remove the shell. Use a paring knife to make a shallow cut along the back of the shrimp to expose the vein.

2 Using the tip of a knife, lift out the vein. Discard the vein by wiping the knife blade against a paper towel.

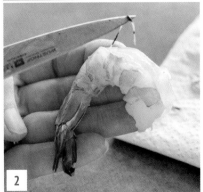

11 CEPHALOPODS

OCTOPUS (pictured, page 17) • SQUID

Octopus and squid are relatives that are "head-footed," which means their legs come from their head. While one (octopus) is much larger—and a bit messier to deal with—than the other (squid), both cephalopods have smooth meat and a somewhat chewy texture that requires breaking down.

Squid

Squid is a bit more versatile than octopus. Its chewy texture becomes tender in braises, but it also breaks down through marinating (see page 355) and is pleasant when battered and fried (see page 352). Its mild taste is the perfect vehicle for a host of bold flavors. We typically separate the body from the tentacles before cutting the body into rings. We also often cut the tentacles in half. See how to prepare squid below.

◀ Preparing Squid

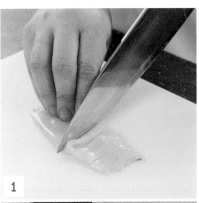

1 Separate the body from the tentacles. Slice the body into rings as specified in the recipe.

2 Halve the tentacles.

Octopus

Octopus takes very well to braising, as it's tough and collagen-rich. The large sack on its head is surrounded by eight sucker-bearing arms. There are more than 300 different species; we've had the most success using frozen octopus from either Spain or Portugal. (Frozen octopus is preferable to fresh because the ice crystals help break down the muscle fibers.) Frozen octopus is cleaned during processing, but it's necessary to rinse the suckers well to rid them of dirt. Octopus is made up of 50 to 80 percent salt water; the finished volume of your dish could be less than half of what you started with and very salty if you don't follow the recipe. For our Red Wine–Braised Octopus (page 316), we like to simmer the octopus first in water to remove some of its salty juices. A bonus: The octopus is easier to clean and cut after this step.

◀ Preparing Octopus

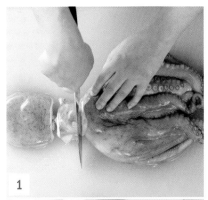

1 *Using a sharp knife, separate the octopus mantle (large sac) and body (lower section with tentacles) from the head (midsection containing eyes); discard the head.*

2 *After simmering in water, use a paring knife to cut the mantle into quarters (or halves), then trim and scrape away the skin and interior fibers. Using your fingers, grasp the skin at the base of each tentacle and pull toward the tips to remove. Be careful not to remove the suction cups from the tentacles.*

3 *Cut the tentacles from around the core of the body in three sections; discard the core. Separate the tentacles.*

---

12 TINNED FISH

Not all the seafood we eat is fresh from the sea. There are methods of preserving fish that don't just make it easier to get into our diets, but that make it delicious—often with remarkably transformed flavor and texture. And both tinned and cured fish are experiencing a bit of a moment, with tinned sardines and bread or potato chip plates and smoked salmon bagel boards almost as common on restaurant menus as charcuterie and cheese. Canned tuna (our favorite is **Wild Planet Wild Albacore Tuna**) has long been a lunchtime staple (see Mediterranean Tuna Salad on page 251). Nutritious, glutamate-rich sardines, herring, and trout are all delicious right from the tin, maybe topping toast, as they're often packed in flavored oil. Anchovies (our favorites are **King Oscar Flat Fillets in Olive Oil**) not only flavor dishes as a background ingredient, but firm, rich fillets can top pizzas and salads (see page 234).

WORKING WITH WHITE FISH

As you've now learned, just because fillets of different fish varieties might look the same—smooth, milky-white, with short muscle segments—doesn't mean they should be treated the same. We began testing essential cooking methods for the fish in this book by cooking every white fish that was accessible to us by our most basic method, pan-roasting (searing the fish, flipping it, and transferring it to the oven to cook through). Some fish took to this traditional technique well; others, we learned, would need different treatment, which led us to categorize fish as you've seen in the preceding pages. And even among those that did work well pan-roasted, flavor and texture differences were noticeable when the fish were tasted side by side, showing the diversity of fish in the sea. Get to know white fish by taking a look at the notes we collected during our blind taste test. You should be able to see the flakes and texture of the cooked fish in the photo.

1. STRIPED BASS

Tasters' Comments: "More fishy" flavor; meaty fish; closer to swordfish and halibut than other white fish tasted here.

Pan-Roast? NO

2. HADDOCK

Tasters' Comments: Similar to cod in terms of texture/flavor; liked this method for this fish.

Pan-Roast? YES

3. POLLOCK

Tasters' Comments: Smaller flakes of white flesh; most neutral-tasting fish; this method seemed to work well; similar to cod overall.

Pan-Roast? YES

4. HALIBUT

Tasters' Comments: Short fibers, spongy, meaty texture; good color; feels dry and not best method for halibut; exudes no liquid.

Pan-Roast? NO

5. COD

Tasters' Comments: Firm, silky but "bouncy/springy" texture; has large flakes; buttery flavor; lots of color; loses liquid while resting.

Pan-Roast? YES

6. HAKE

Tasters' Comments: "Shellfish-like" flavor (like scallops); moist and flaky; thick and meaty like cod.

Pan-Roast? YES

7. BLACK SEA BASS

Tasters' Comments: Moist; cooked quickly; large flakes like cod; exuded lots of liquid while resting.

Pan-Roast? YES

8. MAHI-MAHI

Tasters' Comments: "Tastes like chicken," meaty, tuna/swordfish-like fibers; feels overcooked with this method and to this temp.

Pan-Roast? NO

9. RED SNAPPER

Tasters' Comments: Stringier/ meatier texture; has a tuna-ish texture and flavor; feels overcooked/ dried out using this method.

Pan-Roast? NO

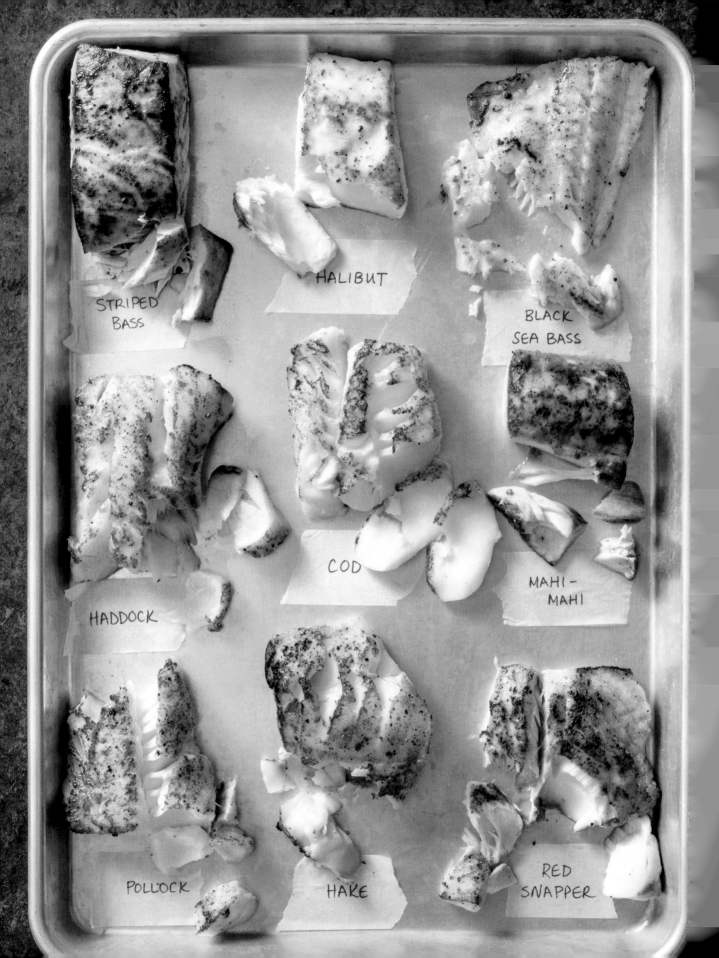

STRIPED
BASS

HALIBUT

BLACK
SEA BASS

HADDOCK

COD

MAHI-
MAHI

POLLOCK

HAKE

RED
SNAPPER

FISH TO EAT WHOLE

Fillets of the fish in the preceding pages make it into our weekly rotation. They're approachable and quick and easy to cook. But whole fish shouldn't intimidate the seafood cook, and while we find their beautiful presentation suitable for special occasions (see our impressive Salt-Baked Branzino on page 302 or our Grilled Whole Trout with Orange and Fennel on page 264), they're not too difficult to prepare anytime. We like cooking black sea bass, branzino, mackerel, red snapper, and trout whole, and all five of these are easy to find at a good fish counter. Here are some pointers to take the fear out of fish with fins.

1

2

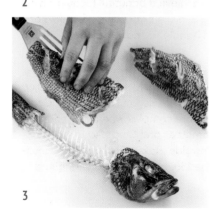

3

Black sea bass, branzino (European sea bass), and red snapper are all of comparable size and should be filleted after cooking (see below) to serve. Mackerel and trout are nice because each fish serves one.

Customarily, these fish will come to you scaled and gutted (certainly ask your fishmonger if this is not automatic); you may just need to snip off the fins with kitchen scissors before cooking.

Trout also often comes butterflied and boned, convenient when you'd like to make a recipe that displays trout this way, like our Roasted Trout with White Bean and Tomato Salad (page 129). (You can also easily cut the trout into fillets when it arrives like this.)

Unless you're salt-crusting your branzino (see page 302), cooking whole fish by roasting or grilling is a fairly streamlined process; serving it as fillets is simple if you follow our steps (unless folks just want to dig in with their own forks and knives, which is fine, too). And be sure to look out for translucent pin bones when eating—part of the whole-fish experience.

◀ Serving Whole Fish

1 *Make a vertical cut just behind the head from the top of the fish to the belly. Make another cut along the top of the fish from the head to the tail.*

2 *Starting at the head and working toward the tail, gently slide a spatula between the top fillet and bones to separate; transfer the fillet, skin side up, to a serving platter.*

3 *Gently lift the tail and peel the skeleton and head from the bottom fillet; discard the head and skeleton. Transfer the second fillet, skin side up, to the platter.*

EVERY WAY IS THE BEST WAY TO COOK FISH

Fish is delicate and should be handled with care, but it's also incredibly versatile: With the exception of microwaving (be kind to your household or officemates), nearly any method of cooking that exists works for fish. Some fish, like meaty salmon, take well to any cooking method you throw at them; others work well in certain situations. But none of the fish we cook can be prepared only one way. If this book inspires you to put more fish in your rotation, you'll certainly never be bored; here are the major methods of preparing fish.

BRINING FISH

While this isn't a necessary step, fish benefits from brining (unless you're looking to achieve crispy skin). Fish, even fattier salmon, can benefit from some extra moisture during pan-searing, as can shrimp. Fillets often have a thicker and a thinner end; fish that is perfectly cooked at its thickest point can be overcooked and dry at the thinner end. Brining prevents this drying. We've found that you can brine any species of fish—and fast. That's because the brine more quickly penetrates the short muscle fibers and does its job at a faster clip than for meat. For up to six 1-inch-thick fish steaks or fillets, use 5 tablespoons of salt dissolved in 2 quarts of water and brine for 15 minutes. For up to 2 pounds of shell-on shrimp, use 2 tablespoons of salt dissolved in 1 quart of water and brine for 15 minutes.

There is one case where we strongly recommend brining fish: when you're freezing it. This makes up for any potential hits to quality that freezing fish can take. See page 29 for more information on freezing fish.

Roasting

Cooking fish in the oven at a high temperature is the most hands-off and, therefore one of the simplest way of handling it. Fish is delicate, however, so it can also lead to dried-out fish if you don't do it right. In our basic recipe for Roasted Salmon Fillets (page 37), we preheat the baking sheet for the fillets in a 500-degree oven and (carefully) add the fillets to this sheet to jump-start the process of rendering fat from the skin when it hits, then we lower the oven temperature to 275 degrees. By finishing in a more moderate oven, the fillets cook gently and evenly for silky flesh. For something more impressive for company, you can roast a large center-cut fillet (page 289).

Roasting isn't our preferred method for ultralean white fish, although we do employ it in some situations, like Crunchy Oven-Fried Fish Fillets (page 51), to quickly drive off moisture that would make for a soggy crust. Even shrimp works well in the oven, the shrimp shells protecting the meat—and caramelizing deliciously if you choose to eat them (see page 86). And mussels, which come in a range of sizes and therefore open up at different times, actually benefit more from this method (see page 88) over traditional but more uneven steaming in a pot. Roasting achieves browning and deepens the flavor of whole fish, like Whole Roast Snapper with Citrus Vinaigrette (page 300).

Broiling

The top-down cooking of broiling is great for recipes where you want to get color or crust on the surface. We use it to achieve a beautiful lacquer on our Miso-Marinated Salmon (page 38) and to achieve browning on bluefish or mackerel fillets—these fatty, oily fish can handle the heat.

Baking

Lower the oven temperature on fish that needs a delicate touch—the flaky, white fish (see page 7)—and achieve instant classics like Nut-Crusted Cod Fillets (page 52). Meals can also become more complex when they enter the baking dish: Baked Halibut with Cherry Tomatoes and Chickpeas (page 134) surrounds spiced halibut with a comforting side. Baked Scallops with Couscous, Leeks, and Orange Vinaigrette (page 156) is a spin on New England baked scallops.

Fish is susceptible to overcooking, so reheating previously cooked fillets is something that might make a cook balk. But since almost everyone has leftover fish from time to time, we figured out the best approach to warming it up. As we suspected, we had far more success reheating thick fillets and steaks than thin ones. Both swordfish steaks and halibut fillets reheated nicely, retaining their moisture well and with no detectable change in flavor. Likewise, salmon reheated well, but be aware that thanks to the oxidation of its abundant fatty acids into strong-smelling aldehydes, doing so brought out a bit more of the fish's pungent aroma. There was little we could do to prevent thin fish (see page 8) from drying out and overcooking when heated a second time.

To reheat thicker fish fillets, use this gentle approach: Place the fillets on a wire rack set in a rimmed baking sheet, cover with foil (to prevent the exteriors of the fish from drying out), and heat them in a 275-degree oven until they register 125 to 130 degrees, about 15 minutes for 1-inch-thick fillets (timing varies according to fillet size). We recommend serving leftover cooked thin fish in cold applications like salads.

Pan-Searing

Hot flame, hot pan, sizzling fish—pan-searing cooks fish fast for minimal moisture loss and maximum browning. This is ideal for fish that's cooked to rare or medium-rare, like salmon (see page 41) or tuna (see page 74). It also delivers crispy skin on fish where it's appealing—black sea bass, arctic char, bluefish, or salmon (see page 57). For fish cooked to higher temperatures, or those that don't have lubricating fat, though, the method can dry out the fish before it cooks through. Our solution for flaky white fish is a dual method: **pan-roasting**. We first sear on one side for browning, then finish cooking gently in the oven. (See page 22 for more information.)

And for thick, meaty white fish that need to be cooked through but whose muscle structure is too tight for heat to penetrate efficiently, we flip the fish frequently when pan-searing (see page 77). A hot skillet cooks food from the bottom up. When a protein is flipped, the seared side, which is then facing up, is also quite hot. Some of its heat dissipates into the air, and some of it cooks the protein from the top down. The more frequently a protein is flipped, the more it will cook from both the bottom up and the top down—evenly. Note that this method causes more carryover cooking. And at such a high temperature, the proteins can shrink and squeeze out juices, so we pull the seafood early and let it rest to rise to temperature.

Pan-searing isn't just for fillets of fish. We also sear seafood burgers and cakes (see pages 214–220) and quick-cooking shrimp (see page 84) in the pan.

Steaming

Steaming cooks fish with vapor. While we steam clams on the stove (see page 91)—a quick, efficient process—we like to use the oven to evenly steam fish. We do this with a method known as cooking *en papillote,* or in packets. To do this you enclose the fish—like the halibut fillets in our Thai-Style Halibut and Creamy Coconut Couscous Packets (page 115)—in a package (we like foil because it's easy to crimp) and bake at a moderate temperature. The packets trap the moisture emitted from the fish, steaming the fish (and any vegetable or grain accompaniments) in its own moisture for a concentrated flavor. And we steam four fillets of fish in foil at the same time for our Oven-Steamed Fish with Scallions and Ginger (page 49), allowing the sauced fish to rest in a baking dish within the foil.

Poaching

Poaching also involves cooking seafood gently in a moist environment, but here the fish comes in contact with liquid. We find it to be the best method for cooking (and infusing flavor into) shrimp when we don't want browning but rather plump, tender shellfish for Shrimp Cocktail (page 327) or Spring Rolls with Shrimp (page 350). You can cook many fish with this healthful technique (see page 55). In traditional French cooking, the poaching liquid is *court bouillon* (French for "short stock," as it can be made relatively quickly when compared with poultry or meat stocks), or water that has been infused with herbs and aromatic vegetables and fortified with wine or vinegar. Plain water would simply dilute the flavor of fish; the court bouillon helps season it. Traditional poaching calls for fully submerging foods in the liquid, but we choose to only partially submerge fish fillets, raising them from the bottom of the pan with lemon slices for a sort of hybrid poaching-steaming method that prevents the flavor of the fish's natural juices from washing away in the liquid.

A variation on traditional poaching is oil-poaching—yes, cooking fish in a pan of olive oil. This renders silky, supple flesh in Oil-Poached Snapper with Tomato Vinaigrette (page 294). Poaching in oil leads to remarkably moist, velvety results. This is because oil has roughly half the thermal capacity of water, which means it requires half the amount of energy to reach the same temperature as an equal volume of water. This, in turn, means it has less energy to transfer to food and will cook it more slowly. And while you might expect that fish poached in fat would be greasy, it actually absorbs very little oil. Why? For the oil to penetrate the fish, moisture must exit first. But because oil and water repel each other, it's very difficult for moisture inside the fish to readily enter the oil. Hence, more of the juices stay in the fish.

Braising

Braising—cooking an ingredient in a closed environment to break down its proteins and achieve ultratender results—might not be the first cooking technique that comes to mind for delicate fish, but the ocean's the limit when it comes to braising fish and seafood. Braising simmers and steams anything from lean, meaty halibut fillets to shellfish to perfection. It's gentle and forgiving, guaranteeing moist fish. We consider fish and shellfish soups and stews to be braises, and chapter 3 is full of them (see page 166).

A variation on braising in a pot is cooking *en cocotte* (French for covered cooking "in a casserole"). Here the liquid released from the fish itself creates a moist environment, in effect braising the item in its own juices. The muscle fibers break down and a shallow sauce forms, ultraconcentrated in flavor.

Frying

Fried seafood is undeniably delicious—a treat from fish and clam shacks along the coasts or the fish fries of the South. Frying cooks fish quickly so there's little chance of drying out, and it crisps up an appealing coating on the outside. Fish and Chips (page 298) and Fried Calamari (page 352) are fun projects to do at home—it's satisfying to re-create these restaurant favorites.

◀ ## Grilling

Flipping fish on the grill or even preparing oysters on the half shell (see page 280) is a summer pleasure. Delicate fish—fillets or whole—easily pick up char from the grill, so the flavor imparted is tremendous. We also smoke salmon on the grill to achieve wood-smoked flavor (see page 269).

Some folks fear grilling fish, and that's because it's notorious for sticking. We've developed a method for preparing the grill that ensures protein won't stick. (For more information, see page 257.) If, by chance, your fish skin still sticks, slide a metal spatula between the skin and the flesh and remove the fish to serve skinless.

1 *Heat the grill according to the recipe. Fold several paper towels into a compact wad. Holding the paper towels with tongs, dip in oil and then wipe the grate. Dip the paper towels in the oil again and wipe the grate a second time.*

2 *Cover the grill and heat it to 500 degrees, about 5 minutes longer.*

3 *Uncover and wipe the grate twice more with the oiled paper towels.*

THE EDUCATED SEAFOOD SHOPPER

No matter what cooking technique you're using, there are some universal considerations when purchasing fish, whether you're getting it from your small local fishmonger or a big chain grocery store (make sure the store, no matter the size, has high turnover). Here are our tips for buying quality fish so your meals are tasteful and fresh.

EQUIPMENT

Fish cookery requires the same arsenal of tools that you'd use for any other savory cooking, but there are a few fish-specific items that you should invest in.

Boning Knife

A chef's knife and a paring knife are all you need for most cutting jobs in the kitchen. But a boning knife can make it easier to perform certain tasks, as its thin, narrow, razor-like blade is ideal for slipping under skin or butchering fish steaks. It allows you to trim away only what you don't want, with little or no waste. The **Zwilling Pro 5.5" Flexible Boning Knife** ($110) makes every task seem effortless; the Victorinox Swiss Army Fibrox Pro 6" Flexible Boning Knife ($28) is our Best Buy.

Oyster Knife

You could wait for a night out to enjoy the briny pleasure of a fresh, raw oyster, but with the right tool and some practice you can shuck oysters at home for a fraction of restaurant prices. Regular knives are unsuitable for opening oysters because they're too sharp and flexible; the thick, dull blades of oyster knives function as levers to pry shells apart without cutting into them. To find the best all-purpose

continues ▶

Buying Fillets and Steaks

Fish fillets and steaks should be sold on (but not buried in) ice. Whenever possible, we portion individual fillets from larger center-cut fillets (ones measuring the total poundage called for in the recipe). Larger fillets keep longer and allow for more consistent sizing. Not only do precut portions often have different thicknesses, their proportions could be different, making for a less attractive presentation. Don't be afraid to be picky at the counter; a ragged piece of hake or a tail end of sea bass will be difficult to cook properly. It's important to keep your fish cold, so if you have a long ride, ask your fishmonger for a bag of ice. The fish should smell sweet like the sea (not "fishy" or sour)—though your chances of being able to pre-sniff your fish are slim. The surface should be shiny and bright and uniform in color. The flesh should be firm and elastic; when you press into it, the indentation shouldn't remain.

Buying Whole Fish

Unlike fillets and steaks, whole fish should be buried in ice at the seafood counter. The skin should be bright and reflective, without damage. The smell again should be faintly sweet. You are likely buying a whole fish from a *person*, not an unattended case, so instruct the fishmonger to do what you'd like: gut, scale, and snip off the fins (if these tasks are not already taken care of).

Buying Frozen Fish

Around 85 percent of the seafood consumed in the United States is imported. Seafood's high perishability means that a lot of the seafood you eat—yes, even the "fresh" fish you buy at the seafood counter—has been frozen. Does that make a difference? Modern flash-freezing methods cause less damage to tissue, leading to less moisture loss when thawed and better texture. Most fish is also frozen at the peak of freshness, so some argue that frozen fish is even "fresher" than fresh-caught fish that's been sitting on ice for more than a day. However, this doesn't always mean that you'll be happy with the frozen fish you buy. Here are our recommendations for frozen fish.

Assess the quality of frozen fish.

Inspect the fillets for signs of poor handling: tears or punctures in packaging that could let in air, ice crystals on the fish ("freezer burn") or in the packaging, liquid inside the packaging, discolored or soft (partially defrosted) flesh.

Ask for frozen fillets.

Instead of buying thawed previously frozen fish at the seafood counter, ask if you can get a frozen piece so you have control over how it is thawed. Store it in the coldest part of your freezer, and use it within four months.

CRUSTACEANS

Baked Crab Dip (325)

Baked Shrimp and Orzo with Feta and Tomatoes (146)

Baked Stuffed Shrimp (336)

Best Crab Cakes (216)

Boiled Lobster (307)

Brazilian Shrimp and Fish Stew (*Moqueca*) (195)

Cóctel de Camarón (348)

Crab Louis Salad (252)

Fried Brown Rice with Pork and Shrimp (155)

Garlicky Roasted Shrimp with Cilantro and Lime (86)

Garlicky Roasted Shrimp with Parsley and Anise (86)

Grilled Caribbean Shrimp Skewers (282)

Grilled Jalapeño and Lime Shrimp Skewers (282)

Grilled Lobsters (285)

Grilled Paella (314)

Grilled Red Chile and Ginger Shrimp Skewers (282)

Gumbo (188)

Lemony Linguine with Shrimp and Spinach (149)

Linguine with Seafood (313)

Lobster and Corn Chowder (204)

Lobster Fettuccine with Fennel and Tarragon (311)

New England Lobster Rolls (211)

One-Pan Shrimp Pad Thai (145)

Popcorn Shrimp (328)

Rich and Velvety Shrimp Bisque (169)

Roasted Stuffed Lobster Tails (308)

Roasted Stuffed Lobster Tails with Fennel and Pernod (308)

Seafood and Chorizo Stew (191)

Shrimp and Arugula Salad with Lemon Vinaigrette (246)

Shrimp Burgers (214)

Shrimp and Cabbage Potstickers (340)

Shrimp Cocktail (327)

Shrimp Fra Diavolo with Linguine (150)

Shrimp Po' Boys (213)

Shrimp Risotto (141)

Shrimp Salad (248)

Shrimp Salad with Corn and Chipotle (248)

Shrimp Salad with Wasabi and Pickled Ginger (248)

Shrimp Tacos (230)

Sizzling Garlic Shrimp (320)

Sizzling Saigon Crêpes (*Bánh Xèo*) (222)

Spicy Shrimp Lettuce Wraps (233)

Spring Rolls with Shrimp (350)

Stir-Fried Shrimp and Broccoli (153)

Thai-Style Hot-and-Sour Soup with Shrimp and Rice Vermicelli (186)

Tuscan Shrimp and Beans (142)

CEPHALOPODS

Calamari Stew (200)

Fried Calamari (352)

Linguine with Seafood (313)

Red Wine–Braised Octopus (316)

CURED FISH

Buckwheat Blini with Smoked Salmon (333)

Fennel and Apple Salad with Smoked Mackerel (240)

Mediterranean Couscous Salad with Smoked Trout (243)

Salt Cod Fritters (342)

Smoked Salmon Niçoise Salad (239)

TINNED FISH

Caesar Salad (234)

Garlicky Spaghetti with Clams (163)

Mediterranean Tuna Salad (251)

Provençal-Style Anchovy Dip (323)

WHOLE FISH

Grilled Whole Red Snapper (266)

Grilled Whole Trout with Orange and Fennel (264)

Roasted Trout with White Bean and Tomato Salad (129)

Salt-Baked Branzino (302)

Whole Roast Mackerel (305)

Whole Roast Snapper with Citrus Vinaigrette (300)

CHAPTER 1

everyday essentials

ROASTED SALMON FILLETS | SERVES 4

SUBSTITUTIONS ARCTIC CHAR • WILD SALMON

4 (6- to 8-ounce) skin-on salmon fillets, 1 inch thick

2 teaspoons vegetable oil

½ teaspoon table salt

¼ teaspoon pepper

WHY THIS RECIPE WORKS

Salmon fillets are one of the top cuts of fish to cook, and there's good reason for that. They're a weeknight workhorse—rich and satisfying, nutritious, and easy to jazz up for interest. To get dinner on the table with ease, while firing up some sides to round out the plate, we turn to this dual-temperature roasting technique; it's a hands-off way to serve up fish with a nicely browned exterior. Rather than sear the fillets on the stovetop, we preheat a baking sheet in a 500-degree oven. While the pan heats up, we ready the fillets for roasting, slashing the skin so the fat renders in the oven. We drop the temperature to 275 degrees just before placing the fillets on the hot pan and into the oven. The initial contact with the hot pan crisps the skin (as searing would), and the heat of the gradually cooling oven cooks the fillets gently, ensuring silky fish every time. If your knife is not sharp enough to cut through the skin easily, try a serrated knife. It is important to keep the skin on during cooking; remove it afterward if desired. If using arctic char or wild salmon, cook the fillets to 120 degrees (for medium-rare) and start checking for doneness after 4 minutes. The salmon is pictured with Almond Vinaigrette (page 71).

1 | Adjust oven rack to lowest position, place aluminum foil–lined rimmed baking sheet on rack, and heat oven to 500 degrees. Make 4 or 5 shallow slashes, about 1 inch apart, on skin side of each fillet, being careful not to cut into flesh. Pat salmon dry with paper towels, rub with oil, and sprinkle with salt and pepper.

2 | Reduce oven temperature to 275 degrees and use oven mitts to remove sheet from oven. Carefully place salmon skin side down on hot sheet. Roast until center is still translucent when checked with tip of paring knife and registers 125 degrees (for medium-rare), 8 to 12 minutes. Transfer salmon to platter and serve.

MISO-MARINATED SALMON | SERVES 4

SUBSTITUTIONS ARCTIC CHAR • WILD SALMON

1 cup white miso paste

¼ cup sugar

3 tablespoons sake

3 tablespoons mirin

4 (6- to 8-ounce) skin-on salmon fillets, 1 inch thick

WHY THIS RECIPE WORKS

The Japanese technique of marinating fish in miso started as a way to preserve a fresh catch without refrigeration during its long journey inland. Now the dish is delicacy, not necessity. The technique is quite simple. Miso (a paste made by fermenting soybeans and sometimes other grains with salt and a grain- or bean-based starter called koji) is combined with sugar, sake, and mirin (a sweet Japanese rice wine) to make a marinade that essentially cures the fish: The miso, sugar, and alcohol all work to season and pull moisture out of the flesh, resulting in a firmer, denser texture. Miso also adds flavor benefits: sweetness, acidity, and water-soluble compounds such as glutamic acid that, over time, penetrate the proteins and lend them deeply complex flavor. Once we marinate the fish in our miso mixture, we scrape the fish clean and broil it, producing meaty-textured, well-seasoned fillets with a lacquered savory-sweet glaze. Note that the fish needs to marinate for at least 6 hours before cooking. It is important to keep the skin on during cooking; remove it afterward if desired. Yellow, red, or brown miso paste can be used instead of white. If using arctic char or wild salmon, cook the fillets to 120 degrees (for medium-rare) and start checking for doneness after 6 minutes.

1 | Whisk miso, sugar, sake, and mirin in bowl until sugar and miso are dissolved. Pat salmon dry with paper towels, then place in 1-gallon zipper-lock bag; pour marinade over top. Seal bag, pressing out as much air as possible, then flip bag to ensure fish is well coated. Place bag on large plate and refrigerate for at least 6 hours or up to 24 hours, flipping bag occasionally to ensure salmon marinates evenly.

2 | Adjust oven rack 8 inches from broiler element and heat broiler. Place wire rack in rimmed baking sheet and cover rack with aluminum foil. Remove salmon from marinade and scrape miso mixture from fillets (do not rinse). Place salmon, skin side down, on foil, leaving 1 inch between fillets.

3 | Broil salmon until deeply browned and center is still translucent when checked with tip of paring knife and registers 125 degrees (for medium-rare), 8 to 12 minutes, rotating sheet halfway through cooking and shielding fillets with foil if browning too quickly. Transfer salmon to platter and serve.

PAN-SEARED SALMON STEAKS | SERVES 4

4 (8- to 10-ounce) salmon steaks, 1 inch thick
½ teaspoon table salt
¼ teaspoon pepper
¼ cup cornstarch
2 tablespoons vegetable oil

WHY THIS RECIPE WORKS

If you want salmon with lots of crisp browning, salmon steaks are a good way to go. Because neither side of a steak has skin, its larger fleshy surface promises plenty of crisp exterior to contrast with the silky interior. Also, whereas a fillet has a thick end and a tapered end, which can lead to uneven cooking, a steak is generally uniformly thick. To make sure this is the case, we debone and then tie each steak into a round to produce a structurally sound parcel that cooks evenly and develops a nice crust. To bolster the color of the crust, we decided to coat the steaks with a starch. A quick dredge in flour made the crust crispier, but coverage was spotty. Finer cornstarch proved better; we used a pastry brush to gently sweep away the excess so that only a translucent dusting remained. The medallions emerged with perfectly even and beautifully crisp browned exteriors encasing moist, buttery flesh. For photographed steps on cutting and tying the salmon steaks, see page 10.

1 | Pat salmon dry with paper towels. Place 1 salmon steak on counter with belly flaps facing you. Locate white line at top of salmon steak. Using sharp paring knife, cut along 1 side of white line, around spine, then along membrane inside belly flap. Repeat process on other side of white line.

2 | Using kitchen shears and sharp paring knife, cut out spine and membrane; discard. Remove any pin bones using tweezers. Using sharp paring knife, separate bottom 1½ inches of skin from salmon on 1 flap of steak, then discard skin. Tuck skinned portion into center of steak. Wrap other flap around steak and tie kitchen twine around circumference of salmon. Repeat with remaining steaks.

3 | Sprinkle both sides of salmon with salt and pepper. Spread cornstarch in even layer on large plate. Lightly press both sides of salmon into cornstarch. Using pastry brush, remove excess cornstarch.

4 | Heat oil in 12-inch nonstick skillet over medium-high heat until shimmering. Place salmon in skillet and cook until first side is browned, about 3 minutes. Flip salmon and cook until second side is browned, about 3 minutes. Continue to cook, flipping salmon every 2 minutes, until center is still translucent when checked with tip of paring knife and register 125 degrees, 2 to 6 minutes longer. Transfer salmon to platter and discard twine. Serve.

PAN-ROASTED COD | SERVES 4

SUBSTITUTIONS BLACK SEA BASS • HADDOCK • HAKE • POLLOCK

4 (6- to 8-ounce) skinless cod fillets, 1 inch thick
½ teaspoon table salt
¼ teaspoon pepper
½ teaspoon sugar
1 tablespoon vegetable oil

WHY THIS RECIPE WORKS

There's not much more pristine than a perfectly portioned moist white fish fillet sporting a chestnut-brown crust with some crispness—and nothing more convenient than its minutes-long cooking time. But lean cod is also easy to over-cook at home and rarely turns out as in a restaurant. So for a cooking method that reliably turned out delicious flaky white fish fillets, we used a common technique borrowed from professional kitchens: Sear the fillets in a hot pan, flip, then transfer to an oven to continue cooking rather than finishing on the stove. (For more information on this technique, see page 22.) To brown the fish quickly before the hot pan had a chance to dry out the fish's exterior, we turned to a sprinkling of sugar, which accelerated browning for supersavory—not sweet—flavor. A well-browned crust appeared in around a minute, giving the interior time to turn succulent in the oven. We love this technique for white fish that's good just about anytime. You will need a 12-inch ovensafe nonstick skillet for this recipe. The cod is pictured with Grapefruit-Basil Relish (page 69).

1 | Adjust oven rack to middle position and heat oven to 425 degrees. Pat cod dry with paper towels, sprinkle with salt and pepper, and sprinkle sugar lightly over 1 side of each fillet.

2 | Heat oil in 12-inch ovensafe nonstick skillet over medium-high heat until just smoking. Lay fillets sugared side down in skillet and, using spatula, lightly press fillets for 20 to 30 seconds to ensure even contact with skillet. Cook until browned on first side, 1 to 2 minutes.

3 | Using 2 spatulas, flip fillets, then transfer skillet to oven. Roast until fish flakes apart when gently prodded with paring knife and registers 135 degrees, 7 to 10 minutes. Transfer cod to platter and serve.

BUTTER-BASTED FISH FILLETS WITH GARLIC AND THYME | SERVES 2

SUBSTITUTIONS BLACK SEA BASS • HADDOCK • HAKE • POLLOCK

2 (6- to 8-ounce) skinless cod fillets, 1 inch thick
½ teaspoon kosher salt
⅛ teaspoon pepper
1 tablespoon vegetable oil
3 tablespoons unsalted butter, cut into ½-inch cubes
2 garlic cloves, crushed and peeled
4 sprigs fresh thyme
Lemon wedges

WHY THIS RECIPE WORKS

Butter basting sounds like music to the ears: The technique involves repeatedly spooning sizzling butter over food as it cooks. The butter bath, which is also a classic method for cooking big beef steaks, is great for mild, lean, flaky fish. It's a good alternative to Pan-Roasted Cod (page 44), because it distributes heat almost like an oven: The hot butter helps cook the top of the fillet as the skillet heats the bottom, allowing you to flip the delicate fish only once and early in the cooking process before the flesh has become too fragile. Throughout the process, the butter browns and coats the mild fish in savory flavor, adding richness. We add thyme sprigs and crushed garlic cloves to the pan, which infuse the butter as it heats and makes for an aromatic dish. Lemon wedges are a must; the brightness of the lemon juice cuts through the butter's richness.

1 | Pat all sides of fillets dry with paper towels. Sprinkle on all sides with salt and pepper. Heat oil in 12-inch nonstick skillet over medium-high heat until just smoking. Reduce heat to medium and place cod skinned side down in skillet. Using fish spatula, gently press on each fillet for 5 seconds to ensure good contact with skillet. Cook cod, without moving it, until underside is light golden brown, 4 to 5 minutes.

2 | Using 2 spatulas, gently flip fillets and cook for 1 minute. Scatter butter around cod. When butter is melted, tilt skillet slightly toward you so that butter pools at front of skillet. Using large spoon, scoop up melted butter and pour over cod repeatedly for 15 seconds. Place skillet flat on burner and continue to cook 30 seconds longer. Tilt skillet and baste for 15 seconds. Place skillet flat on burner and take temperature of thickest part of each fillet. Continue to alternate basting and cooking until fillets reach 130 degrees. Add garlic and thyme sprigs to skillet at 12 o'clock position (butter will spatter). When spattering has subsided, continue basting and cooking until fillets reach 135 degrees at thickest point. (Total cooking time will range from 8 to 10 minutes.)

3 | Transfer fillets to individual plates. Discard garlic. Top each fillet with thyme sprigs, pour butter over cod, and serve with lemon wedges.

OVEN-STEAMING COD

1 Place sling lengthwise on top of aromatics in pan, with extra foil hanging over ends of pan, then place cod on sling.

2 Whisk soy sauce, rice wine, sesame oil, sugar, salt, and white pepper together in bowl, then pour around cod in pan.

3 Cover pan tightly with foil and bake until fish registers 130 degrees, 12 to 14 minutes. Carefully transfer sling and cod to deep platter.

OVEN-STEAMED FISH WITH SCALLIONS AND GINGER | SERVES 4

SUBSTITUTIONS BLACK SEA BASS • HADDOCK • HAKE • POLLOCK

- 8 scallions, trimmed, divided
- 1 (3-inch) piece ginger, peeled
- 3 garlic cloves, sliced thin
- 4 (6- to 8-ounce) skinless cod fillets, 1 inch thick
- 3 tablespoons soy sauce
- 2 tablespoons Chinese rice wine or dry sherry
- 1½ teaspoons toasted sesame oil
- 1½ teaspoons sugar
- ¼ teaspoon table salt
- ¼ teaspoon white pepper
- 2 tablespoons vegetable oil
- ⅓ cup fresh cilantro leaves and thin stems

WHY THIS RECIPE WORKS

Both Chinese and French cuisines have classic approaches to steaming fish, which we think deserve more attention. Steaming is a delicate method for cooking a delicate protein that leads to supremely moist, tender results. It's fast enough to do on a weeknight but also offers company-worthy elegance. We mashed up the Chinese method (bold, fresh flavors for the fish and a finishing drizzle of hot oil that sizzles on the fish, releasing aromas) and the French method (oven-steaming to produce a flavorful, concentrated fish jus) for a new technique that's easy and impressive. For a simple setup, we placed the skinless fillets on a foil sling in a baking pan that we cover, which allows the fish to flavor the cooking liquid (soy sauce, rice wine, sesame oil, and seasonings), and vice versa. The sling makes it easy to transfer the fish to a platter without the fillets falling apart. Removing the fish from the oven before it's fully cooked—130 degrees rather than the typical 135—prevents it from overcooking at the end, when we pour over the sizzling ginger-infused oil (which raises its temperature). If using a glass baking dish, add 5 minutes to the cooking time.

1 | Adjust oven rack to middle position and heat oven to 450 degrees. Chop 6 scallions coarse and scatter over bottom of 13 by 9-inch baking pan. Slice remaining 2 scallions thin on bias and set aside until ready to serve. Coarsely chop 2 inches ginger and add to pan with scallions, then sprinkle with garlic. Slice remaining 1 inch ginger into matchsticks; set aside.

2 | Fold 18 by 12-inch piece of aluminum foil lengthwise to create 18 by 6-inch sling and spray lightly with vegetable oil spray. Place sling lengthwise on top of aromatics in pan, with extra foil hanging over ends of pan, then place cod on sling, spaced evenly apart. (If fillets vary in thickness, place thinner fillets in middle and thicker fillets at ends.)

3 | Whisk soy sauce, rice wine, sesame oil, sugar, salt, and white pepper together in bowl, then pour around cod in pan. Cover pan tightly with foil and bake until fish registers 130 degrees, 12 to 14 minutes.

4 | Grasping sling at both ends, carefully transfer sling and cod to deep platter. Place spatula at 1 end of fillets to hold in place and carefully slide out sling from under cod, leaving cod behind on platter. Strain remaining cooking liquid from pan through fine-mesh strainer set over bowl, pressing on solids to extract liquid; discard solids. Pour strained liquid over cod, then sprinkle with reserved scallions. Heat vegetable oil in 8-inch skillet over high heat until shimmering. Reduce heat to low, add reserved ginger, and cook, stirring, until ginger begins to brown and crisp, 20 to 30 seconds. Drizzle oil and ginger over cod (oil will crackle), then sprinkle with cilantro. Serve.

CRUNCHY OVEN-FRIED FISH FILLETS

| SERVES 4

SUBSTITUTIONS BLACK SEA BASS • COD • HAKE • POLLOCK

---

2 large eggs

¼ cup mayonnaise

¼ cup all-purpose flour

2 teaspoons grated lemon zest

½ teaspoon table salt

¼ teaspoon pepper

2 cups panko bread crumbs

2 tablespoons vegetable oil

4 (6- to 8-ounce) skinless haddock fillets, 1 inch thick

WHY THIS RECIPE WORKS

Batter-fried fish is a summertime treat (see our recipe for Fish and Chips on page 298), but frying is a special-occasion activity for us. We wanted a recipe for moist, flavorful fish fillets with a crunchy crust as good as fried—but from the oven. Panko bread crumbs crisp right up in a hot oven and create a crunchy crust. Pretoasting them maximizes that crunch; doing so in the microwave maximizes ease. We dipped the fillets first in a sticky wash of mayonnaise, flour, and eggs and then applied the browned crumbs for a thick, satisfying crust. Placing the coated fish on a wire rack for baking allowed air to circulate, crisping all sides for fish that's just as good as fried. To delight all eaters, we also created a fish stick variation for the freezer—they're at the ready to dunk into Classic Tartar Sauce (page 70).

1 | Adjust oven rack to middle position and heat oven to 425 degrees. Line rimmed baking sheet with aluminum foil, set wire rack in sheet, and spray with vegetable oil spray. Whisk eggs, mayonnaise, flour, lemon zest, salt, and pepper together in shallow dish.

2 | Toss panko with oil in bowl until evenly coated. Microwave, stirring frequently, until lightly browned, 3 to 5 minutes. Transfer toasted panko to second shallow dish.

3 | Pat haddock dry with paper towels. Working with 1 fillet at a time, dredge haddock in egg mixture, letting excess drip off, then coat with panko mixture, pressing gently to adhere. Transfer fillets to prepared rack.

4 | Bake until crumbs are golden and haddock registers 135 degrees, 12 to 16 minutes, rotating sheet halfway through baking. Transfer haddock to platter and serve.

variation |
CRUNCHY OVEN-FRIED FISH STICKS

We found that cutting the fish into 4-inch-long pieces made for the sturdiest fish sticks. Any longer and they were too delicate to pick up. If you're freezing the fish sticks, we recommend brining the fish before breading and freezing (see page 25). If brining, omit the salt from the egg mixture.

Working with 1 fillet at a time, cut haddock fillets into ¾-inch-wide by 4-inch-long strips. Decrease baking time in step 4 to 10 to 12 minutes. (Raw fish sticks can be frozen for up to 1 month. Do not thaw frozen fish sticks before baking; increase baking time to 12 to 18 minutes.)

NUT-CRUSTED COD FILLETS | SERVES 4

SUBSTITUTIONS BLACK SEA BASS • HADDOCK • HAKE • POLLOCK

½ cup shelled pistachios

2 tablespoons vegetable oil

1 large shallot, minced

¾ teaspoon table salt, divided

1 garlic clove, minced

1 teaspoon minced fresh thyme or ¼ teaspoon dried

½ cup whole-wheat panko bread crumbs

½ teaspoon pepper, divided

2 tablespoons minced fresh parsley

1 tablespoon plain yogurt

1 large egg yolk

½ teaspoon grated lemon zest

4 (6- to 8-ounce) skinless cod fillets, 1 inch thick

WHY THIS RECIPE WORKS

Traditional breading, though delicious, isn't the only coating that can give fish crunch, and a nut crust gives fish not only texture and appeal but also welcome richness in every bite. We made a surprising selection for our nut crust: Ground pistachios offer intriguing fragrance, appealing color, and a gentle sweetness, which emphasize the subtly sweet seafood flavor of the cod. Nuts alone didn't make a cohesive coating, however, so we also added panko bread crumbs—whole-wheat panko enhanced the coating's nuttiness. Toasting the two components with aromatics brought out their flavors, introduced some more, and ensured the topping remained extra crisp. To adhere this substantial crust to the fillets, we brushed the fish with a mixture of yogurt, egg yolk, and lemon zest before pressing on the crumbs. Because our crust is so flavorful, we coated only the tops of the fillets (but we still baked them on a wire rack set in a sheet pan to ensure even cooking). Any nut will work for the topping, but we particularly like the fragrance of pistachios and hazelnuts.

1 | Adjust oven rack to middle position and heat oven to 300 degrees. Set wire rack in rimmed baking sheet and spray with vegetable oil spray. Process pistachios in food processor until finely chopped, 20 to 30 seconds. Heat oil in 12-inch nonstick skillet over medium heat until shimmering. Add shallot and ¼ teaspoon salt and cook until softened, about 3 minutes. Stir in garlic and thyme and cook until fragrant, about 30 seconds. Reduce heat to medium-low, add pistachios, panko, and ¼ teaspoon pepper and cook, stirring frequently, until well browned and crisp, about 8 minutes. Transfer nut mixture to shallow dish and let cool for 10 minutes. Stir in parsley; set aside.

2 | Whisk yogurt, egg yolk, and lemon zest together in bowl. Pat cod dry with paper towels and sprinkle with remaining ½ teaspoon salt and remaining ¼ teaspoon pepper. Brush tops of fillets evenly with yogurt mixture. Working with 1 fillet at a time, press coated side in nut mixture, pressing gently to adhere. Transfer cod, crumb side up, to prepared rack and repeat with remaining fillets.

3 | Bake until fish flakes apart when gently prodded with paring knife and registers 135 degrees, 20 to 25 minutes, rotating sheet halfway through baking. Transfer cod to platter and serve.

PERFECT POACHED FISH | SERVES 4

SUBSTITUTIONS ARCTIC CHAR • BLACK SEA BASS • COD • HADDOCK • HAKE • HALIBUT • MAHI-MAHI • POLLOCK • RED SNAPPER • SWORDFISH • WILD SALMON

1 lemon, sliced into thin rounds

4 sprigs fresh parsley

1 shallot, sliced thin

½ cup dry white wine

4 (6- to 8-ounce) skinless salmon fillets, 1 inch thick

½ teaspoon table salt

¼ teaspoon pepper

WHY THIS RECIPE WORKS

As you learned in our introduction, every category of fish has different properties—taste, texture, nutrition, and more. But is there a method that works to cook a majority of fish fillets, regardless of cooking category? There is, and not only is it reliable, foolproof, and dead-simple, but it makes each fish taste delicate and distinctly like itself: poaching. (For more information on poaching, see page 26.) Heating fish with liquid produces steam that delicately cooks the fish—if done right. A low cooking temperature would prevent overcooking, but it doesn't create enough steam to evenly cook the fish. High heat would overcook the fish. Our solution isn't obvious: We increased the ratio of wine to water in our poaching liquid. The additional alcohol lowers the liquid's boiling point, producing more vapor even at lower temperatures. For better flavor we do not fully submerge the fish; we rest the fillets on some lemon slices to avoid overcooking on the bottoms. You will need a 12-inch skillet with a tight-fitting lid for this recipe. If using arctic char or wild salmon, cook the fillets to 120 degrees (for medium-rare) and start checking for doneness after 8 minutes. If using black sea bass, cod, haddock, hake, or pollock, cook the fish to 135 degrees. If using halibut, mahi-mahi, red snapper, or swordfish, cook the fish to 130 degrees and let rest, tented with foil, for 10 minutes before serving.

1 | Arrange lemon slices in single layer across bottom of 12-inch skillet. Top with parsley sprigs and shallot, then add wine and ½ cup water. Pat salmon dry with paper towels, sprinkle with salt and pepper, and place, skinned side down, on top of lemon slices in skillet. Bring to simmer over medium-high heat. Cover, reduce heat to low, and cook, adjusting heat as needed to maintain gentle simmer, until salmon registers 125 degrees (for medium-rare), 11 to 16 minutes.

2 | Remove skillet from heat and, using spatula, carefully transfer salmon and lemon slices to paper towel–lined plate to drain. (Discard poaching liquid.) Carefully lift and tilt fillets to remove lemon slices and transfer to platter. Serve.

CRISPY PAN-SEARED BLACK SEA BASS

| SERVES 4

SUBSTITUTIONS ARCTIC CHAR • BLUEFISH • FARMED OR WILD SALMON • RED SNAPPER

¾ teaspoon plus ⅛ teaspoon table salt, divided

¾ teaspoon sugar

4 (6- to 8-ounce) skin-on black sea bass fillets, 1 inch thick

2 tablespoons vegetable oil

WHY THIS RECIPE WORKS

Serving fish skin-on is a way to instantly elevate it, creating succulence and textural contrast as well as an elegant presentation. If you're going to do it, you want potato-chip-thin/crisp skin covering ultramoist fish. For restaurant-quality fish, we salt the fillets before we cook them. Why? First, the salt seasons the flesh deeply by diffusion. Second, salt actually dissolves some of the proteins in the fish and forms a gel that can hold on to more moisture so the portions near the outside don't overcook in the pan. The second secret is going low and slow: Start the fish in a hot pan, then drop the flame to maintain an even, steady sear. Cooking the fish most of the way on the skin side—an old-school, fancy French technique dubbed "unilateral" cooking—ensures that the skin gets incredibly crispy while the flesh stays moist. This recipe works well with fish fillets, 1-inch thick, that have skin that is pleasant to eat. Do not use fillets thicker than 1 inch for this recipe as they are difficult to cook through without scorching the skin or overcooking the bottom layer of flesh. If using arctic char or wild salmon, cook the fillets to 120 degrees (for medium-rare). If using farmed salmon, cook the fillets to 125 degrees (for medium-rare). If using bluefish, cook the fillets to 130 degrees (for medium-rare). The bass is pictured with Green Olive, Almond, and Orange Relish (page 69) and Oregano–Black Olive Relish (page 70).

1 | Combine ¾ teaspoon salt and sugar in bowl. Using sharp knife, make 3 or 4 shallow slashes, about ½ inch apart, in skin side of each fillet, being careful not to cut into flesh and leaving ½ inch of skin at the edges intact. Sprinkle flesh side of fillets evenly with salt mixture and place, skin side up, on wire rack set in rimmed baking sheet. Sprinkle skin side with remaining ⅛ teaspoon salt. Refrigerate for at least 45 minutes or up to 1½ hours.

2 | Pat fillets dry with paper towels. Heat oil in 12-inch nonstick skillet over high heat until just smoking. Place fillets, skin side down, in skillet. Immediately reduce heat to medium-low and, using fish spatula, firmly press fillets for 20 to 30 seconds to ensure even contact between skin and skillet. Continue to cook until skin is well browned and flesh is opaque except for top ¼ inch, 6 to 12 minutes. (If at any time during searing, oil starts to smoke, or sides of fish start to brown, reduce heat so that oil is sizzling but not smoking.)

3 | Off heat, flip fillets with 2 spatulas and continue to cook using residual heat of skillet until bass registers 135 degrees, 30 seconds to 1 minute longer. Transfer bass, skin side up, to platter and serve.

SAUTÉED TILAPIA | SERVES 4

SUBSTITUTIONS CATFISH • FLOUNDER • SOLE

4 (6- to 8-ounce) skinless tilapia fillets, split lengthwise down natural seam

½ teaspoon table salt

2 tablespoons vegetable oil
Lemon wedges

WHY THIS RECIPE WORKS

Thin white tilapia has a distinct personality, but the flavor isn't that far off from thicker fillets like cod or haddock. That doesn't mean it can be cooked the same. Consider the anatomy of thin white fish: The thick half of a thin, wide fillet rests flat on the pan and browns nicely during sautéing, but the thin half tilts up, hardly making contact at all. The only way around this was to split them at their seams and cook the thick halves in one batch and the thin halves in a second. The move actually enhanced rather than detracted from their aesthetic: We prefer uniform, evenly browned fish fillets any day. High heat got the fish, both thick and thin pieces, remarkably brown and evenly crisp on both sides. If at any time during cooking, the oil begins to smoke, reduce the heat as needed. The tilapia is pictured with Cilantro Chimichurri (page 71).

1 | Sprinkle tilapia with salt and let sit at room temperature for 15 minutes. Pat tilapia dry with paper towels.

2 | Heat oil in 12-inch nonstick skillet over high heat until just smoking. Add thick halves of fillets to skillet and cook, tilting and gently shaking skillet occasionally to distribute oil, until golden brown, 2 to 3 minutes. Using 2 spatulas, flip fillets and cook until second sides are golden brown, 2 to 3 minutes. Transfer tilapia to serving platter.

3 | Return skillet to high heat. When oil is just smoking, add thin halves of fillets and cook until golden brown, about 1 minute. Flip and cook until second sides are golden brown, about 1 minute. Transfer tilapia to platter and serve with lemon wedges.

PAN-FRIED SOLE | SERVES 4

SUBSTITUTIONS CATFISH • FLOUNDER • TILAPIA

4 (6- to 8-ounce) skinless sole fillets, split lengthwise down natural seam

½ teaspoon table salt

¼ teaspoon pepper

½ cup all-purpose flour

2 tablespoons vegetable oil, divided

2 tablespoons unsalted butter, cut into 2 pieces, divided

Lemon wedges

WHY THIS RECIPE WORKS

Lightly browned thin fillets of sole are a classic for a reason, and a floured piece of fish is a grand vehicle for soaking up a bright contrasting sauce (see our classic meunière preparation)—unless the coating is soggy and wan. We found that omitting heavy eggs or bread crumbs from our coating was key, and the perfect crust came from simply drying the fillets, seasoning them with salt and pepper, and then dredging them in flour. As with our Sautéed Tilapia (page 58), we got the most even cooking and best browning by splitting the fish down the natural seam. Try to purchase fillets that are of similar size. If using smaller fillets (3 ounces each), serve two fillets per person and reduce the cooking time on the second side to about 1 minute. You will need to cook smaller fillets in three or four batches and wipe out the skillet with paper towels after the second and third batches to prevent any browned bits from scorching.

1| Adjust oven rack to middle position and heat oven to 200 degrees. Pat sole dry with paper towels and sprinkle with salt and pepper. Spread flour in shallow dish. Dredge fillets in flour, shaking off excess, and transfer to large plate.

2| Heat 1 tablespoon oil in 12-inch nonstick skillet over medium-high heat until shimmering. Add 1 tablespoon butter and swirl until melted. Add thick halves of fillets to skillet and cook until golden on first side, about 3 minutes. Using 2 spatulas, flip fillets and cook until second sides are golden and fish flakes apart when gently prodded with paring knife, about 2 minutes. Transfer to ovensafe platter and keep warm in oven. Wipe skillet clean with paper towels and repeat with remaining 1 tablespoon oil, remaining 1 tablespoon butter, and thin halves of fillets. Serve with lemon wedges.

variation |
SOLE MEUNIÈRE
Omit lemon wedges. Before serving, melt 4 tablespoons unsalted butter in medium saucepan over medium-high heat. Continue to cook, swirling saucepan constantly, until butter is golden brown and has nutty aroma, 1 to 1½ minutes longer. Remove saucepan from heat, add 1½ tablespoons lemon juice, and season with salt to taste. Spoon sauce over sole and sprinkle with 2 tablespoons chopped fresh parsley. Serve immediately.

FRIED CATFISH | SERVES 4 TO 6

SUBSTITUTIONS FLOUNDER • SOLE • TILAPIA

2 cups buttermilk

1 teaspoon hot sauce

2 cups cornmeal, divided

2 teaspoons pepper

2 teaspoons granulated garlic

1½ teaspoons table salt

1 teaspoon cayenne pepper

4 (6- to 8-ounce) catfish fillets, split lengthwise down natural seam

2 quarts peanut or vegetable oil

WHY THIS RECIPE WORKS

You can serve catfish sautéed (see page 58) or pan-fried (see page 60), but you're probably most familiar with it deep-fried—especially if you're from the South. In fact, the dish rarely makes appearances north of the Delta, where fish eaters assume catfish tastes "pondy." We wanted to ship sweet Southern catfish in an ultracrunchy and deeply flavored crust everywhere. Dunking the catfish in a flavorful mixture of buttermilk and hot sauce before rolling each fillet in cornmeal made the coating stay put. As with other thin fish, we sliced the catfish fillets in half, both to make frying more manageable and to increase each piece's surface area, which upped our coating-to-fish ratio. Using a combination of coarse cornmeal and cornmeal that we finely ground produced the best texture: crunchy but not too hard or gritty. On top of the spicy kick we got from the hot sauce–buttermilk dunk, we boosted flavor further by adding salt, pepper, garlic, and cayenne to the cornmeal blend—and by making Comeback Sauce (page 70), which is a cross between rémoulade and Thousand Island Dressing) it's often served with. Use a Dutch oven that holds 6 quarts or more. If your spice grinder is small, grind the cornmeal in batches or process it in a blender for 60 to 90 seconds.

1 | Adjust oven rack to middle position and heat oven to 200 degrees. Set wire rack in rimmed baking sheet and line half of rack with triple layer of paper towels. Whisk buttermilk and hot sauce together in shallow dish. Process 1 cup cornmeal in spice grinder to fine powder, 30 to 45 seconds. Whisk pepper, granulated garlic, salt, cayenne, remaining 1 cup cornmeal, and ground cornmeal together in second shallow dish.

2 | Pat catfish dry with paper towels. Working with 1 piece at a time, dip fillets in buttermilk mixture, letting excess drip back into dish. Dredge fillets in cornmeal mixture, shaking off excess, and transfer to large plate.

3 | Add oil to Dutch oven until it measures about 1½ inches deep and heat over medium-high heat to 350 degrees. Working with 4 fillets at a time, add fish to hot oil. Adjust burner, if necessary, to maintain oil temperature between 325 and 350 degrees. Cook catfish until golden brown and crispy, about 5 minutes. Transfer catfish to paper towel–lined side of prepared rack and let drain for 1 minute, then move to unlined side of rack and season with salt and pepper to taste; keep warm in oven. Return oil to 350 degrees and repeat with remaining catfish. Serve.

PECAN-CRUSTED TROUT | SERVES 4

SUBSTITUTIONS NONE

1 cup pecans

¼ cup panko bread crumbs

1 teaspoon grated lemon zest, plus lemon wedges for serving

1¼ teaspoons table salt, divided

1 teaspoon pepper, divided

⅛ teaspoon cayenne pepper

1 large egg

1 teaspoon Dijon mustard

3 (8- to 10-ounce) boneless, butterflied whole trout, halved between fillets

¼ cup vegetable oil, divided

WHY THIS RECIPE WORKS

You can serve flavorful, versatile trout unadorned (see pages 126 and 129), but pecan-crusted fish is a commonplace dish across the American South, where pecans are plentiful and trout is both economical and easy to find. It's a good center-of-the-plate staple. In restaurants, you're likely to encounter a deep-fried version, but we make this multitextured dish easy by pan-frying in a nonstick skillet. We combine the pecans with panko in the food processor; the bread crumbs absorb some fat and moisture from the nuts to help this pecan-heavy coating adhere. A teaspoon of lemon zest, a bit of cayenne, and some salt and pepper flavor the crust. Because trout is thin, we coat just one side so the fish flavor isn't obscured by the rich coating. The trout is pictured with Creamy Lemon-Garlic Sauce (page 71).

1 | Adjust oven rack to middle position and heat oven to 200 degrees. Set wire rack in rimmed baking sheet. Process pecans and panko in food processor until pecans are finely chopped and mixture resembles coarse meal, 10 to 12 pulses. Transfer to shallow dish and stir in lemon zest, ½ teaspoon salt, ½ teaspoon pepper, and cayenne. Whisk egg, mustard, ¼ teaspoon salt, and ¼ teaspoon pepper together in second shallow dish.

2 | Pat trout dry with paper towels and sprinkle with remaining ½ teaspoon salt and remaining ¼ teaspoon pepper. Working with 1 fillet at a time, dredge flesh side of trout in egg mixture, letting excess drip back into dish. Press coated side of trout in nut mixture, pressing gently to adhere. Transfer trout, pecan side up, to large plate and repeat with remaining fillets.

3 | Heat 2 tablespoons oil in 12-inch nonstick skillet over medium heat until shimmering. Place 3 fillets in skillet, pecan side down (alternating thick and thin ends to fit fillets in skillet in 1 layer), and cook until pecan coating is browned and fragrant, 3 to 4 minutes. Flip fillets using 2 spatulas and continue to cook until skin is browned and trout flakes apart when gently prodded with paring knife, 2 to 3 minutes longer. Transfer trout, pecan side up, to prepared rack and keep warm in oven.

4 | Wipe skillet clean with paper towels. Repeat with remaining 2 tablespoons oil and remaining 3 fillets. Serve.

PAN-ROASTED MONKFISH | SERVES 4

SUBSTITUTIONS NONE

4   (6- to 8-ounce) skinless
    monkfish fillets, 1 inch thick,
    trimmed
½   teaspoon sugar
½   teaspoon table salt
¼   teaspoon pepper
2   tablespoons vegetable oil

WHY THIS RECIPE WORKS

Monkfish has a firm, lobsterlike texture and slightly sweet flavor—without a lobsterlike price tag. Unlike other white fish, the chewier flesh of monkfish fillets comes from the hardworking tail, rather than the central body, which means it has long, sinewy muscle fibers that run its length, so it requires different cooking. Cooked to the normal 135 degrees for white fish, pan-roasted monkfish was unappealingly fibrous, mealy, and spongy. To improve the texture, we tested cooking the fish to incrementally higher temperatures and found 160 degrees to be ideal—this higher temperature made the fish tender, flaky even, while still retaining moisture and a firm and meaty texture. This made sense: Much like cooking cuts of meat from active muscles, such as pork butt or beef chuck, more cooking was needed to soften and break down the muscle fibers for tender results. Monkfish fillets are surrounded by a thin membrane that needs to be removed before cooking. Your fishmonger can do this for you, or you can remove it yourself (see page 13). The monkfish is pictured with Oregano–Black Olive Relish (page 70).

1 | Adjust oven rack to middle position and heat oven to 425 degrees. Pat monkfish dry with paper towels, then sprinkle with sugar, salt, and pepper.

2 | Heat oil in 12-inch ovensafe skillet over medium-high heat until just smoking. Place monkfish in skillet and, using fish spatula, lightly press fillets for 20 to 30 seconds to ensure even contact with skillet. Cook until browned on first side, about 2 minutes.

3 | Using 2 spatulas, flip fillets and cook until browned on second side, about 2 minutes. Transfer skillet to oven and roast until monkfish is opaque in center and registers 160 degrees, 8 to 12 minutes. Transfer monkfish to platter, tent loosely with aluminum foil, and let rest for 5 minutes. Serve.

SAUCES FOR FISH AND SHELLFISH

Simply seasoned fish can be the base to any great meal. And while lemon wedges are a classic accompaniment, a great sauce or relish can transform a basic preparation into a lively main dish. We photograph fish throughout the book with sauces we enjoy pairing them with, but feel free to experiment as you like. In general, oily fish benefit from bright, acidic sauces to cut through their richness, and leaner fish benefit from creamier sauces or those with briny elements to punch up their flavors.

PICTURED ABOVE Caper-Currant Relish (page 69), Classic Tartar Sauce (page 70), Salsa Verde (page 72), Mignonette Sauce (page 72), and Tarragon-Lime Compound Butter (page 73)

These brightly flavored medleys of vegetables or fruits and flavorings—sometimes cooked, sometimes simply stirred together—add style to any type of simple seafood dish. They can also provide contrasting texture, which is often a welcome addition to delicate seafood.

CAPER-CURRANT RELISH
MAKES ½ CUP

We like this salty-sweet relish with rich, skin-on fish.

- 3 tablespoons minced fresh parsley
- 3 tablespoons extra-virgin olive oil
- 2 tablespoons capers, rinsed and chopped fine
- 2 tablespoons dried currants, chopped fine
- 1 garlic clove, minced
- 1 teaspoon grated lemon zest plus 2 tablespoons juice

Combine all ingredients in bowl. Let sit at room temperature for at least 20 minutes before serving. (Relish can be refrigerated for up to 2 days.)

FRESH TOMATO RELISH
MAKES ABOUT 1 CUP

Be sure to use super-ripe tomatoes in this simple relish.

- 2 tomatoes, cored, seeded, and cut into ¼-inch pieces
- 1 small shallot, minced
- 1 small garlic clove, minced
- 2 tablespoons chopped fresh basil
- 1 tablespoon extra-virgin olive oil
- 1 teaspoon red wine vinegar

Combine all ingredients in bowl; let sit for 15 minutes. Season with salt and pepper to taste. (Relish can be refrigerated for up to 2 days.)

GRAPEFRUIT-BASIL RELISH
MAKES ABOUT 1 CUP

This tangy, aromatic relish pairs just as well with rich salmon as it does with pan-roasted white fish.

- 2 red grapefruits
- 1 small shallot, minced
- 2 tablespoons chopped fresh basil
- 2 teaspoons lemon juice
- 2 teaspoons extra-virgin olive oil

Cut away peel and pith from grapefruits. Cut grapefruits into 8 wedges, then slice crosswise into ½-inch-thick pieces. Place grapefruits in strainer set over bowl and let drain for 15 minutes; measure out and reserve 1 tablespoon drained juice. Combine reserved juice, shallot, basil, lemon juice, and oil in bowl. Stir in grapefruits and let sit for 15 minutes. Season with salt, pepper, and sugar to taste. (Relish can be refrigerated for up to 2 days.)

variations |
TANGERINE-GINGER RELISH

Substitute 4 tangerines for grapefruits; quarter tangerines before slicing crosswise. Substitute 1½ teaspoons grated fresh ginger for shallot, and 1 thinly sliced scallion for basil.

ORANGE-AVOCADO RELISH

Substitute 1 large orange for grapefruits; quarter orange before slicing crosswise. Substitute 2 tablespoons minced fresh cilantro for basil, and 4 teaspoons lime juice for lemon juice.

Add 1 diced avocado and 1 small minced jalapeño chile to juice mixture with orange.

GREEN OLIVE, ALMOND, AND ORANGE RELISH
MAKES 1 CUP

If the olives are marinated, rinse and drain them before chopping. This relish provides a trifecta of flavor: brininess, richness, and sweetness.

- ½ cup slivered almonds, toasted
- ½ cup green olives, pitted and chopped coarse
- 1 garlic clove, minced
- 1 teaspoon grated orange zest plus ¼ cup juice
- ¼ cup extra-virgin olive oil
- ¼ cup minced fresh mint
- 2 teaspoons white wine vinegar
  Cayenne pepper

Pulse almonds, olives, garlic, and orange zest in food processor until nuts and olives are finely chopped, 10 to 12 pulses. Transfer to bowl and stir in orange juice, oil, mint, and vinegar. Season with salt and cayenne to taste. (Relish can be refrigerated for up to 2 days.)

SPICY CUCUMBER RELISH
MAKES ABOUT 1 CUP

For a spicier relish, add some of the serrano chile seeds. This relish is a refreshing topping for meaty seared tuna.

1 cucumber, peeled, halved lengthwise, seeded, and cut into ¼-inch pieces

1 small shallot, minced

1 serrano chile, stemmed, seeded, and minced

2 tablespoons minced fresh mint

1 tablespoon lime juice, plus extra to taste

Combine all ingredients in bowl, let sit for 15 minutes, and season with salt and extra lime juice to taste.

MANGO-MINT CHUTNEY
MAKES ABOUT 1¼ CUPS

Chutneys marry fresh fruits with spices in a sweet-tart-savory profile and add intrigue to simple fish dishes.

1 shallot, minced

1 tablespoon vegetable oil

1 teaspoon grated fresh ginger

½ teaspoon ground coriander

¼ teaspoon dry mustard

¼ teaspoon ground turmeric

⅛ teaspoon cayenne pepper

1 ripe but firm mango, peeled, pitted, and cut into ½-inch pieces (1½ cups)

2 tablespoons white wine vinegar

1 tablespoon dried currants

1 tablespoon packed light brown sugar

2 tablespoons coarsely chopped mint

1 | Combine shallot and 2 cups water in bowl; set aside. Heat 1 tablespoon oil in small saucepan over medium heat until shimmering. Add ginger, coriander, mustard, turmeric, and cayenne and cook until fragrant, about 30 seconds. Stir in mango, ¼ cup water, vinegar, currants, sugar, and ¼ teaspoon salt. Bring to simmer and cook, stirring occasionally, until mixture is thickened and reduced to about 1 cup, 10 to 15 minutes.

2 | Drain shallot; stir into chutney. Let chutney cool completely, about 30 minutes. Stir in mint. Season with salt and pepper to taste. (Chutney can be refrigerated for up to 2 days.)

OREGANO–BLACK OLIVE RELISH
MAKES ⅓ CUP

We like this assertive relish with sweet-fleshed fish like monkfish.

2 tablespoons extra-virgin olive oil

1 tablespoon minced fresh oregano

2 tablespoons red wine vinegar

1 small shallot, minced

1 teaspoon Dijon mustard

¼ teaspoon pepper

¼ cup pitted kalamata olives, minced

Combine oil and oregano in medium bowl and microwave until bubbling, about 30 seconds. Let mixture steep for 5 minutes, then whisk in vinegar, shallot, mustard, and pepper. Stir in olives. (Relish can be refrigerated for up to 2 days.)

2 | CREAMY SAUCES

These easy homemade sauces made with mayonnaise or yogurt add richness and creaminess to fish dishes.

CLASSIC TARTAR SAUCE
MAKES ABOUT 1 CUP

Be sure to rinse the capers before mincing them or else the sauce will have a strong, briny flavor. This is a classic with fried white fish but it pairs nicely with baked fish, too.

¾ cup mayonnaise

1½ teaspoons minced shallot

2 tablespoons capers, rinsed and minced

2 tablespoons sweet pickle relish

1½ teaspoons white vinegar

½ teaspoon Worcestershire sauce

Combine all ingredients in bowl, let sit for 15 minutes, and season with salt and pepper to taste. (Sauce can be refrigerated for up to 5 days.)

COMEBACK SAUCE
MAKES ABOUT 1 CUP

Good whenever you want to add richness and zippy heat to a fish dish, this Southern sauce is traditional with fried fish.

½ cup mayonnaise

⅓ cup chopped onion

2 tablespoons vegetable oil

2 tablespoons chili sauce

1 tablespoon ketchup

2½ teaspoons Worcestershire sauce

2½ teaspoons hot sauce

1 teaspoon yellow mustard

1 teaspoon lemon juice

1 garlic clove, minced

¾ teaspoon pepper

⅛ teaspoon paprika

Process all ingredients in blender until smooth, about 30 seconds. (Sauce can be refrigerated for up to 5 days.)

LEMON-GARLIC SAUCE
MAKES ABOUT ½ CUP

This creamy sauce includes classic fish pairings: lemon, garlic, and herbs.

- ½ cup mayonnaise
- 1 tablespoon minced fresh parsley
- ½ teaspoon grated lemon zest
- 1 small garlic clove, minced

Combine all ingredients in bowl; refrigerate for 15 minutes. (Sauce can be refrigerated for up to 3 days.)

HERB YOGURT SAUCE
MAKES ½ CUP

This sauce adds elegant richness to poached fish.

- ½ cup plain yogurt
- 2 tablespoons minced fresh dill, tarragon, basil, cilantro, or parsley
- ½ teaspoon grated lemon or lime zest plus 2 teaspoons juice
- 1 small garlic clove, minced

Combine all ingredients in bowl; refrigerate for 15 minutes. Season with salt and pepper to taste. (Sauce can be refrigerated for up to 2 days.)

OLD BAY DIPPING SAUCE
MAKES ABOUT ¾ CUP

Old Bay seasoning, a seafood favorite of the Mid-Atlantic states, can be found in the spice aisle.

- ½ cup plain Greek yogurt
- ¼ cup mayonnaise
- 1 tablespoon Dijon mustard
- 1 tablespoon Old Bay seasoning

Combine all ingredients in bowl, let sit for 15 minutes, and season with salt and pepper to taste. (Sauce can be refrigerated for up to 5 days.)

RÉMOULADE
MAKES ABOUT 1¼ CUP

This sauce is classic with crab cakes or grilled seafood. The egg yolks in this recipe are not cooked. If you prefer, ¼ cup Egg Beaters may be substituted.

- 2 large egg yolks
- 2 tablespoons water, plus extra as needed
- 4 teaspoons lemon juice
- 1 teaspoon Dijon mustard
- 1 small garlic clove, minced
- ¼ teaspoon table salt
- ¾ cup vegetable oil
- 1 tablespoon capers, rinsed
- 1 tablespoon minced fresh parsley
- 1 tablespoon sweet pickle relish

Process egg yolks, water, lemon juice, mustard, garlic, and salt in blender until combined, about 10 seconds, scraping down sides of blender jar as needed. With blender running, slowly add oil and process until sauce is emulsified, about 2 minutes. Add capers, parsley, and relish and pulse until combined but not smooth, about 10 pulses. Adjust consistency with extra water as needed. Season with salt and pepper to taste. (Rémoulade can be refrigerated for up to 3 days.)

---

3   HERB SAUCES

Bright, fragrant, and colorful, herb sauces are a vibrant choice for any fish dish.

ALMOND VINAIGRETTE
MAKES ABOUT ½ CUP

Almonds add richness and intriguing crunch to a traditional vinaigrette for dressing fish.

- ⅓ cup almonds, toasted
- 2 teaspoons honey
- 1 teaspoon Dijon mustard
- 4 teaspoons white wine vinegar
- 1 shallot, minced
- ⅓ cup extra-virgin olive oil
- 1 tablespoon cold water
- 1 tablespoon chopped fresh tarragon leaves

Place almonds in zipper-lock bag and, using rolling pin, pound until no pieces larger than ½ inch remain. Combine pounded almonds, honey, mustard, vinegar, and shallot in bowl. While whisking constantly, slowly drizzle in olive oil until combined. Add water and tarragon and whisk to combine, then season with salt and pepper to taste. Serve.

CILANTRO CHIMICHURRI
MAKES ABOUT ¾ CUP

Briefly soaking the dried oregano helps soften it and release its flavor. Chimichurri pairs well with meaty fish.

- 2 tablespoons hot water
- 2 tablespoons red wine vinegar
- 1 teaspoon dried oregano
- ½ cup minced fresh parsley
- ¼ cup minced fresh cilantro
- 3 garlic cloves, minced
- ½ teaspoon table salt
- ¼ teaspoon red pepper flakes
- ¼ cup extra-virgin olive oil

Combine hot water, vinegar, and oregano in bowl; let stand for 5 minutes. Add parsley, cilantro, garlic, salt, and pepper flakes and stir to combine. Whisk in oil until incorporated. (Sauce can be refrigerated for up to 2 days.)

SALSA VERDE
MAKES 1 CUP

In Europe, salsa verde is a popular with swordfish and grilled fish.

- 3 cups fresh parsley leaves
- 1 cup fresh mint leaves
- ½ cup extra-virgin olive oil
- 3 tablespoons white wine vinegar
- 2 tablespoons capers, rinsed
- 3 anchovy fillets, rinsed
- 1 garlic clove, minced
- ⅛ teaspoon table salt

Pulse all ingredients in food processor until mixture is finely chopped (mixture should not be smooth), about 10 pulses, scraping down sides of bowl as needed. Transfer mixture to bowl and serve. (Sauce can be refrigerated for up to 2 days; bring to room temperature before serving.)

GREEN ZHOUG
MAKES ABOUT ½ CUP

Zhoug is an Israeli hot sauce. Our vibrant green version is made with fresh herbs, chiles, and spices. Serve this sauce with rich fish like bluefish.

- 6 tablespoons extra-virgin olive oil
- ½ teaspoon ground coriander
- ¼ teaspoon ground cumin
- ¼ teaspoon ground cardamom
- ¼ teaspoon table salt
  Pinch ground cloves
- ¾ cup fresh cilantro leaves
- ½ cup fresh parsley leaves
- 2 green Thai chiles, stemmed and chopped
- 2 garlic cloves, minced

1 | Microwave oil, coriander, cumin, cardamom, salt, and cloves in covered bowl until fragrant, about 30 seconds; let cool to room temperature.

2 | Pulse oil-spice mixture, cilantro, parsley, chiles, and garlic in food processor until coarse paste forms, about 15 pulses, scraping down sides of bowl as needed. (Zhoug can be refrigerated for up to 4 days.)

ORANGE-LIME DRESSING
MAKES ½ CUP

Dressings like this one are a nice, refreshing alternative to creamy sauces for seared fish or to browned butter for scallops.

- ¼ cup extra-virgin olive oil
- 2 tablespoons orange juice
- 2 tablespoons lime juice
- 1 small shallot, minced
- 1 tablespoon minced fresh cilantro
- ⅛ teaspoon red pepper flakes

Whisk all ingredients together in bowl and season with salt and pepper to taste. Serve. (Dressing can be refrigerated for up to 2 days.)

4 | SAUCES FOR SHELLFISH

Raw or grilled bivalves taste like the sea, and while they're crisp and clean-tasting with just lemon juice and/or a small spoonful of a bright tomato salsa, you can elevate their sweet brininess with a splash of one of these traditional or rich, unique sauces.

MIGNONETTE SAUCE
MAKES ABOUT ¾ CUP

You can drizzle the sauce over the seafood or remove the meat of the shellfish with small forks and dip it into this tangy, potent sauce.

- ½ cup red wine vinegar
- 2 shallots, chopped fine
- 2 tablespoons lemon juice
- 2 tablespoons fresh parsley

Combine all ingredients in bowl.

SPICY LEMON BUTTER
MAKES ABOUT ¼ CUP

- 4 tablespoons unsalted butter
- 1 tablespoon hot sauce
- 1 teaspoon lemon juice
- ¼ teaspoon salt

Melt butter in small saucepan over medium-low heat. Off heat, add hot sauce, lemon juice, and salt. Cover and keep warm until serving.

TANGY SOY-CITRUS SAUCE
MAKES ABOUT ½ CUP

- ¼ cup low-sodium soy sauce
- 1½ teaspoons lemon juice
- 1½ teaspoons lime juice
- 1 scallion, sliced thin
- ½ teaspoon grated fresh ginger

Combine all ingredients in bowl.

5 COMPOUND BUTTERS

Compound butters—butter mixed with aromatic ingredients and spices—are a great accompaniment to simple roasted fish. As a dollop melts on the warm seafood, it becomes its own sauce. We like to make a double or triple batch, roll it into a log, and store it in the freezer so that flavored butter is always just a slice away.

TO MAKE COMPOUND BUTTER

Whip 8 tablespoons softened unsalted butter in bowl with fork until light and fluffy. Mix in any of the ingredient combinations listed below and season with salt and pepper to taste. Cover in plastic wrap and let rest so flavors blend, about 10 minutes, or roll into log and refrigerate. (Makes about ½ cup. Butter can be refrigerated in airtight container for up to 4 days or frozen, wrapped tightly in plastic wrap, for up to 2 months.)

CHIPOTLE-CILANTRO COMPOUND BUTTER

- 2 teaspoons minced canned chipotle chile in adobo sauce, plus 2 teaspoons adobo sauce
- 4 teaspoons minced fresh cilantro
- 2 garlic cloves, minced
- 2 teaspoons honey
- 2 teaspoons grated lime zest

CHIVE-LEMON MISO COMPOUND BUTTER

- ¼ cup white miso
- 2 teaspoons grated lemon zest plus 4 teaspoons juice
- ¼ teaspoon pepper
- ¼ cup minced fresh chives

PARSLEY-CAPER COMPOUND BUTTER

- ¼ cup minced fresh parsley
- 4 teaspoons capers, rinsed and minced

PARSLEY-LEMON COMPOUND BUTTER

- ¼ cup minced fresh parsley
- 4 teaspoons grated lemon zest

TARRAGON-LIME COMPOUND BUTTER

- ¼ cup minced scallion
- 2 tablespoons minced fresh tarragon
- 4 teaspoons lime juice

TAPENADE COMPOUND BUTTER

- 10 oil-cured black olives, pitted and chopped fine
- 1 anchovy fillet, rinsed and minced
- 1 tablespoon brandy
- 2 teaspoons minced fresh thyme
- 2 garlic cloves, minced
- ¼ teaspoon grated orange zest

PAN-SEARED TUNA STEAKS | SERVES 4

SUBSTITUTIONS NONE

4 (6- to 8-ounce) tuna steaks,
   1 inch thick
½ teaspoon table salt
¼ teaspoon pepper
½ teaspoon sugar
1 tablespoon vegetable oil

WHY THIS RECIPE WORKS

Moist and rare in the middle, with a delectable crust, pan-seared tuna is a popular entrée in restaurants. Make it at home, though, and the center is often cooked through while the exterior is pale. After testing ¾-inch-thick steaks, we found that a thickness of at least 1 inch is necessary to achieve both good browning on the exterior of the tuna and a rare center. A sprinkle of sugar, a very hot skillet to get a good quick sear, and 1 tablespoon of oil finish the job of creating a superior crust. A doneness temperature of 110 degrees may seem low, but tuna, like beef, continues to climb in temperature from residual heat as it's taken off the stove, so it was just right. A variation with a sesame seed coating gives the steaks an appealing crunchy crust to contrast the rare interior. Rubbing the fish with oil before coating helps the seeds adhere.

1 | Pat tuna dry with paper towels and sprinkle with salt and pepper. Sprinkle sugar evenly over 1 side of each steak.

2 | Heat oil in 12-inch nonstick skillet over medium-high heat until just smoking. Place steaks, sugared sides down, in skillet and cook, flipping every 1 to 2 minutes, until center is translucent red when checked with tip of paring knife and registers 110 degrees (for rare), 2 to 4 minutes. Transfer steaks to cutting board and slice ½ inch thick. Serve.

variation |
SESAME-CRUSTED PAN-SEARED TUNA STEAKS

Omit sugar. Spread ¾ cup sesame seeds in shallow dish. After patting tuna dry with paper towels, rub steaks all over with 1 tablespoon vegetable oil. After seasoning oiled steaks with salt and pepper, press both sides of each steak in sesame seeds to coat. Proceed with step 2 of recipe.

PAN-SEARED SWORDFISH STEAKS | SERVES 4

SUBSTITUTIONS HALIBUT • MAHI-MAHI • RED SNAPPER • STRIPED BASS

2 teaspoons vegetable oil

4 (6- to 8-ounce) skinless swordfish steaks, 1 inch thick

¾ teaspoon table salt

WHY THIS RECIPE WORKS

Most types of fish require a delicate touch; swordfish (and other firm white fish), on the other hand, is a fish for meat lovers. This fish's distinctive texture, combined with a sweet, mild flavor, could excite even a staunch carnivore—that is, when it doesn't turn out with soft, mushy flesh. Fast cooking is the way to go: Enzymes in swordfish called cathepsins snip the proteins that hold the muscle fibers together. In fish, cathepsins are highly active at 130 degrees. When swordfish is cooked very slowly, its cathepsins have a long time to turn its flesh soft and mushy. The fastest way to cook the swordfish indoors is in a skillet, but the exteriors overcooked quickly when we tried conventional searing, so we turned to frequent flipping. When a protein is flipped, the seared side, which is then facing up, is also quite hot. Some of its heat dissipates into the air, and some of it cooks the protein from the top down. The more often a protein is flipped, the more it will cook from both the bottom up and the top down. This method cooks the steaks throughout while also giving them golden-brown crusts. We've found that skin-on swordfish often buckles in the hot skillet. Ask your fishmonger to remove the skin or trim it yourself with a thin, sharp knife.

1 | Heat oil in 12-inch nonstick skillet over medium-high heat until shimmering. While oil heats, pat steaks dry with paper towels and sprinkle with salt.

2 | Place steaks in skillet and cook, flipping every 2 minutes, until golden brown and centers register 130 degrees, 7 to 11 minutes. Transfer to platter and let rest for 10 minutes. Serve.

HALIBUT EN COCOTTE WITH ROASTED GARLIC AND CHERRY TOMATOES | SERVES 4

SUBSTITUTIONS MAHI-MAHI • RED SNAPPER • STRIPED BASS • SWORDFISH

¼ cup extra-virgin olive oil, divided

2 garlic cloves, sliced thin

⅛ teaspoon red pepper flakes

Pinch plus ½ teaspoon table salt, divided

12 ounces cherry tomatoes, quartered

1 tablespoon capers, rinsed

1 teaspoon minced fresh thyme

4 (6- to 8-ounce) skinless halibut fillets, 1 inch thick

¼ teaspoon pepper

WHY THIS RECIPE WORKS

Cooking *en cocotte* (in a casserole) is a French technique that's a variation on braising: It uses a covered pot, a low oven temperature, and an extended cooking time to yield tender results—with no liquid in the pan. The cover seals in the juices so the fish cooks in them. Halibut is meaty, lean, and relatively high in collagen, with a tremendously clean flavor that benefitted from the technique. We created a bold sauce with a combination of olive oil, garlic, thyme, capers, red pepper flakes, and tomatoes that serves as a bright, briny counterpoint to the succulent halibut. Cooking sliced garlic in olive oil drew out its flavor, and once the garlic was golden brown, we stirred in the cherry tomatoes and placed the halibut on top. As the fish cooked, the tomatoes began to break down, releasing their juices and helping to build the sauce. Finishing with a splash of extra-virgin olive oil rounded out the flavors and gave the dish a lush feel.

1 | Adjust oven rack to lowest position and heat oven to 250 degrees. Cook 2 tablespoons oil, garlic, pepper flakes, and pinch salt in Dutch oven over medium-low heat until garlic is light golden, 2 to 4 minutes. Off heat, stir in tomatoes, capers, and thyme.

2 | Pat halibut dry with paper towels, sprinkle with remaining ½ teaspoon salt and pepper, and lay on top of tomatoes in pot. Place large piece of aluminum foil over pot and cover tightly with lid; transfer pot to oven. Cook until fish flakes apart when gently prodded with paring knife and registers 130 degrees, 35 to 40 minutes.

3 | Transfer halibut to platter and let rest for 10 minutes. Meanwhile, bring tomato mixture to simmer over medium-high heat until slightly thickened, about 2 minutes. Off heat, stir in remaining 2 tablespoons oil and season with salt and pepper to taste. Spoon sauce over halibut and serve.

variation |
SALMON EN COCOTTE

If using arctic char or wild salmon, cook the fillets to 120 degrees (for medium-rare).

Substitute 4 (6- to 8-ounce) 1-inch-thick skinless salmon fillets for halibut. Cook until center of salmon is still translucent when checked with tip of paring knife and registers 125 degrees (for medium-rare), reducing cooking time in step 2 to 25 to 35 minutes and skipping rest time in step 3.

GARLICKY ROASTED SHRIMP WITH PARSLEY AND ANISE | SERVES 4 TO 6

SUBSTITUTIONS NONE

2 pounds shell-on jumbo shrimp (16 to 20 per pound)

4 tablespoons unsalted butter, melted

¼ cup extra-virgin olive oil

6 garlic cloves, minced

1 teaspoon anise seeds

½ teaspoon table salt

½ teaspoon red pepper flakes

¼ teaspoon pepper

2 tablespoons minced fresh parsley

Lemon wedges

WHY THIS RECIPE WORKS
The flavor of sweet shrimp concentrates and deepens through roasting, but those benefits are only worth it if the quick-cooking flesh stays tender and moist in the process. For an ideal balance of profound flavor, we butterflied the shrimp. And although we slice through the shells, we don't remove them. These steps offered an easy route to flavor-infused flesh that was protected from the oven's heat by the shells. In fact, the shells are almost the best part, boosting flavor while also adding a layer of protection. After tossing the shrimp in melted butter and olive oil infused with garlic, spices, and herbs, we elevated them on a wire rack set in a rimmed baking sheet and slid them under the broiler. Within minutes, our shrimp emerged tender and deeply fragrant beneath flavorful, browned shells that you can choose to eat or remove.

1 | Adjust oven rack 4 inches from broiler element and heat broiler. Using kitchen shears or sharp paring knife, cut through shell of shrimp and devein but do not remove shell. Using paring knife, continue to cut shrimp ½ inch deep, taking care not to cut in half completely. Pat shrimp dry with paper towels.

2 | Combine melted butter, oil, garlic, anise seeds, salt, pepper flakes, and pepper in large bowl. Add shrimp and parsley to butter mixture and toss well, making sure butter mixture gets into interior of shrimp. Arrange shrimp in single layer on wire rack set in rimmed baking sheet.

3 | Broil shrimp until opaque and shells are beginning to brown, 2 to 4 minutes, rotating sheet halfway through broiling. Flip shrimp and continue to broil until second side is opaque and shells are beginning to brown, 2 to 4 minutes longer, rotating sheet halfway through broiling. Transfer shrimp to platter. Serve with lemon wedges.

variation |
GARLICKY ROASTED SHRIMP WITH CILANTRO AND LIME
Annatto powder, also called achiote, can be found with the Latin American foods at your supermarket. An equal amount of paprika can be substituted.

Omit butter and increase oil to ½ cup. Omit anise seeds and pepper. Add 2 teaspoons lightly crushed coriander seeds, 2 teaspoons grated lime zest, and 1 teaspoon annatto powder to oil mixture in step 2. Substitute ¼ cup minced fresh cilantro for parsley and lime wedges for lemon wedges.

ROASTED MUSSELS | SERVES 2 TO 4

SUBSTITUTIONS NONE

1 tablespoon extra-virgin olive oil

3 garlic cloves, minced

Pinch red pepper flakes

1 cup dry white wine

3 sprigs fresh thyme

2 bay leaves

4 pounds mussels, scrubbed and debearded

¼ teaspoon table salt

2 tablespoons unsalted butter, cut into 4 pieces

2 tablespoons minced fresh parsley

WHY THIS RECIPE WORKS

Ask almost anyone how to prepare mussels and they will no doubt recite the standard stovetop steaming steps. But in the test kitchen, we've learned that roasting them is far better. Mussels come in a range of sizes, making it a real challenge to cook them evenly, so rather than piling them into a Dutch oven (where the mussels closest to the stove's burner will inevitably overcook), we roast them en masse in the generous space afforded by a roomy roasting pan. After infusing white wine with garlic, thyme, and bay leaves on the stovetop, we stir in the mussels and seal them under a sheet of aluminum foil. The all-encompassing heat of a 500-degree oven gently heats the shellfish through so the majority of the mussels, both big and small, yawn open in about 15 minutes, their liquid mingling with the reduced wine for an irresistibly briny-sweet broth. A hit of butter melted into the concentrated cooking liquid before serving offers a rich complement to these simple but spectacular mussels. Discard any mussel with an unpleasant odor or with a cracked shell or a shell that won't close. Serve with crusty bread.

1 | Adjust oven rack to lowest position and heat oven to 500 degrees. Heat oil, garlic, and pepper flakes in large roasting pan over medium heat (over 2 burners, if possible) and cook, stirring constantly, until fragrant, about 30 seconds. Stir in wine, thyme sprigs, and bay leaves and boil until wine is slightly reduced, about 1 minute.

2 | Stir in mussels and salt. Cover pan tightly with aluminum foil and transfer to oven. Roast until most mussels have opened (a few may remain closed), 15 to 18 minutes.

3 | Remove pan from oven. Push mussels to sides of pan. Being careful of hot pan handles, add butter to center and whisk until melted. Discard thyme sprigs and bay leaves and stir in parsley. Serve.

variation |

ROASTED MUSSELS WITH LEEKS AND PERNOD

Omit pepper flakes and increase oil to 3 tablespoons. Cook oil; 1 pound leeks, white and light green parts only, halved lengthwise, sliced thin, and washed thoroughly; and garlic in roasting pan until leeks are wilted, about 3 minutes. Proceed with recipe as directed, omitting thyme sprigs and substituting ½ cup Pernod and ¼ cup water for wine, ¼ cup crème fraîche for butter, and chives for parsley.

CLANS STEAMED IN WHITE WINE | SERVES 4 TO 6

SUBSTITUTIONS NONE

1½ cups dry white wine

3 shallots, minced

4 garlic cloves, minced

1 bay leaf

4 pounds littleneck or cherrystone clams, scrubbed

3 tablespoons extra-virgin olive oil

2 tablespoons minced fresh parsley

WHY THIS RECIPE WORKS

It doesn't take a lot of embellishment to turn fresh clams into an exceptional dish, but it does take proper technique, as clams quickly turn from tender to tough and rubbery. Unlike mussels (see page 88), clams can cook evenly on the stovetop. This is because per pound there are fewer clams than mussels, so even if you are cooking 4 pounds of them, there aren't that many in the pot to deal with. This allows for easy stirring and more even cooking. To flavor our clams, we made a broth by quickly infusing wine with shallots, garlic, and bay leaf. As the clams steamed in the flavorful liquid, they opened up and released their juices into the pot, enhancing the broth. A drizzle of olive oil and some parsley finished the dish. Discard any clams with an unpleasant odor or with a cracked shell or a shell that won't close.

1 | Bring wine, shallots, garlic, and bay leaf to simmer in Dutch oven over medium-high heat and cook for 3 minutes. Add clams, cover, and cook, stirring twice, until clams open, 4 to 8 minutes. Using slotted spoon, transfer clams to serving bowl, discarding any that refuse to open.

2 | Off heat, whisk oil into cooking liquid until combined. Pour sauce over clams and sprinkle with parsley. Serve.

variation |
CLAMS STEAMED IN BEER
Substitute 2 cups mild lager for white wine.

CHAPTER 2

easy weeknight dinners

ROASTED SALMON AND BROCCOLI RABE WITH PISTACHIO GREMOLATA | SERVES 4

SUBSTITUTIONS ARCTIC CHAR • WILD SALMON

¼ cup shelled pistachios, toasted and chopped fine

2 tablespoons minced fresh parsley

2 garlic cloves, minced, divided

1 teaspoon grated lemon zest

1 pound broccoli rabe, trimmed and cut into 1½-inch pieces

2 tablespoons plus 2 teaspoons extra-virgin olive oil, divided

¾ teaspoon table salt, divided

½ teaspoon pepper, divided
  Pinch red pepper flakes

4 (6- to 8-ounce) skinless salmon fillets, 1 inch thick

WHY THIS RECIPE WORKS

Quick-cooking and, often, low-prep fish is an appealing dinner choice for the busy cook who needs a healthful, satisfying, and, of course, delicious dinner on the table. Streamlining things further and combining fish with a side in a one-pan dinner, then, is the ultimate in convenience—and appeal! Salmon pairs well with many quick-cooking vegetables because it doesn't emit a lot of rendered juices during cooking. We like it with broccoli rabe; the pleasant bitterness of this deeply green vegetable counterbalances the supremely rich salmon. We reinforced the broccoli rabe's bite with some red pepper flakes and minced garlic and then relegated it to one half of the sheet pan, resting the salmon on the other half. Roasted in a hot oven, the fillets cooked through to a silky medium-rare right as the broccoli rabe turned tender. To bring the dish together, we sprinkled a fresh, nutty pistachio gremolata over the top before serving. Broccoli rabe is sometimes called rapini. If using arctic char or wild salmon, cook the fillets to 120 degrees (for medium-rare) and start checking for doneness after 4 minutes.

1 | Adjust oven rack to middle position and heat oven to 450 degrees. Combine pistachios, parsley, half of garlic, and lemon zest in small bowl; set gremolata aside until ready to serve.

2 | Toss broccoli rabe, 2 tablespoons oil, ¼ teaspoon salt, ¼ teaspoon pepper, pepper flakes, and remaining garlic together in bowl. Arrange on half of rimmed baking sheet. Pat salmon dry with paper towels, rub with remaining 2 teaspoons oil, and sprinkle with remaining ½ teaspoon salt and remaining ¼ teaspoon pepper. Arrange salmon skinned side down on empty half of sheet.

3 | Roast until center of salmon is still translucent when checked with tip of paring knife and registers 125 degrees (for medium-rare) and broccoli rabe is tender, 8 to 12 minutes. Sprinkle salmon with gremolata and serve.

LEMON-HERB ROASTED COD WITH CRISPY GARLIC POTATOES | SERVES 4

SUBSTITUTIONS BLACK SEA BASS • HADDOCK • HAKE • POLLOCK

- 3 tablespoons extra-virgin olive oil, divided
- 1½ pounds russet potatoes, unpeeled, sliced into ¼-inch-thick rounds
- 3 garlic cloves, minced
- ¾ teaspoon table salt, divided
- ½ teaspoon pepper, divided
- 4 (6- to 8-ounce) skinless cod fillets, 1 inch thick
- 3 tablespoons unsalted butter, cut into ¼-inch pieces
- 4 sprigs fresh thyme
- 4 thin lemon slices

WHY THIS RECIPE WORKS

White fish and potatoes may most famously mingle in Fish and Chips (page 298), but the combination is equally delicious in this ingenious recipe, which delivers perfectly roasted cod and potatoes—all in one sheet pan. We roasted fillets in elegant fashion, atop beds of shingled sliced spuds, which gave the quick-cooking fish some insulation from the sheet pan. Slicing and microwaving starchy russets with garlic and oil before roasting jump-started their cooking so the potatoes and fish finished at the same time. To infuse the mild cod with flavor, we topped each fillet with butter, thyme sprigs, and slices of lemon, allowing the three components to gently baste and season the cod as it roasted. In the end, we were met with four beautiful portions of rich, tender cod and fragrant, crisp potatoes.

1 | Adjust oven rack to lower-middle position and heat oven to 425 degrees. Brush rimmed baking sheet with 1 tablespoon oil. Combine potatoes, garlic, remaining 2 tablespoons oil, ¼ teaspoon salt, and ¼ teaspoon pepper in bowl. Microwave until potatoes are just tender, 12 to 14 minutes.

2 | Shingle potatoes into 4 rectangular piles that measure roughly 4 by 6 inches on prepared sheet. Pat cod dry with paper towels, sprinkle with remaining ½ teaspoon salt and remaining ¼ teaspoon pepper, and lay 1 fillet skinned side down on each potato pile. Place butter, thyme sprigs, and lemon slices on top of cod.

3 | Roast until fish flakes apart when gently prodded with paring knife and registers 135 degrees, 15 to 18 minutes. Slide spatula underneath potatoes and cod, gently transfer to individual plates, and serve.

ROASTED COD WITH ARTICHOKES AND SUN-DRIED TOMATOES | SERVES 4

SUBSTITUTIONS BLACK SEA BASS • HADDOCK • HAKE • POLLOCK

3 cups jarred whole baby artichokes packed in water, halved, rinsed, and patted dry

¾ cup oil-packed sun-dried tomatoes, drained, ¼ cup oil reserved, divided

¾ teaspoon table salt, divided

½ teaspoon pepper, divided

½ cup pitted kalamata olives, chopped coarse

1 teaspoon grated lemon zest plus 1 tablespoon juice

4 (6- to 8-ounce) skinless cod fillets, 1 inch thick

2 tablespoons chopped fresh basil

WHY THIS RECIPE WORKS

A meal from a casserole dish doesn't mean bland and old-fashioned. This roasted cod dish is bold and bright, inspired by the flavors of the Mediterranean. Using a pantry-friendly combination of tender jarred baby artichokes, sweet sun-dried tomatoes, and briny kalamata olives strategically as our base for the fish kept prep work light and promised to infuse the mild fish with multiple layers of flavor. We roasted the artichokes first, tossing them with the tomatoes' packing oil to deepen their subtle flavor. We stirred in the sun-dried tomatoes and chopped olives as well as some grated lemon zest before finally nestling in the cod fillets, brushing them with more of the potent tomato oil. By the end of its brief roasting time, this fuss-free cod dinner boasted incredible complexity, with fish infusing vegetables and vegetables infusing fish. While we prefer the flavor and texture of jarred whole baby artichokes, you can substitute 18 ounces frozen artichoke hearts, thawed and patted dry.

1| Adjust oven rack to middle position and heat oven to 450 degrees. Toss artichokes with 2 tablespoons tomato oil, ¼ teaspoon salt, and ¼ teaspoon pepper in bowl, then spread into even layer in 13 by 9-inch baking dish. Roast artichokes until lightly browned, about 15 minutes.

2| Remove baking dish from oven and stir in olives, lemon zest, tomatoes, and 1 tablespoon tomato oil. Pat cod dry with paper towels and nestle into vegetables in dish. Brush cod with remaining 1 tablespoon tomato oil and sprinkle with remaining ½ teaspoon salt and ¼ teaspoon pepper.

3| Roast until fish flakes apart when gently prodded with paring knife and registers 135 degrees, 15 to 18 minutes. Drizzle with lemon juice and sprinkle with basil. Serve.

HAKE IN SAFFRON BROTH WITH CHORIZO AND POTATOES | SERVES 4

SUBSTITUTIONS BLACK SEA BASS • COD • HADDOCK • POLLOCK

1 tablespoon extra-virgin olive oil, plus extra for drizzling

1 onion, chopped fine

3 ounces Spanish-style chorizo sausage, sliced ¼ inch thick

4 garlic cloves, minced

¼ teaspoon saffron threads, crumbled

1 (8-ounce) bottle clam juice

¾ cup water

½ cup dry white wine

4 ounces small red potatoes, unpeeled, sliced ¼ inch thick

1 bay leaf

4 (6- to 8-ounce) skinless hake fillets, 1 inch thick

½ teaspoon table salt

¼ teaspoon pepper

1 teaspoon lemon juice

2 tablespoons minced fresh parsley

WHY THIS RECIPE WORKS

Saffron's distinctive aroma and bright yellow-orange color pair particularly well with delicate seafood; we wanted to utilize the exquisite spice in a Spanish-inspired seafood dish. Versatile, mild hake, a favorite white fish in Spain, was the perfect stage for the saffron. We created a flavorful saffron broth with aromatics, white wine, and clam juice in which we braised the fish, and then we ladled the broth over the fillets before serving. For additional flavor, we added spicy Spanish-style chorizo to the pan with the onion and sautéed the sausage until browned. This lent a subtle but not overwhelming heat—more of a smoky flavor—to the broth. Then we looked for a starchy element to round out the meal. Waxy red potatoes, sliced into coins to mirror the slices of chorizo, brought in just the right creaminess to soak up the flavorful broth. A hit of lemon added brightness to the broth at the end of cooking, and a sprinkle of parsley and drizzle of olive oil on the flaky fish, swimming in the fragrant saffron liquid, brought it all together. Use small red potatoes measuring 1 to 2 inches in diameter. You will need a 12-inch skillet with a tight-fitting lid for this recipe. Serve with crusty bread.

1 | Heat oil in 12-inch skillet over medium heat until shimmering. Add onion and chorizo and cook until onion is softened and lightly browned, 5 to 7 minutes. Stir in garlic and saffron and cook until fragrant, about 30 seconds. Stir in clam juice, water, wine, potatoes, and bay leaf and bring to simmer. Reduce heat to medium-low, cover, and cook until potatoes are almost tender, about 10 minutes.

2 | Pat hake dry with paper towels and sprinkle with salt and pepper. Nestle hake skinned side down into skillet and spoon some broth over top. Bring to simmer, cover, and cook until potatoes are tender and fish flakes apart when gently prodded with paring knife and registers 135 degrees, 10 to 12 minutes.

3 | Carefully transfer hake to individual shallow bowls. Using slotted spoon, divide potatoes and chorizo evenly among bowls. Discard bay leaf. Stir lemon juice into broth and season with salt and pepper to taste. Spoon broth over hake, sprinkle with parsley, and drizzle with extra oil. Serve.

SEARED BREADED HADDOCK WITH BROCCOLI AND VINAIGRETTE | SERVES 4

SUBSTITUTIONS BLACK SEA BASS • COD • HAKE • POLLOCK

1 pound broccoli florets, cut into 2-inch pieces

½ cup extra-virgin olive oil, divided

1 teaspoon table salt, divided

¾ teaspoon pepper, divided

2 tablespoons minced fresh oregano

2 tablespoons minced fresh parsley

1 tablespoon lemon juice

1 small garlic clove, minced

½ cup panko bread crumbs

4 (6- to 8-ounce) skinless haddock fillets, 1 inch thick

4 teaspoons mayonnaise

WHY THIS RECIPE WORKS

Breaded haddock is a classic baked affair, but the breading process, while effective, dirties a couple too many dishes for a weeknight, and the lower oven temperature required isn't usually hospitable to side dishes. We took the fish out of the oven, searing bread crumbs onto its top surface to browned, golden perfection. Cooking the fish with the panko side down toasted the crumbs and used heat to seal them to the fish so all we needed was a spread of binding mayonnaise to make the crumbs stick rather than go through the drudge of a wet dredge. And the stovetop cooking freed up the oven for pretty much anything; we chose to roast satisfying broccoli to pair with the light fish. A vinaigrette brought the two components together with brightness and an earthy herbal aroma from fresh oregano, a surprising but welcome change to the lighter herbs (like parsley and dill) typically served with fish. This completed the transformation of the typical baked New England dinner.

1 | Adjust oven rack to lowest position and heat oven to 450 degrees. Toss broccoli with 2 tablespoons oil, ¼ teaspoon salt, and ¼ teaspoon pepper on rimmed baking sheet. Roast until browned and tender, 14 to 16 minutes; transfer to platter and tent with aluminum foil to keep warm.

2 | Meanwhile, combine oregano, parsley, lemon juice, garlic, ¼ cup oil, ¼ teaspoon salt, and ¼ teaspoon pepper in bowl; set aside. Spread panko in shallow dish. Pat haddock dry with paper towels and sprinkle with remaining ½ teaspoon salt and remaining ¼ teaspoon pepper. Spread 1 teaspoon mayonnaise on 1 side of each fillet. Press mayonnaise-coated sides of fillets into panko.

3 | Heat remaining 2 tablespoons oil in 12-inch nonstick skillet over medium heat until shimmering. Place fillets panko side down in skillet and cook until browned, about 7 minutes. Flip fillets and cook until fish flakes apart when gently prodded with paring knife and registers 135 degrees, about 2 minutes. Add haddock to platter with broccoli and whisk vinaigrette to recombine. Serve with vinaigrette.

COD BAKED IN FOIL WITH LEEKS AND CARROTS | SERVES 4

SUBSTITUTIONS BLACK SEA BASS • HADDOCK • HAKE • POLLOCK

4 tablespoons unsalted butter, softened

1 teaspoon minced fresh thyme

2 garlic cloves, minced, divided

1¼ teaspoons grated lemon zest, divided, plus lemon wedges for serving

1 teaspoon table salt, divided

½ teaspoon pepper, divided

2 tablespoons minced fresh parsley

2 carrots, peeled and cut into matchsticks

1 pound leeks, white and light green parts only, halved lengthwise, washed thoroughly, and cut into matchsticks

¼ cup dry white wine

4 (6- to 8-ounce) skinless cod fillets, 1 inch thick

WHY THIS RECIPE WORKS

Cooking fish *en papillote*, or folded in a pouch, is a classic French technique that, in addition to being incredibly easy (and virtually cleanup-free), allows the fish to steam in its own juices and thus emerge moist and flavorful. We found that foil was easier to work with than parchment and created a leakproof seal. Placing the packets on the lower-middle rack of the oven, close to the heat source, concentrated the exuded liquid in the packets and deepened its flavor. Vegetable selection was important: Hardier vegetables like potatoes and squash failed to cook evenly in the packets, and more water-absorbing vegetables like eggplant turned to mush when enclosed. Carrots and leeks, cut into elegant matchsticks, cooked at the same rate as the fish and made a nice presentation as a bed for the fish when everything emerged from the packets. A zesty compound butter topping the fish added richness and flavor (and color contrast to the fish) as it melted. Open each packet promptly after baking to prevent overcooking. To test for doneness without opening the foil packets, use a permanent marker to mark an "X" on the outside of the foil where the fish fillet is the thickest, then insert an instant-read thermometer through the "X" into the fish to measure its internal temperature.

1 | Adjust oven rack to lower-middle position and heat oven to 450 degrees. Mash butter, thyme, half of garlic, ¼ teaspoon lemon zest, ¼ teaspoon salt, and ⅛ teaspoon pepper in bowl. Combine parsley, remaining garlic, and remaining 1 teaspoon lemon zest in second bowl. Combine carrots, leeks, ¼ teaspoon salt, and ⅛ teaspoon pepper in third bowl.

2 | Lay four 16 by 12-inch rectangles of aluminum foil on counter with short sides parallel to counter edge. Divide vegetable mixture evenly among foil rectangles, arranging in center of lower half of each sheet of foil. Mound vegetables slightly and sprinkle with wine. Pat cod dry with paper towels, sprinkle with remaining ½ teaspoon salt and remaining ¼ teaspoon pepper, and place on top of vegetables. Spread butter mixture over fillets. Fold top half of foil over fish, then tightly crimp edges into rough 9 by 6-inch packets.

3 | Place packets on rimmed baking sheet (they may overlap slightly) and bake until cod registers 135 degrees, about 15 minutes. Carefully open packets, allowing steam to escape away from you. Using thin metal spatula, gently slide cod and vegetables, and any accumulated juices, onto individual plates. Sprinkle with parsley mixture and serve with lemon wedges.

ASSEMBLING FOIL PACKETS

1 | Divide ingredients among aluminum foil rectangles, arranging in center of lower half of each sheet of foil.

2 | Fold top half of foil over fish, then tightly crimp edges into rough 9 by 6-inch packets.

THAI-STYLE HALIBUT AND CREAMY COCONUT COUSCOUS PACKETS | SERVES 4

SUBSTITUTIONS MAHI-MAHI • RED SNAPPER • STRIPED BASS • SWORDFISH

1½ cups couscous

2 cups boiling water plus ¼ cup room-temperature water

1 cup canned coconut milk

¼ cup chopped fresh cilantro

2 tablespoons fish sauce

1 tablespoon grated fresh ginger

3 garlic cloves, minced

⅛ teaspoon red pepper flakes

4 (6- to 8-ounce) skinless halibut fillets, 1 inch thick

2 tablespoons rice vinegar

WHY THIS RECIPE WORKS

For an interesting spin on the simple technique of cooking fish in a packet (see page 112), we decided to cook halibut fillets on a grain, and we chose a bed of fluffy couscous (since it's super-quick-cooking) with a zesty Thai-inspired sauce to modernize the delicate French technique. We mixed coconut milk, ginger, garlic, fish sauce, a little cilantro (for a fresh herbal touch), and red pepper flakes (for a subtle hint of heat). The bold sauce transformed the couscous into a rich and creamy side and infused the fish with flavor. We found that if we used too much sauce during cooking, the couscous soaked up all of the liquid and ended up gummy while the fish tasted bland. So we reserved some of the sauce to drizzle over the fish before serving. For an accurate measurement of boiling water, bring a full kettle of water to a boil and then measure out the desired amount. To test for doneness without opening the foil packets, use a permanent marker to mark an "X" on the outside of the foil where the fish fillet is the thickest, then insert an instant-read thermometer through the "X" into the fish to measure its internal temperature.

1 | Adjust oven rack to middle position and heat oven to 400 degrees. Combine couscous and boiling water in bowl, cover with plastic wrap, and let sit until liquid is absorbed and couscous is tender, about 5 minutes. Fluff couscous with fork and season with salt and pepper to taste. Combine room-temperature water, coconut milk, cilantro, fish sauce, ginger, garlic, and pepper flakes in small bowl.

2 | Lay four 16 by 12-inch rectangles of aluminum foil on counter with short sides parallel to counter edge. Divide couscous evenly among foil rectangles, arranging in center of lower half of each sheet of foil. Pat halibut dry with paper towels, place on top of couscous, and spoon 1 tablespoon coconut sauce over top of each fillet; reserve remaining coconut sauce for serving. Fold top half of foil over fish and couscous, then tightly crimp edges into rough 9 by 6-inch packets.

3 | Place packets on rimmed baking sheet (they may overlap slightly) and bake until halibut registers 130 degrees, 15 to 18 minutes. Carefully open packets, allowing steam to escape away from you, then let halibut rest in packets for 10 minutes.

4 | Microwave reserved coconut sauce until warmed through, about 1 minute, then stir in rice vinegar. Using thin metal spatula, gently slide halibut and couscous onto individual plates, drizzle with sauce, and serve.

ROASTED SNAPPER AND VEGETABLES WITH MUSTARD SAUCE | SERVES 4

SUBSTITUTIONS HALIBUT • MAHI-MAHI • STRIPED BASS • SWORDFISH

- 6 tablespoons plus 2 teaspoons extra-virgin olive oil, divided
- ¼ cup minced fresh chives
- 2 tablespoons whole-grain mustard
- 1 tablespoon honey, divided
- 1 teaspoon grated lemon zest plus 2 teaspoons juice
- 1 teaspoon plus pinch table salt, divided
- ¾ teaspoon plus pinch pepper, divided
- 1 pound small red potatoes, unpeeled, halved
- 1 pound broccoli florets, cut into 2-inch pieces
- ½ teaspoon paprika
- 4 (6- to 8-ounce) skinless red snapper fillets, 1 inch thick

WHY THIS RECIPE WORKS

Looking for a from-the-sea swap for typical meat and potatoes? Try this easy one-pan meal of hearty red snapper, golden potatoes, and charred broccoli. We started by tossing halved red potatoes and broccoli florets with oil, salt, and pepper separately and placing each on one side of a baking sheet to roast in a hot oven. We removed the broccoli once it was just tender and attractively charred, and added our fillets of red snapper to the freed-up side of the sheet, dropping the oven temperature to allow the fish to cook more gently and the browned potatoes to continue cooking through. A simple mix of lemon zest, honey, and paprika brushed on before roasting the fillets added just enough flavor and color to the fish, and paired beautifully with a bright sauce of chives and grainy mustard. Use small red potatoes measuring 1 to 2 inches in diameter.

1 | Adjust oven rack to lowest position and heat oven to 500 degrees. Combine 2 tablespoons oil, chives, mustard, 1 teaspoon honey, lemon juice, pinch salt, and pinch pepper in bowl; set mustard sauce aside until ready to serve. Brush rimmed baking sheet with 1 tablespoon oil.

2 | Toss potatoes with 1 tablespoon oil, ¼ teaspoon salt, and ¼ teaspoon pepper in bowl. Place potatoes, cut sides down, on half of sheet. In now-empty bowl, toss broccoli with 2 tablespoons oil, ¼ teaspoon salt, and ¼ teaspoon pepper, then place on empty side of sheet. Roast until potatoes are golden brown and broccoli is spotty brown and tender, 12 to 14 minutes, rotating sheet halfway through roasting.

3 | While potatoes and broccoli roast, combine 1 teaspoon oil, lemon zest, paprika, remaining 2 teaspoons honey, remaining ½ teaspoon salt, and remaining ¼ teaspoon pepper in small bowl; microwave until bubbling and fragrant, 10 to 15 seconds. Pat red snapper dry with paper towel, brush skinned sides of fillets with remaining 1 teaspoon oil, then brush tops of fillets with honey mixture.

4 | Remove sheet from oven and reduce oven temperature to 275 degrees. Transfer broccoli to platter and tent with aluminum foil to keep warm. Place red snapper, skinned side down, on now-empty side of sheet. Continue to roast until fish flakes apart when gently prodded with paring knife and registers 130 degrees, 6 to 8 minutes longer, rotating sheet halfway through roasting.

5 | Transfer potatoes and red snapper to platter with broccoli. Tent with foil and let sit for 10 minutes. Serve with mustard sauce.

THAI CURRY RICE WITH MAHI-MAHI | SERVES 4

SUBSTITUTIONS HALIBUT • RED SNAPPER • STRIPED BASS • SWORDFISH

1 tablespoon vegetable oil

1½ cups long-grain white rice, rinsed

8 ounces white mushrooms, trimmed and sliced thin

1 (8-ounce) can sliced bamboo shoots, rinsed

2 teaspoons grated fresh ginger

3 scallions, white and green parts separated and sliced thin on bias

2¼ cups water

1 teaspoon table salt, divided

¾ cup canned coconut milk

3 tablespoons red curry paste

4 (6- to 8-ounce) skinless mahi-mahi fillets, 1 inch thick

¼ teaspoon pepper

Lime wedges

WHY THIS RECIPE WORKS

Mahi-mahi is meaty, lean, and mild, perfect for pairing with the rich and aromatic flavors of Thai curry. To create an entire Thai-inspired meal without lots of prep and multiple pans, we layered the components of both the fish curry and rice all in one skillet and timed everything just right for maximum flavor with minimum effort. The rice component became a multidimensional medley when we sautéed it (and therefore toasted it) with meaty mushrooms, crunchy bamboo shoots, uniquely spicy ginger, and fresh scallions. After adding water to the skillet and giving the rice a 10-minute head start, we placed the mahi-mahi fillets on top of the simmering rice and drizzled everything with a simple mixture of coconut milk and Thai curry paste. The fish finished cooking at the same time that the rice got irresistibly crispy on the bottom. All we needed was a sprinkle of more scallions, a few spoonfuls of sauce, and a squeeze of lime to get this impressive dinner on the table. You will need a 12-inch nonstick skillet with a tight-fitting lid for this recipe.

1 | Heat oil in 12-inch nonstick skillet over medium heat until shimmering. Add rice, mushrooms, bamboo shoots, ginger, and scallion whites. Cook, stirring often, until edges of rice begin to turn translucent, about 2 minutes. Add water and ½ teaspoon salt and bring to boil. Cover, reduce heat to low, and simmer for 10 minutes.

2 | Whisk coconut milk and curry paste together in bowl. Pat mahi-mahi dry with paper towels and sprinkle with remaining ½ teaspoon salt and pepper. Lay fillets, skinned side down, on top of rice mixture in skillet and drizzle with one-third of coconut-curry sauce. Cover skillet and cook until liquid is absorbed, rice is tender, and fish flakes apart when gently prodded with paring knife and registers 130 degrees, 10 to 12 minutes. Remove from heat and let sit, covered, for 10 minutes.

3 | Microwave remaining coconut-curry sauce mixture until warm, about 1 minute. Drizzle remaining coconut-curry sauce over fish and rice mixture and sprinkle with scallion greens. Serve with lime wedges.

SAUTÉED TILAPIA WITH BLISTERED GREEN BEANS AND PEPPER RELISH | SERVES 4

SUBSTITUTIONS CATFISH • FLOUNDER • SOLE

4 (6- to 8-ounce) skinless tilapia fillets, halved lengthwise down natural seam

1¼ teaspoons table salt, divided

1 cup jarred roasted red peppers, patted dry and chopped fine

¼ cup whole almonds, toasted and chopped fine

¼ cup extra-virgin olive oil, divided

1 tablespoon chopped fresh basil

1 teaspoon sherry vinegar

⅛ teaspoon plus ¼ teaspoon pepper, divided

1 pound green beans, trimmed

¼ cup water

WHY THIS RECIPE WORKS

Readily available, economical, and sustainable, tilapia has a lot going for it before it even hits your plate. But even better, the firm fillets are easy to handle and flip during sautéing, and this mild fish becomes golden and crispy on the outside but stays moist on the inside. To create a meal centered around tilapia, we first made a simple, flavorful relish of jarred roasted red peppers, crunchy almonds, and basil that would add color, brightness and contrasting texture to the fish. Then we quickly steamed green beans until tender, letting them continue to cook uncovered to get attractive and flavorful browning. Setting the beans aside, we finished our meal by sautéing the tilapia in the same skillet until golden and perfectly cooked. Draining and drying the peppers keeps the relish from becoming watery. You will need a 12-inch nonstick skillet with a tight-fitting lid for this recipe.

1 | Sprinkle tilapia with ½ teaspoon salt and let sit at room temperature for 15 minutes. Meanwhile combine red peppers, almonds, 1 tablespoon oil, basil, vinegar, ¼ teaspoon salt, and ⅛ teaspoon pepper in bowl; set aside relish until ready to serve.

2 | Combine green beans, water, 1 tablespoon oil, remaining ½ teaspoon salt, and remaining ¼ teaspoon pepper in 12-inch nonstick skillet. Cover and cook over medium-high heat, shaking pan occasionally, until water has evaporated, 6 to 8 minutes. Uncover and continue to cook until green beans are blistered and browned, about 2 minutes longer. Transfer to platter and tent with foil to keep warm.

3 | Pat tilapia dry with paper towels. Heat remaining 2 tablespoons oil in now-empty skillet over high heat until just smoking. Add thick halves of tilapia fillets to skillet and cook, tilting and gently shaking skillet occasionally to distribute oil, until golden brown, 2 to 3 minutes. Using 2 spatulas, flip fillets and cook until second sides are golden brown, 2 to 3 minutes; transfer to platter with green beans.

4 | Return skillet to high heat. When oil is just smoking, add thin halves of fillets and cook until golden brown, about 1 minute. Flip and cook until second sides are golden brown, about 1 minute. Transfer tilapia to platter with green beans. Serve with relish.

MOROCCAN FISH AND COUSCOUS PACKETS | SERVES 4

SUBSTITUTIONS CATFISH • FLOUNDER • SOLE

½ cup minced fresh cilantro, divided

¼ cup extra-virgin olive oil

2 tablespoons grated fresh ginger

4 teaspoons smoked paprika

4 garlic cloves, minced

4 teaspoons grated lemon zest, divided, plus 2 tablespoons juice

2 teaspoons ground cumin

1½ teaspoons table salt, divided

½ teaspoon pepper, divided

½ teaspoon brown sugar

¼ teaspoon red pepper flakes

1½ cups couscous

2 cups boiling water

4 (6- to 8-ounce) skinless tilapia fillets, ¾ inch thick

WHY THIS RECIPE WORKS

Moroccan chermoula is a spice and herb mixture that's at once bright, herbaceous, and earthy, packing a punch of flavor wherever it's used. Pairing it with quick-cooking tilapia and couscous baked in foil made an incredibly flavorful, fragrant meal effortless. We placed mounds of fluffy, lemony couscous on the foil and then topped them with chermoula-slathered tilapia fillets before sealing the packets. For an accurate measurement of boiling water, bring a full kettle of water to a boil and then measure out the desired amount. To test for doneness without opening the foil packets, use a permanent marker to mark an "X" on the outside of the foil where the fish fillet is the thickest, then insert an instant-read thermometer through the "X" into the fish to measure its internal temperature. If using catfish, flounder, or sole, you may need to tuck the tapered ends under to achieve a more uniform thickness for even cooking. For catfish, start checking for doneness at 26 minutes; for flounder, start checking for doneness at 16 minutes; for sole, start checking for doneness at 23 minutes.

1 | Adjust oven rack to middle position and heat oven to 400 degrees. Combine 6 tablespoons cilantro, oil, ginger, paprika, garlic, 1 tablespoon lemon zest, lemon juice, cumin, ½ teaspoon salt, ¼ teaspoon pepper, sugar, and pepper flakes in bowl; set chermoula aside.

2 | Combine couscous, ½ teaspoon salt, and boiling water in bowl, cover with plastic wrap, and let sit until liquid is absorbed and couscous is tender, about 5 minutes. Fluff couscous with fork, stir in remaining 1 teaspoon lemon zest, and season with salt and pepper to taste.

3 | Lay four 16 by 12-inch rectangles of aluminum foil on counter with short sides parallel to counter edge. Divide couscous evenly among foil rectangles, arranging in center of lower half of each foil sheet. Pat tilapia dry with paper towels and sprinkle with remaining ½ teaspoon salt and remaining ¼ teaspoon pepper. Place tilapia on top of couscous and spoon 1 tablespoon chermoula over top of each fillet; reserve remaining chermoula for serving. Fold top half of foil over fish and couscous, then tightly crimp edges into rough 9 by 6-inch packets.

4 | Place packets on rimmed baking sheet (they may overlap slightly) and bake until fish registers 135 degrees, 20 to 24 minutes. Carefully open packets, allowing steam to escape away from you. Using thin metal spatula, gently slide couscous and tilapia onto individual plates, then sprinkle with remaining 2 tablespoons cilantro. Serve with remaining chermoula.

CORNMEAL CATFISH AND SOUTHWESTERN CORN | SERVES 4

SUBSTITUTIONS FLOUNDER • SOLE • TILAPIA

2 tablespoons unsalted butter

8 ounces Spanish-style chorizo sausage, diced

1 red bell pepper, stemmed, seeded, and chopped fine

1 jalapeño chile, stemmed, seeded, and minced

1 shallot, minced

1 garlic clove, minced

1 teaspoon table salt, divided

4 cups frozen corn

2 teaspoons minced fresh cilantro

½ cup all-purpose flour

½ cup cornmeal

4 (6- to 8-ounce) skinless catfish fillets, split lengthwise down natural seam

¼ teaspoon pepper

1 cup vegetable oil

WHY THIS RECIPE WORKS

Deep-fried catfish (like anything deep-fried) is a treat (see page 63), but sometimes we want the cornmeal crunch of coated catfish as the centerpiece of a simple weeknight meal. Frying in a shallow skillet gave the catfish a crispy coating, and we needed only to coat the fish pieces in a one-step dry dredge since they wouldn't be jumping into a pot of bubbling oil. Pairing the catfish with a corn side brought out the sweet, buttery flavor of the coating; for more interest, we spiced it up with chorizo and ingredients common to Southwestern cooking like bell pepper, chile, and cilantro. We were able to shallow-fry the fish in the same skillet we'd sautéed the corn in, giving "fish fry" a new definition.

1 | Adjust oven rack to middle position and heat oven to 200 degrees. Melt butter in 12-inch nonstick skillet over medium-high heat. Add chorizo and cook until lightly browned, about 2 minutes. Stir in bell pepper, jalapeño, shallot, garlic, and ½ teaspoon salt and cook until bell pepper begins to brown, about 5 minutes. Stir in corn and cook until warmed through, about 2 minutes. Stir in cilantro and season with salt and pepper to taste; transfer to ovensafe bowl, cover with aluminum foil, and keep warm in oven.

2 | Meanwhile, whisk flour and cornmeal together in shallow dish. Pat catfish dry with paper towels and season with remaining ½ teaspoon salt and pepper. Working with 1 fillet at a time, dredge in cornmeal mixture, pressing gently to adhere; transfer to large plate and repeat with remaining pieces.

3 | Wipe out now-empty skillet with paper towels and line ovensafe platter with triple layer of paper towels. Heat oil over medium-high heat until shimmering. Carefully place 4 fillets in skillet and cook until golden on both sides, about 2 minutes per side. Transfer catfish to prepared platter to drain, then transfer platter to oven to keep warm. Repeat with remaining 4 pieces. Serve with corn mixture.

PAN-SEARED TROUT WITH BRUSSELS SPROUTS AND BACON | SERVES 4

SUBSTITUTIONS NONE

1 pound Brussels sprouts, trimmed and halved

1 teaspoon table salt, divided

½ teaspoon pepper, divided

3 slices bacon, cut into ½-inch pieces

1 shallot, minced

2 garlic cloves, minced

½ teaspoon minced fresh thyme

3 tablespoons cornstarch

3 (8- to 10-ounce) boneless, butterflied whole trout, halved between fillets

¼ cup vegetable oil, divided

WHY THIS RECIPE WORKS

You don't often see hardy Brussels sprouts in seafood recipes, but we love the heft they provide to an otherwise delicate dish—and trout, especially when given a crispy skin, has a presence that easily stands up to the sprouts. Smoky bacon, a classic with Brussels sprouts, also paired well with the trout and tied the dish together; we used the rendered fat from the crispy bits to sauté the Brussels sprouts, which we jump-started in the microwave to get tender enough to cook through in the skillet. A little cornstarch on the trout helped it achieve extra-crispy skin to complement the texture of the Brussels sprouts.

1 | Adjust oven rack to middle position and heat oven to 200 degrees. Combine Brussels sprouts, 1 tablespoon water, ½ teaspoon salt, and ¼ teaspoon pepper in bowl. Microwave, covered, until sprouts are just tender, about 5 minutes; drain.

2 | Meanwhile, cook bacon in 12-inch nonstick skillet over medium-high heat until crispy, about 5 minutes. Using slotted spoon, transfer bacon to paper towel–lined plate. Add shallot to fat left in skillet and cook until softened, about 2 minutes. Stir in garlic and thyme and cook until fragrant, about 30 seconds. Add drained sprouts and cook until lightly browned, about 3 minutes; transfer to ovensafe platter and keep warm in oven.

3 | Spread cornstarch in shallow dish. Pat trout dry with paper towels, sprinkle with remaining ½ teaspoon salt and remaining ¼ teaspoon pepper, then dredge in cornstarch, pressing gently to adhere. Wipe out now-empty skillet with paper towels, add 2 tablespoons oil, and heat over high heat until shimmering. Lay 3 pieces trout skin side down in skillet and reduce heat to medium-high. Cook until golden on both sides and fish flakes apart when gently prodded with paring knife, about 4 minutes per side; transfer to platter with sprouts and keep warm in oven.

4 | Wipe out now-empty skillet with paper towels and repeat with remaining 2 tablespoons oil and remaining 3 trout pieces. Serve with Brussels sprouts and sprinkle with bacon.

LEMON-POACHED HALIBUT WITH ROASTED FINGERLING POTATOES | SERVES 4

SUBSTITUTIONS MAHI-MAHI • RED SNAPPER • STRIPED BASS • SWORDFISH

1½ pounds fingerling potatoes, halved lengthwise

2 tablespoons extra-virgin olive oil, divided

1 teaspoon table salt, divided

¾ teaspoon pepper, divided

8 ounces grape tomatoes, halved

4 (6- to 8-ounce) skinless halibut fillets, 1 inch thick

½ teaspoon dried oregano

8 thin slices lemon

2 tablespoons minced fresh parsley

WHY THIS RECIPE WORKS

We've learned that potatoes don't cook well *en papillote* (see page 112), so we pair our fish with lighter vegetables in packets so they cook through to the perfect texture. But the concentrated, flavorful broth that's created inside the foil seemed like a lovely medium for tying fish and potatoes together on the plate, so we roasted elegant fingerlings outside the packets—right underneath the parcels on a baking sheet for maximum utilization of the oven (we preroasted the potatoes so they finished at the same time as the packets). Adding grape tomatoes to the packets with the halibut provided pops of brightness. We slid the moist poached fish, infused with lemon and oregano, and colorful tomatoes on top of the beautifully browned fingerlings before serving. Use potatoes of a similar size to ensure consistent cooking. To test for doneness without opening the foil packets, use a permanent marker to mark an "X" on the outside of the foil where the fish fillet is the thickest, then insert an instant-read thermometer through the "X" into the fish to measure its internal temperature.

1 | Adjust oven rack to lower-middle position and heat oven to 450 degrees. Toss potatoes with 2 teaspoons oil, ½ teaspoon salt, and ½ teaspoon pepper. Arrange potatoes cut side down on rimmed baking sheet in even layer. Roast until cut sides begin to brown, about 10 minutes.

2 | Meanwhile, lay four 16 by 12-inch rectangles of foil on counter with short sides parallel to counter edge. Divide tomatoes evenly among foil rectangles, arranging in center of lower half of each sheet of foil, then place 1 fillet on each tomato pile. Sprinkle halibut with oregano, remaining ½ teaspoon salt, and remaining ¼ teaspoon pepper, then top each with 2 lemon slices and 1 teaspoon oil. Fold top half of foil over halibut and tomatoes, then tightly crimp edges into rough 9 by 6-inch packets.

3 | Place packets on top of potatoes on sheet and bake until fish registers 130 degrees, about 15 minutes. Carefully open packets, allowing steam to escape away from you, and let halibut rest in packets for 10 minutes.

4 | Divide potatoes among 4 individual serving bowls. Using thin metal spatula, gently slide halibut and tomatoes onto potatoes, then pour accumulated juices over top. Sprinkle with parsley and serve.

BAKED HALIBUT WITH CHERRY TOMATOES AND CHICKPEAS | SERVES 4

SUBSTITUTIONS MAHI-MAHI • RED SNAPPER • STRIPED BASS • SWORDFISH

- 2 (15-ounce) cans chickpeas, rinsed
- 12 ounces cherry tomatoes, halved
- 2 shallots, minced
- 5 tablespoons extra-virgin olive oil, divided
- ¼ cup chicken or vegetable broth
- 5 garlic cloves, minced
- 1 tablespoon grated lemon zest plus 1 tablespoon juice
- 2 teaspoons ground coriander, divided
- 2 teaspoons paprika, divided
- 1 teaspoon table salt, divided
- ½ teaspoon pepper
- 4 (6- to 8-ounce) skinless halibut fillets, 1 inch thick
- ⅛ teaspoon cayenne pepper
- 2 tablespoons chopped fresh cilantro

WHY THIS RECIPE WORKS

We wanted to infuse a white fish like halibut with robust flavors it doesn't often see and bake it with a savory side dish for a quick, complete dinner. We focused first on a rich spice rub for the halibut that would impart flavor as it sat. An oil-based rub with coriander and paprika provided aromatic flavor and nice color, and a little bit of cayenne added just the right amount of subtle heat. We tried many accompaniments, from green beans to potatoes, to pair with this spiced fish, but our favorite turned out to be a combination of chickpeas and cherry tomatoes. The chickpeas soaked up the spiced broth, and some of the tomatoes broke down in the oven, creating a bright sauce that complemented the halibut nicely. We flavored the chickpeas and tomatoes with more coriander and paprika—plus shallots, garlic, and lemon to brighten all of the warmth. We simply nestled the halibut fillets into the chickpea-tomato mixture before baking. When the halibut was cooked through, we drizzled it with some fruity olive oil and sprinkled it with fresh cilantro for an herbal note.

1 | Adjust oven rack to middle position and heat oven to 400 degrees. Combine chickpeas, tomatoes, shallots, 1 tablespoon oil, broth, garlic, lemon zest and juice, 1 teaspoon coriander, 1 teaspoon paprika, ½ teaspoon salt, and pepper in 13 by 9-inch baking dish.

2 | Pat halibut dry with paper towels. Combine 2 tablespoons oil, remaining 1 teaspoon coriander, remaining 1 teaspoon paprika, remaining ½ teaspoon salt, and cayenne in bowl. Add halibut and gently turn to coat. Nestle halibut into chickpea mixture in dish and bake until fish flakes apart when gently prodded with paring knife and registers 130 degrees, 20 to 30 minutes. Remove baking dish from oven, tent with aluminum foil, and let rest for 10 minutes.

3 | Drizzle with remaining 2 tablespoons oil and sprinkle with cilantro. Serve.

SEARED TUNA STEAKS WITH WILTED FRISÉE AND MUSHROOM SALAD | SERVES 4

SUBSTITUTIONS NONE

3 tablespoons harissa, divided
1 tablespoon lemon juice
6 tablespoons extra-virgin olive oil, divided
1–3 tablespoons hot water (110 degrees)
1 shallot, halved and sliced thin
1¼ pounds cremini mushrooms, trimmed and halved if small or quartered if large
12 ounces shiitake mushrooms, stemmed and sliced ½ inch thick
1 teaspoon table salt, divided
1 head frisée (6 ounces), cut into 1-inch pieces
4 (6- to 8-ounce) tuna steaks, 1 inch thick
¼ teaspoon pepper
½ teaspoon sugar
2 tablespoons chopped fresh mint

WHY THIS RECIPE WORKS

Our Tuna Steaks with Cucumber-Peanut Salad (page 136) are a great summer meal; here we warm up the flavors for colder months, pairing harissa-drizzled sliced tuna with an elegant and earthy frisée and mushroom salad for a simple dish with multiple layers of flavor and textures. The North African harissa works well with the meaty tuna steaks and earthy mushrooms in this dish. We cooked the mushrooms—a mix of cremini and shiitake for even more complex flavor—first and wilted the frisée simply by adding hot harissa-coated mushrooms to it; this also transported some of their flavor. Use harissa paste for this recipe rather than harissa sauce; note that spiciness will vary greatly by brand. You will need a 12-inch nonstick skillet with a tight-fitting lid for this recipe.

1 | Whisk 2 tablespoons harissa, lemon juice, and 1 tablespoon oil together in bowl. Whisk in hot water, 1 tablespoon at a time, until sauce is pourable; set aside until ready to serve.

2 | Heat 2 tablespoons oil in 12-inch nonstick skillet over medium heat until shimmering. Add shallot and cook until softened, about 2 minutes. Add cremini mushrooms, shiitake mushrooms, and ½ teaspoon salt, cover, and cook, stirring occasionally, until mushrooms have released their liquid, 8 to 10 minutes.

3 | Uncover skillet, add 2 tablespoons oil, and cook, stirring occasionally, until mushrooms are deep golden brown and tender, 10 to 12 minutes. Add remaining 1 tablespoon harissa and cook until fragrant, about 30 seconds. Transfer mushrooms to large bowl, add frisée, and toss to combine; set aside. Wipe skillet clean with paper towels.

4 | Pat tuna dry with paper towels and sprinkle with remaining ½ teaspoon salt and pepper. Sprinkle sugar evenly over 1 side of each steak. Heat remaining 1 tablespoon oil in now-empty skillet over medium-high heat until just smoking. Place steaks sugared sides down in skillet and cook, flipping every 1 to 2 minutes, until center is translucent red when checked with tip of paring knife and registers 110 degrees (for rare), 2 to 4 minutes.

5 | Transfer steaks to cutting board and slice ½ inch thick. Sprinkle mint over mushroom mixture and season with salt and pepper to taste. Drizzle tuna with reserved harissa sauce and serve with salad.

SHRIMP RISOTTO | SERVES 4 TO 6

1 pound extra-large shrimp (21 to 25 per pound), peeled, deveined, and tails removed, shells reserved

1¾ teaspoons table salt, divided

1 tablespoon vegetable oil

7 cups water

15 black peppercorns

2 bay leaves

4 tablespoons unsalted butter, divided

1 onion, chopped fine

1 fennel bulb, stalks discarded, bulb halved, cored, and chopped fine

⅛ teaspoon baking soda

2 garlic cloves, minced

1½ cups Arborio rice

¾ cup dry white wine

1 ounce Parmesan cheese, grated (½ cup), plus extra for serving

¼ cup minced fresh chives

½ teaspoon grated lemon zest plus 1 tablespoon juice, plus lemon wedges for serving

WHY THIS RECIPE WORKS

Risotto can contain any number of shellfish, but for a simplified dish, we selected shrimp—our favorite here, as bites of sweet shrimp are a nice relief from the richness of the surrounding creamy rice. We seared shrimp shells to extract their flavorful compounds, added water and seasonings, and simmered for just 5 minutes to make a seafood broth for cooking our risotto. Meanwhile, we salted the shrimp to ensure they would remain plump and juicy through the cooking process. We simmered the risotto covered to help it cook evenly due to the natural agitation of starches when grain hit grain in the pot—no frequent stirring or sore wrists here for a creamy product. Adding the chopped shrimp off the heat allowed them to cook very gently and retain their delicate texture. Final additions of butter, lemon, chives, and Parmesan contributed complexity while keeping things light.

1 | Cut each shrimp crosswise into thirds, then toss with ½ teaspoon salt; set aside. Heat oil in Dutch oven over high heat until shimmering. Add reserved shrimp shells and cook, stirring frequently, until shells begin to turn spotty brown, 2 to 4 minutes. Add water, peppercorns, bay leaves, and 1 teaspoon salt and bring to boil. Reduce heat to low and simmer for 5 minutes. Strain stock through fine-mesh strainer set over large bowl, pressing on solids with rubber spatula to extract as much liquid as possible; discard solids.

2 | Melt 2 tablespoons butter in now-empty pot over medium heat. Add onion, fennel, baking soda, and remaining ¼ teaspoon salt. Cook, stirring frequently, until vegetables are softened but not browned, 8 to 10 minutes (volume will be dramatically reduced and onion will have mostly disintegrated). Add garlic and stir until fragrant, about 30 seconds. Add rice and cook, stirring frequently, until grains are translucent around edges, about 3 minutes.

3 | Add wine and cook, stirring constantly, until fully absorbed, 2 to 3 minutes. Stir 4 cups stock into rice mixture; reduce heat to medium-low, cover, and simmer until almost all liquid has been absorbed and rice is just al dente, 16 to 18 minutes, stirring twice during simmering.

4 | Add ¾ cup stock to risotto and stir gently and constantly until risotto becomes creamy, about 3 minutes. Stir in Parmesan and shrimp. Cover pot and let sit off heat for 5 minutes.

5 | Gently stir chives, lemon zest and juice, and remaining 2 tablespoons butter into risotto. Season with salt and pepper to taste. Stir in additional stock to loosen texture of risotto, if desired. Serve, passing lemon wedges and extra Parmesan separately.

TUSCAN SHRIMP AND BEANS | SERVES 4 TO 6

SUBSTITUTIONS NONE

- ¼ cup extra-virgin olive oil, divided
- 1 pound large shell-on shrimp (26 to 30 per pound), peeled, deveined, and tails removed, shells reserved
- 1 cup water
- 1 onion, chopped fine
- 4 garlic cloves, peeled, halved lengthwise, and sliced thin
- 2 anchovy fillets, rinsed, patted dry, and minced
- ½ teaspoon table salt
- ¼ teaspoon red pepper flakes
- ⅛ teaspoon pepper
- 2 (15-ounce) cans cannellini beans (1 can drained and rinsed, 1 can left undrained)
- 1 (14.5-ounce) can diced tomatoes, drained
- ¼ cup shredded fresh basil
- ½ teaspoon grated lemon zest plus 1 tablespoon juice

WHY THIS RECIPE WORKS

Brothy white bean dishes are commonplace in Tuscany, and we love a version with shrimp included—the tender bite of the shrimp is a nice foil to the creamy beans. These beans are typically quite fragrant with aromatics, but to give them fuller seafood flavor, we made a quick concentrated shrimp-shell stock and used it to simmer the beans. We also cooked the shrimp with the beans rather than separately (we added the shrimp late in the cooking process, and reduced the heat so they cooked gently) and sautéed minced anchovies with the aromatics. Canned beans and canned tomatoes make this dish fast and doable at any time of year; plus, the liquid from one of the cans of beans lends the dish nice body. Plenty of fresh basil plus lemon juice and zest provide freshness and nice acidity. You will need a 12-inch skillet with a tight-fitting lid for this recipe. Serve with crusty bread.

1 | Heat 1 tablespoon oil in 12-inch skillet over medium heat until shimmering. Add shrimp shells and cook, stirring frequently, until they begin to turn spotty brown and skillet starts to brown, 5 to 6 minutes. Remove skillet from heat and carefully add water. When bubbling subsides, return skillet to medium heat and simmer gently, stirring occasionally, for 5 minutes. Strain mixture through fine-mesh strainer set over large bowl, pressing on solids with rubber spatula to extract as much liquid as possible; discard solids (you should have about ¼ cup liquid). Wipe skillet clean with paper towels.

2 | Heat 2 tablespoons oil, onion, garlic, anchovies, salt, pepper flakes, and pepper in now-empty skillet over medium-low heat. Cook, stirring occasionally, until onion is softened, about 5 minutes. Add 1 can drained beans, 1 can beans and their liquid, tomatoes, and shrimp stock and bring to simmer. Simmer, stirring occasionally, for 15 minutes.

3 | Reduce heat to low, add shrimp, cover, and cook, stirring once during cooking, until shrimp are just opaque, 5 to 7 minutes. Remove skillet from heat and stir in basil and lemon zest and juice. Season with salt and pepper to taste. Transfer to serving dish, drizzle with remaining 1 tablespoon oil, and serve.

ONE-PAN SHRIMP PAD THAI | SERVES 4

SUBSTITUTIONS NONE

8 ounces (⅜-inch-wide) rice noodles

⅓ cup lime juice (3 limes)

⅓ cup packed brown sugar

¼ cup fish sauce

1 pound extra-large shrimp (21 to 25 per pound), peeled, deveined, and tails removed

2 tablespoons vegetable oil

4 garlic cloves, minced

8 ounces (4 cups) mung bean sprouts

¼ cup chopped fresh cilantro

¼ cup dry-roasted peanuts, chopped

WHY THIS RECIPE WORKS

With its sweet-and-sour, salty-spicy sauce; plump, sweet shrimp; and tender rice noodles, pad thai is Thailand's best-known noodle dish. But making it at home can be a chore, thanks to lengthy ingredient lists with hard-to-find items. We found we could achieve just the right balance of flavors for a satisfying supper even after streamlining the recipe to its most crucial components. There's no tamarind required in our sauce, which uses a simple combination of fish sauce, lime juice, and brown sugar. And shrimp alone was enough to give this dish heft—no need for dried shrimp in addition, or eggs. The dish boasts great texture as well, with crisp-fresh mung beans and chopped peanuts providing crunch against the juicy shrimp and just-chewy-enough rice noodles. To get the texture of the rice noodles just right, we first soaked them in hot water so they'd start to soften, then stir-fried them in the pan. Do not substitute other types of noodles for the rice noodles here. This dish progresses quickly after step 2; have your ingredients ready to go by then.

1 | Soak noodles in 3 quarts boiling water until softened and pliable but not fully tender, stirring occasionally, about 15 minutes. Drain noodles and rinse under cold running water until water runs clear. Drain well and set aside.

2 | Whisk lime juice, sugar, and fish sauce together in bowl. Pat shrimp dry with paper towels. Heat oil in 12-inch nonstick skillet over medium heat until just beginning to smoke. Add shrimp and garlic and cook, stirring occasionally, until shrimp are just opaque, about 4 minutes. Transfer to plate and tent loosely with aluminum foil.

3 | Add noodles and lime juice mixture to now-empty skillet and cook over medium heat until sauce is thickened slightly, about 4 minutes. Add sprouts and shrimp to skillet and cook until shrimp are opaque throughout and noodles are well coated and tender, about 3 minutes. Sprinkle with cilantro and peanuts and serve.

BAKED SHRIMP AND ORZO WITH FETA AND TOMATOES | SERVES 4

SUBSTITUTIONS NONE

1 tablespoon extra-virgin olive oil

1 red onion, chopped fine

1 red bell pepper, stemmed, seeded, and cut into ½-inch pieces

4 garlic cloves, minced

2 teaspoons minced fresh oregano or ½ teaspoon dried

2 cups orzo

Pinch saffron threads, crumbled

3 cups chicken or vegetable broth

1 (14.5-ounce) can diced tomatoes, drained with juice reserved

1 pound extra-large shrimp (21 to 25 per pound), peeled, deveined, and tails removed

½ teaspoon table salt

¼ teaspoon pepper

½ cup frozen peas

3 ounces feta cheese, crumbled (¾ cup)

2 scallions, sliced thin

Lemon wedges

WHY THIS RECIPE WORKS

This dish has a lot going for it, and the sum is an amazing composition of its harmonious parts: creamy pasta, juicy shrimp, fresh-tasting peas, briny feta cheese. Power ingredients like pleasantly assertive oregano, floral saffron, canned tomatoes, and the aforementioned cheese bring plenty of Mediterranean flavor to the dish. To guarantee perfectly cooked shrimp and pasta, we settled on a combined stovetop-oven cooking method. Sautéing the orzo in the aromatics unlocked its toasty notes; we then stirred in chicken broth and the drained juice from a can of diced tomatoes. As the orzo cooked to al dente, its released starch (similar to a risotto) created a sauce with a subtly creamy texture. To prevent the shrimp from overcooking, we stirred them right into the orzo, along with the reserved tomatoes and frozen peas, and transferred the skillet to the oven to cook through gently. Sprinkling on the feta at this point delivered an appealing browned, cheesy crust. Make sure that the orzo is al dente, or slightly firm to the bite; otherwise it may overcook in the oven. You will need a 12-inch ovensafe nonstick skillet for this recipe.

1 | Adjust oven rack to middle position and heat oven to 375 degrees. Heat oil in 12-inch ovensafe nonstick skillet over medium heat until shimmering. Add onion and bell pepper and cook until vegetables are softened, 5 to 7 minutes. Stir in garlic and oregano and cook until fragrant, about 30 seconds. Stir in orzo and saffron and cook, stirring often, until orzo is lightly browned, about 4 minutes.

2 | Stir in broth and reserved tomato juice, bring to simmer, and cook, stirring occasionally, until orzo is al dente, 10 to 12 minutes.

3 | Pat shrimp dry with paper towels and sprinkle with salt and pepper. Stir shrimp, tomatoes, and peas into orzo mixture in skillet, then sprinkle feta evenly over top. Transfer skillet to oven and bake until shrimp are opaque throughout and feta is lightly browned, about 20 minutes.

4 | Carefully remove skillet from oven and sprinkle scallions over top. Serve with lemon wedges.

LEMONY LINGUINE WITH SHRIMP AND SPINACH | SERVES 4 TO 6

SUBSTITUTIONS NONE

5 tablespoons extra-virgin olive oil, divided

2 teaspoons grated lemon zest plus ¼ cup juice (2 lemons)

1 garlic clove, minced

½ teaspoon table salt

1 ounce Parmesan cheese, grated (½ cup)

1 pound jumbo shrimp (16 to 20 per pound), peeled, deveined, and shells reserved

2½ cups dry white wine

2½ cups water

1 (8-ounce) bottle clam juice

1 pound linguine

5 ounces (5 cups) baby spinach

¼ cup shredded fresh basil

2 tablespoons unsalted butter, softened

WHY THIS RECIPE WORKS

Sweet shrimp, bright lemon, and tender spinach come together seamlessly in this one-pan seafood-supplemented interpretation of the Italian classic *spaghetti al limone*. As with many of Italy's favorite dishes, the original is a lesson in simplicity, where a few simple ingredients contribute to an intensely flavored dish. To coax the most flavor out of every component in this unique version, we simmered the shrimp shells with wine and then enhanced this quick stock with clam juice. This liquid was used both to poach our shrimp and to cook our pasta, which became infused with briny flavor as the sauce reduced. We found the flat, wide strands of linguine stood up better to the shrimp and spinach than did more traditional spaghetti. Baby spinach wilted immediately when stirred into the warm pasta along with our shrimp. To add plenty of lemon flavor, we whisked up a lemon-Parmesan dressing, using the citrus's zest as well as its juice, and poured this over the still-hot pasta to maximize absorption and create a nutty, creamy sauce. Finally, we finished the dish with a healthy pat of butter and a sprinkle of fresh basil.

1 | Whisk ¼ cup oil, lemon zest and juice, garlic, and salt together in bowl, then stir in Parmesan until thick and creamy; set aside.

2 | Heat remaining 1 tablespoon oil in Dutch oven over medium heat until shimmering. Add shrimp shells and cook, stirring frequently, until beginning to turn spotty brown, 2 to 4 minutes. Stir in wine and simmer until reduced slightly, about 5 minutes. Strain mixture through fine-mesh strainer set over large bowl, pressing on solids with rubber spatula to extract as much liquid as possible; discard solids.

3 | Return reduced wine mixture to pot, add water and clam juice, and bring to gentle simmer over medium heat. Stir in shrimp and cook until just opaque, about 2 minutes. Using slotted spoon, transfer shrimp to clean bowl.

4 | Add pasta to liquid left in pot, increase heat to high, and bring to boil. Reduce heat to medium and simmer vigorously, stirring often, until pasta is tender, 12 to 14 minutes.

5 | Off heat, stir in spinach and shrimp and let sit until spinach is wilted and shrimp are opaque throughout, about 30 seconds. Stir in lemon sauce, basil, and butter until butter is melted and pasta is well coated. Season with salt and pepper to taste and serve.

SHRIMP FRA DIAVOLO WITH LINGUINE

| SERVES 4 TO 6

SUBSTITUTIONS NONE

1 pound large shrimp (26 to 30 per pound), peeled, deveined, and tails removed

6 tablespoons extra-virgin olive oil, divided

1½ teaspoons table salt, divided, plus salt for cooking pasta

1 teaspoon red pepper flakes, divided

¼ cup cognac or brandy

12 garlic cloves, minced, divided

1 (28-ounce) can diced tomatoes, drained

1 cup dry white wine

½ teaspoon sugar

1 pound linguine

¼ cup minced fresh parsley

WHY THIS RECIPE WORKS

Shrimp fra diavolo, the 20th-century Italian American combo of shrimp, tomatoes, garlic, and hot pepper served over pasta is, at its best, lively and piquant, the tangy tomatoes countering the sweet and briny shrimp, and the pepper and garlic providing a spirited—and, yes, devilish—kick. The key is to achieve this without being so heavy-handed with the spice that it overwhelms the dish. We began by searing the shrimp briefly to help them caramelize and enrich their sweetness, then added red pepper flakes, which took on a toasty, earthy note. Then we flambéed the shrimp with cognac—the combined forces of cognac and flame further brought out the shrimp's sweet notes and imbued our fra diavolo with the cognac's richness and complexity. We sautéed the garlic slowly for mellow, nutty flavor, and reserved some raw garlic for a last-minute punch of heat and spice. Simmered diced tomatoes and some white wine (balanced by a bit of sugar) completed our perfect fra diavolo. Before flambéing, roll up long sleeves, tie back long hair, and turn off the exhaust fan and lit burners; use a long match or wooden skewer. This dish is fairly spicy; to make it milder, reduce the amount of pepper flakes.

1 | Toss shrimp with 1 tablespoon oil, ¾ teaspoon salt, and ½ teaspoon pepper flakes in bowl. Heat 1 tablespoon oil in 12-inch skillet over high heat until just smoking. Add shrimp mixture in single layer and cook, without stirring, until shrimp is spotty brown, about 30 seconds. Off heat, flip shrimp, add cognac, and let warm through, about 5 seconds. Wave lit match over pan until cognac ignites, then shake pan to distribute flames. When flames subside, transfer shrimp mixture to clean bowl.

2 | Let now-empty skillet cool slightly, about 3 minutes. Cook 3 tablespoons oil and three-quarters garlic in cooled skillet over low heat, stirring constantly, until garlic foams and is sticky and straw-colored, about 10 minutes. Stir in tomatoes, wine, sugar, remaining ¾ teaspoon salt, and remaining ½ teaspoon pepper flakes. Increase heat to medium-high and simmer until thickened, about 8 minutes.

3 | Meanwhile, bring 4 quarts water to boil in large pot. Add pasta and 1 tablespoon salt and cook, stirring often, until al dente. Reserve ½ cup cooking water, then drain pasta and return it to pot.

4 | Stir shrimp and any accumulated juices, remaining garlic, and parsley into sauce and bring to brief simmer to warm shrimp through, about 1 minute. Off heat, stir in remaining 1 tablespoon oil. Add several large spoonfuls of sauce (without shrimp) to pasta and toss to combine. Season with salt to taste and add reserved cooking water as needed to adjust consistency. Divide pasta among individual bowls. Top each bowl with remaining sauce and shrimp. Serve.

STIR-FRIED SHRIMP AND BROCCOLI

| SERVES 4

⅓ cup dry sherry

2 tablespoons oyster sauce

2 tablespoons water

1 tablespoon soy sauce

2 teaspoons Asian chili-garlic sauce

2 teaspoons cornstarch

1 tablespoon vegetable oil

2 scallions, white and green parts separated and sliced thin

1 tablespoon grated fresh ginger

2 garlic cloves, minced

1 pound broccoli, florets cut into 1-inch pieces, stalks peeled and sliced ¼ inch thick

1 pound extra-large shrimp (21 to 25 per pound), peeled, deveined, and tails removed

WHY THIS RECIPE WORKS

Quick-cooking shrimp should be a perfect match for stir-fries, which by definition come together quickly. But "quick cooking" can become "quickly overcooked" if you're not careful. In fact, instead of actually stir-frying shrimp in a hot skillet, which can result in rubbery, dry shrimp, we preferred poaching them gently in the sauce for shrimp that stayed plump, moist, and tender. Hearty broccoli was a bright green counterpoint to the sweet shrimp. Aromatics—ginger, scallions, and garlic—contributed depth to the sauce of savory dry sherry, umami-rich oyster sauce and soy sauce, and a hit of Asian chili-garlic for pleasant spiciness. You will need a 12-inch nonstick skillet with a tight-fitting lid for this recipe. The stir-fry portion of this recipe moves quickly, so be sure to have all your ingredients in place before starting.

1 | Whisk sherry, oyster sauce, water, soy sauce, chili-garlic sauce, and cornstarch together in bowl; set aside.

2 | Cook oil, scallion whites, ginger, and garlic in 12-inch nonstick skillet over high heat, mashing mixture into skillet until fragrant, about 30 seconds. Stir in sherry–oyster sauce mixture, broccoli, and shrimp and bring to simmer. Reduce heat to medium-low, cover, and cook, stirring occasionally, until shrimp are opaque throughout and sauce has thickened, 3 to 5 minutes. Transfer to serving platter and sprinkle with scallion greens. Serve.

FRIED BROWN RICE WITH PORK AND SHRIMP | SERVES 6

SUBSTITUTIONS NONE

2 cups short-grain brown rice

2¾ teaspoons table salt, divided

10 ounces boneless country-style pork ribs, trimmed

1 tablespoon hoisin sauce

2 teaspoons honey

⅛ teaspoon five-spice powder
Small pinch cayenne pepper

4 teaspoons vegetable oil, divided

8 ounces large shrimp (26 to 30 per pound), peeled, deveined, tails removed, and cut into ½-inch pieces

3 eggs, lightly beaten

1 tablespoon toasted sesame oil

6 scallions, white and green parts separated and sliced thin on bias

2 garlic cloves, minced

1½ teaspoons grated fresh ginger

2 tablespoons soy sauce

1 cup frozen peas

WHY THIS RECIPE WORKS

Using the brown variety puts a modern spin on fried rice and provides a hearty base to stand up to the barbecued pork, shrimp, and scrambled eggs in this dish. To balance the nuttier flavor of brown rice, we used more ginger, garlic, and soy sauce than we do for white-rice recipes. Staggering the cooking was key to ensuring every component was perfectly cooked—no rubbery shrimp or eggs. The stir-fry portion of this recipe moves quickly, so be sure to have all your ingredients in place before starting.

1 | Bring 3 quarts water to boil in large pot. Add rice and 2 teaspoons salt. Cook, stirring occasionally, until rice is tender, about 35 minutes. Drain well and return to pot. Cover and set aside.

2 | Meanwhile, cut pork into 1-inch pieces and slice each piece against grain ¼ inch thick. Combine pork with hoisin, honey, five-spice powder, cayenne, and ½ teaspoon salt and toss to coat; set aside.

3 | Heat 1 teaspoon vegetable oil in 12-inch nonstick skillet over medium-high heat until shimmering. Add shrimp in single layer and cook, without moving, until golden brown, about 90 seconds. Stir and continue to cook until opaque throughout, about 90 seconds longer. Push shrimp to 1 side of skillet. Add 1 teaspoon vegetable oil to cleared side of skillet. Add eggs to clearing and sprinkle with remaining ¼ teaspoon salt. Using rubber spatula, stir eggs gently until set but still wet, about 30 seconds. Stir eggs into shrimp and continue to cook, breaking up large pieces of egg, until eggs are fully cooked, about 30 seconds longer. Transfer shrimp-egg mixture to clean bowl.

4 | Heat remaining 2 teaspoons vegetable oil in now-empty skillet over medium-high heat until shimmering. Add pork in even layer. Cook pork, without moving, until well browned, 2 to 3 minutes. Flip pork and cook, without moving, until cooked through and caramelized on second side, 2 to 3 minutes. Transfer to bowl with shrimp-egg mixture.

5 | Heat sesame oil in now-empty skillet over medium-high heat until shimmering. Add scallion whites and cook, stirring frequently, until well browned, about 1 minute. Stir in garlic and ginger and cook until fragrant and beginning to brown, 30 to 60 seconds. Add soy sauce and half of rice and stir until all ingredients are fully incorporated, making sure to break up clumps of ginger and garlic. Reduce heat to medium-low and add remaining rice, pork mixture, and peas. Stir until all ingredients are evenly incorporated and heated through, 2 to 4 minutes. Remove from heat and stir in scallion greens. Transfer to platter and serve.

BAKED SCALLOPS WITH COUSCOUS, LEEKS, AND ORANGE VINAIGRETTE | SERVES 4

SUBSTITUTIONS NONE

1 pound leeks, white and light green parts only, halved lengthwise, sliced thin, and washed thoroughly

1 cup Israeli couscous

5 tablespoons extra-virgin olive oil, divided, plus extra for serving

4 garlic cloves, minced

1⅛ teaspoons table salt, divided

½ teaspoon pepper, divided

Pinch saffron threads (optional)

¾ cup boiling water

¼ cup dry white wine

1½ pounds large sea scallops, tendons removed

2 tablespoons minced fresh tarragon

1 tablespoon white wine vinegar

½ teaspoon Dijon mustard

½ teaspoon grated orange zest plus 1 tablespoon juice

WHY THIS RECIPE WORKS

We love the browned tops of seared scallops, but the tender mollusks also take well to being baked, as they benefit from gentle cooking. You never again have to wonder what to pair your scallops with; cooking them on a bed of Israeli couscous, leeks, and white wine allows the pearls of pasta to absorb the scallops' briny liquid. To ensure that the scallops finished cooking with the rest of the dish, we gave the leeks and couscous some time in the microwave, adding garlic and a pinch of saffron. We stirred in wine and boiling water, which started the dish off hot and shortened the cooking time. Using a hot oven and sealing the baking dish with foil resulted in perfectly cooked scallops that steamed atop the couscous. A tarragon-orange vinaigrette complemented the delicate scallops and leeks without overpowering them. For an accurate measurement of boiling water, bring a full kettle of water to a boil and then measure out the desired amount.

1 | Adjust oven rack to middle position and heat oven to 450 degrees. Combine leeks, couscous, 2 tablespoons oil, garlic, ½ teaspoon salt, ¼ teaspoon pepper, and saffron, if using, in bowl. Microwave, covered and stirring occasionally, until leeks are softened, about 6 minutes. Stir in boiling water and wine, then transfer mixture to 13 by 9-inch baking dish.

2 | Pat scallops dry with paper towels and sprinkle with ½ teaspoon salt and remaining ¼ teaspoon pepper. Nestle scallops into couscous mixture and cover dish tightly with aluminum foil. Bake until couscous is tender, sides of scallops are firm, and centers are opaque, 20 to 25 minutes.

3 | Meanwhile, whisk tarragon, vinegar, mustard, orange zest and juice, remaining ⅛ teaspoon salt, and remaining 3 tablespoons oil together in bowl.

4 | Drizzle vinaigrette over scallops and serve, passing extra oil separately.

SPANISH-STYLE BROTHY RICE WITH CLAMS AND SALSA VERDE | SERVES 4 TO 6

SUBSTITUTIONS NONE

5 tablespoons extra-virgin olive oil, divided

¼ cup minced fresh parsley

1 garlic clove, minced, divided

1 tablespoon white wine vinegar

2 cups dry white wine

2 pounds littleneck clams, scrubbed

5 cups water

1 (8-ounce) bottle clam juice

1 leek, white and light green parts only, halved lengthwise, chopped fine, and washed thoroughly

1 green bell pepper, stemmed, seeded, and chopped fine

½ teaspoon table salt

1½ cups Bomba rice

Lemon wedges

1 recipe Salsa Verde (page 72)

WHY THIS RECIPE WORKS

This traditional rice dish from Spain's Mediterranean coast combines the briny sweetness of clams and their liquor with the verdant flavors of leeks, green pepper, and parsley. Unlike paella-style rice dishes, in which the rice absorbs most or all of the cooking liquid, brothy rice has a higher proportion of liquid to rice, so that the finished rice remains surrounded by flavorful liquid. We found that the key to achieving the best-tasting dish was to coax as much flavor as possible from each of its simple ingredients. We started by opening our clams in wine and using the cooking liquid to build a deeply flavorful broth. We then set the clams aside so they wouldn't overcook and built an aromatic base using leek, green pepper, and garlic. To emphasize these vegetal flavors and the acidic notes of the wine, we finished the dish with a white wine vinegar–enhanced salsa verde. Bomba rice is the most traditional rice for this dish, but you can use any variety of Valencia rice. If you cannot find Valencia rice, you can substitute Arborio rice.

1 | Combine 3 tablespoons oil, parsley, half of garlic, and vinegar in bowl; set aside. Bring wine to boil in large saucepan over high heat. Add clams, cover, and cook, stirring occasionally, until clams open, 5 to 7 minutes.

2 | Using slotted spoon, transfer clams to large bowl, discarding any that refuse to open, and cover to keep warm. Stir water and clam juice into wine and bring to simmer. Reduce heat to low, cover, and keep warm.

3 | Heat remaining 2 tablespoons oil in Dutch oven over medium heat until shimmering. Add leek, bell pepper, and salt and cook until softened, 8 to 10 minutes. Add rice and remaining garlic and cook, stirring frequently, until grain edges begin to turn translucent, about 3 minutes.

4 | Add 2 cups warm broth and cook, stirring frequently, until almost fully absorbed, about 5 minutes. Continue to cook rice, stirring frequently and adding warm broth, 1 cup at a time, every few minutes as liquid is absorbed, until rice is creamy and cooked through but still somewhat firm in center, 12 to 14 minutes.

5 | Off heat, stir in 1 cup warm broth and adjust consistency with extra broth as needed (rice mixture should have thin but creamy consistency; you may have broth left over). Stir in parsley mixture and season with salt and pepper to taste. Nestle clams into rice along with any accumulated juices, cover, and let sit until heated through, 5 to 7 minutes. Serve with lemon wedges and salsa verde.

ISRAELI COUSCOUS WITH CLAMS, LEEKS, AND TOMATOES | SERVES 4

SUBSTITUTIONS NONE

2 tablespoons unsalted butter

1½ pounds leeks, white and light green parts only, halved lengthwise, sliced thin, and washed thoroughly

2 tablespoons minced fresh tarragon, divided

3 garlic cloves, minced

1 cup dry white wine

4 pounds littleneck or cherrystone clams, scrubbed

2½ cups chicken or vegetable broth

2 cups Israeli couscous

3 tomatoes, cored, seeded, and chopped

1 teaspoon grated lemon zest

WHY THIS RECIPE WORKS

A brothy bowl of shellfish and tiny pasta is traditional seaside comfort food in parts of Italy. We set out to create a one-pot dish of the sort, using clams and Israeli couscous. We kept our ingredient list simple; we wanted to ensure that the briny clam flavor was showcased, not overpowered by too many other elements. We started down what seemed like the obvious path, first building a base of leeks, garlic, tarragon, and white wine; next cooking our couscous; and, finally, steaming the clams on top. But by the time the shells opened, the couscous had turned to mush and we couldn't access the little pearls of pasta to fluff them before serving. We reversed the order, first steaming the clams in the aromatic broth until they just opened and then setting them aside so they wouldn't become rubbery. This freed up the pot to cook the couscous in the clam liquid, which we stretched with chicken broth. The couscous came out perfectly, and its starch helped thicken the broth. Tomatoes and lemon zest complemented the briny flavors. We returned the clams to the pot, along with their juices, and let everything warm through before serving. A sprinkling of tarragon was the perfect finish to the dish. Serve with crusty bread.

1 | Melt butter in Dutch oven over medium heat. Add leeks and cook until softened, about 4 minutes. Stir in 1 tablespoon tarragon and garlic and cook until fragrant, about 30 seconds. Stir in wine, increase heat to high, and bring to boil. Add clams, cover, and cook, stirring occasionally, until clams have opened, 5 to 7 minutes.

2 | Using slotted spoon, transfer clams to large bowl and tent with aluminum foil; discard any clams that refuse to open. Reduce heat to medium, add broth and couscous to pot, and bring to simmer. Cover and cook until couscous is nearly tender and some broth remains, 8 to 10 minutes.

3 | Off heat, stir in tomatoes and lemon zest and season with salt and pepper to taste. Nestle clams into couscous mixture along with any accumulated juices. Cover and let sit until warmed through, about 5 minutes. Sprinkle with remaining 1 tablespoon tarragon and serve.

GARLICKY SPAGHETTI WITH CLAMS | SERVES 4

SUBSTITUTIONS NONE

2 tablespoons plus ½ teaspoon minced garlic, divided

¼ cup extra-virgin olive oil

¼ teaspoon red pepper flakes

1 pound spaghetti
Table salt for cooking pasta

2 (6½-ounce) cans whole clams, drained and chopped

4 anchovy fillets, rinsed, patted dry, and minced

2 teaspoons lemon juice

1½ ounces Parmesan cheese, grated (¾ cup), plus extra for serving

2 tablespoons chopped fresh parsley

WHY THIS RECIPE WORKS

Fresh clams are great, but you can get the flavor of the sea with ease and delight from canned whole clams for a pantry-friendly seafood pasta. The key was making the most of the garlic to bolster and deepen the flavor of the canned clams. Toasting most of the garlic over low heat in ¼ cup of extra-virgin olive oil ensured that it cooked to a pale golden brown—any darker and its flavor went from delicately buttery and sweet to bitter and harsh. We cooked our spaghetti in just 2 quarts of salted water to make sure that the pasta cooking liquid was loaded with starch. We reserved a portion of this liquid and added it to the spaghetti, along with the oil; the starch helped the oil cling to the pasta and gave the dish a perfect, not greasy, texture. Incorporating ½ teaspoon of raw minced garlic brought some fire. Anchovies and Parmesan, both staples for us, also provided pleasant pungency.

1 | Cook 2 tablespoons garlic and oil in 8-inch nonstick skillet over low heat, stirring occasionally, until garlic is pale golden brown, 9 to 12 minutes. Off heat, stir in pepper flakes; set aside.

2 | Bring 2 quarts water to boil in large pot. Add pasta and 2 teaspoons salt and cook, stirring frequently, until al dente. Reserve 1 cup cooking water, then drain pasta and return it to pot. Add remaining ½ teaspoon garlic, clams, anchovies, lemon juice, reserved garlic-oil mixture, and reserved cooking water. Stir until pasta is well coated with oil and no water remains in bottom of pot. Add Parmesan and parsley and toss to combine. Season with salt and pepper to taste. Serve, passing extra Parmesan separately.

MUSSELS MARINARA WITH SPAGHETTI

| SERVES 4 TO 6

2 (28-ounce) cans whole peeled tomatoes

3 tablespoons extra-virgin olive oil, divided

1 onion, chopped fine

6 garlic cloves, minced

1 anchovy fillet, rinsed and minced

½ teaspoon red pepper flakes

2 cups water

1 (8-ounce) bottle clam juice

1 pound spaghetti

2 pounds mussels, scrubbed and debearded

¼ cup minced fresh parsley

WHY THIS RECIPE WORKS

In this meal, mussels infuse everything else with their briny liquid, providing the base for a great sauce. Here, we give mussels marinara—mussels draped in a spicy tomato sauce and served over pasta—the one-pot treatment, preparing both pasta and mussels directly in the sauce. We gave our sauce plenty of punch by adding finely chopped onion, lots of garlic, minced anchovy, and red pepper flakes, which would stand up well to the mussels. After tasting the sauce, we wanted it to have more seafood character. Substituting clam juice for some of the water pumped up the briny profile. As for the mussels, we added them just as the spaghetti, which we cooked in the sauce, was nearing doneness. Within minutes, the shells gently opened and released their liquor, further bolstering the briny marinara sauce. With a glug of olive oil and a sprinkling of parsley, our simple yet sensational mussels marinara was ready. When adding the spaghetti in step 3, stir gently to avoid breaking the noodles; after a minute or two they will soften enough to be stirred more easily. If necessary, add hot water, 1 tablespoon at a time, to adjust the consistency of the sauce before serving. Discard any mussels with an unpleasant odor or a cracked or broken shell.

1 | Working in 2 batches, pulse tomatoes and their juice in food processor until coarsely chopped and no large pieces remain, 6 to 8 pulses; transfer to bowl.

2 | Heat 2 tablespoons oil in Dutch oven over medium heat until shimmering. Add onion and cook until softened, about 5 minutes. Stir in garlic, anchovy, and pepper flakes and cook until fragrant, about 30 seconds. Stir in processed tomatoes and simmer gently until tomatoes no longer taste raw, about 10 minutes.

3 | Stir in water, clam juice, and pasta, increase heat to high, and bring to boil. Reduce heat to medium, cover, and simmer vigorously, stirring often, for 12 minutes. Stir in mussels, cover, and continue to simmer vigorously until pasta is tender and mussels have opened, 2 to 4 minutes.

4 | Uncover, discard any mussels that refuse to open, reduce heat to low, and stir in remaining 1 tablespoon oil and parsley. Cook, tossing pasta gently, until well coated with sauce, 1 to 2 minutes. Season with salt and pepper to taste and serve.

CHAPTER 3

soups, stews, and chowders

5 | Arrange shrimp evenly over stew, cover, and continue to cook until halibut flakes apart when gently prodded with paring knife, shrimp and scallops are firm and opaque in center, and mussels have opened, about 2 minutes. Off heat, discard bay leaves and any mussels that refuse to open. Gently stir in tarragon and season with salt and pepper to taste. Serve.

COD IN COCONUT BROTH WITH LEMON GRASS AND GINGER | SERVES 4

SUBSTITUTIONS BLACK SEA BASS • HADDOCK • HAKE • POLLOCK

1 tablespoon vegetable oil

1 leek, white and light green parts only, halved lengthwise, sliced thin, and washed thoroughly

1 teaspoon table salt, divided

4 garlic cloves, minced

1 tablespoon grated fresh ginger

1 cup water

2 carrots, peeled and cut into 2-inch-long matchsticks

1 (10-inch) lemon grass stalk, trimmed to bottom 6 inches and bruised with back of knife

4 (6- to 8-ounce) skinless cod fillets, 1 inch thick

¼ teaspoon pepper

⅓ cup canned coconut milk

1 tablespoon lime juice, plus lime wedges for serving

1 teaspoon fish sauce

2 tablespoons chopped dry-roasted peanuts

2 tablespoons fresh cilantro leaves

1 serrano chile, stemmed and sliced thin

WHY THIS RECIPE WORKS

When it's in a soup, mild, flaky cod is often served as it is in New England, swimming in a velvety sauce made from cream and often butter. We liked the idea of bathing cod in something different—a broth that was still rich but didn't obscure the cod. A Thai-style approach draws upon the flavors of coconut soup to build a lush, aromatic broth seasoned with lemon grass, ginger, garlic, fish sauce, and lime. Poaching the cod in this broth ensured the flavors infused the fish and allowed it to cook gently and evenly. Mild leeks and sweet carrots complemented the delicate cod, a little coconut milk added richness, and a garnish of peanuts, cilantro, and a serrano chile added welcome color, aroma, and crunch. Best of all, this dish came together quickly and in just one pan, making it an elegant but weeknight-friendly meal. If you can't find a serrano chile, substitute a red Fresno chile. You can use light coconut milk, but the broth will be noticeably thinner and less rich.

1 | Heat oil in 12-inch nonstick skillet over medium heat until shimmering. Add leek and ½ teaspoon salt and cook, stirring occasionally, until lightly browned, 4 to 6 minutes. Stir in garlic and ginger and cook until fragrant, about 30 seconds.

2 | Stir in water, carrots, and lemon grass and bring to simmer. Pat cod dry with paper towels and sprinkle with remaining ½ teaspoon salt and pepper. Nestle fish into skillet, spoon some cooking liquid over top, and bring to simmer. Cover, reduce heat to low, and cook until fish flakes apart when gently prodded with paring knife and registers 135 degrees, 8 to 12 minutes.

3 | Carefully transfer fish to individual shallow bowls. Discard lemon grass. Using slotted spoon, divide leeks and carrots evenly among bowls. Off heat, whisk coconut milk, lime juice, and fish sauce into broth and season with salt and pepper to taste. Ladle broth over fish. Sprinkle individual portions with peanuts, cilantro, and chile. Serve with lime wedges.

THAI-STYLE HOT-AND-SOUR SOUP WITH SHRIMP AND RICE VERMICELLI | SERVES 4

SUBSTITUTIONS NONE

- 4 ounces rice vermicelli noodles
- 3 cups chicken or vegetable broth
- 3 cups water
- 1 pound large shrimp (26 to 30 per pound), peeled, deveined, and tails removed, shells reserved
- 8 ounces cremini mushrooms, stemmed and quartered, stems reserved
- 2 tomatoes, cored and chopped coarse, divided
- 1 jalapeño chile, stemmed, seeded, and sliced into ¼-inch-thick rings, divided
- 2 sprigs fresh cilantro plus ¼ cup chopped
- 2 tablespoons fish sauce
- 2 garlic cloves, lightly crushed and peeled
- 1 (½-inch) piece ginger, peeled, halved, and smashed
- 1 teaspoon sugar
- 3 tablespoons lime juice, plus lime wedges for serving (2 limes)

WHY THIS RECIPE WORKS

The hot-and-sour Thai soup known as *tom yum* is a bold display of the energetic flavors that Thai cuisine is famous for. To make the soup pantry-friendly without dulling the flavor, we substituted an easy-to-find jalapeño for traditional Thai chiles and lime juice for harder-to-find makrut lime leaves. Then, to enhance the most important flavor in the soup, the shrimp, we saved the shells and added them to a combination of chicken broth and water for a broth with thorough shrimp flavor. We built an intensely aromatic soup while making the most of our short ingredient list by infusing our broth with tomatoes, mushroom stems, jalapeño, garlic, ginger, cilantro stems, fish sauce, and sugar. We strained and poured the flavorful broth over vermicelli rice noodles and topped it with a final burst of tart lime juice and fresh cilantro. To smash the ginger pieces, use the flat side of a chef's knife.

1 | Bring 2 quarts water to boil in large saucepan. Off heat, add noodles and let sit until tender, about 5 minutes. Drain noodles and rinse with cold water until water runs clear. Drain well and set aside.

2 | Bring broth, water, shrimp shells, mushroom stems, half of tomatoes, half of jalapeño rings, cilantro sprigs, fish sauce, garlic, ginger, and sugar to boil in now-empty saucepan. Reduce heat to low, cover, and simmer gently for 20 minutes.

3 | Strain broth through fine-mesh strainer set over large bowl, pressing on solids to extract as much liquid as possible. Return broth to again-empty saucepan and bring to simmer over medium-high heat. Add quartered mushrooms and remaining jalapeño rings and cook for 2 minutes. Stir in shrimp and cook until opaque throughout, about 1 minute.

4 | Off heat, stir in lime juice and season with salt and pepper to taste. Divide noodles, remaining chopped tomatoes, and chopped cilantro among individual serving bowls and ladle soup over top. Serve with lime wedges.

SEAFOOD AND CHORIZO STEW | SERVES 4

SUBSTITUTIONS (for cod) BLACK SEA BASS • HADDOCK • HAKE • POLLOCK

- 1 tablespoon extra-virgin olive oil, plus extra for serving
- 6 ounces chorizo sausage, quartered lengthwise and sliced ½ inch thick
- 1 onion, chopped fine
- 4 garlic cloves, minced
- 1 tablespoon chopped fresh oregano, divided
- 2 (14.5-ounce) cans diced tomatoes
- 1 (8-ounce) bottle clam juice
- 1 pound extra-large shrimp (21 to 25 per pound), peeled, deveined, and tails removed
- 2 (6- to 8-ounce) skinless cod fillets, 1 inch thick, cut into 1-inch pieces
- ½ teaspoon table salt
- ¼ teaspoon pepper

WHY THIS RECIPE WORKS

Seafood stews like Bouillabaisse (page 172) and Cioppino (page 183) can seem like grand, celebratory affairs, with their medley of fresh-catch seafood and rich broths. The ones with the most pizzazz can also be the simplest, however—a stew is just as nice on a weekday for a small family. A quick way to flavor is with spice. We started by cooking chorizo and onion together until browned. The chorizo's bold flavor added heat and interest to sweet shrimp and mild-mannered cod in the stew, and a tomato base brought the lively components together. More complicated seafood stews often require staggering cooking or cooking seafood separate from the broth; by cutting the cod into smaller pieces, they cooked at the same quick rate as the shrimp so we could stir them in together, and we liked the way the firm fish maintained its bite-size shape. A drizzle of oil finished off this impressive, multidimensional fish dish that diners would never guess is a breeze to make.

1 | Heat oil in large saucepan over medium-high heat until shimmering. Add chorizo and onion and cook until lightly browned, 7 to 9 minutes. Stir in garlic and 1 teaspoon oregano and cook until fragrant, about 30 seconds. Add tomatoes and their juice and clam juice, scraping up any browned bits, and bring to simmer. Cook until slightly thickened, about 10 minutes.

2 | Pat shrimp and cod dry with paper towels and sprinkle with salt and pepper. Gently stir seafood into stew and cook until cod flakes apart when gently prodded with paring knife and registers 135 degrees and shrimp is opaque throughout, about 5 minutes. Stir in remaining 2 teaspoons oregano and season with salt and pepper to taste. Portion stew into individual serving bowls and drizzle with extra oil. Serve.

EASTERN NORTH CAROLINA FISH STEW

| SERVES 8

SUBSTITUTIONS (for cod) BLACK SEA BASS • HADDOCK • HAKE • POLLOCK

6 slices thick-cut bacon, sliced crosswise ½ inch thick

2 onions, halved and sliced thin

1½ teaspoons table salt

½ teaspoon red pepper flakes

6 cups water

1 (6-ounce) can tomato paste

1 pound red potatoes, unpeeled, sliced ¼ inch thick

1 bay leaf

1 teaspoon Tabasco sauce, plus extra for serving

2 pounds skinless cod fillets, 1 inch thick, cut into 2-inch pieces

8 large eggs

WHY THIS RECIPE WORKS

A hearty, tomatoey, bacon-infused fish stew has been a standard of locals on the riverbanks of Eastern North Carolina for decades. The bacon (or sometimes salt pork), a key ingredient, gives the dish deep savory notes and flavorful fat. There are always chunks of a firm, meaty white fish and slices of red potatoes, plus an ingredient that really sticks out from other fish stews: eggs. Yes, when the stew's nearly done, the cook cracks eggs into it to poach until just cooked through. While most local recipes call for incorporating the uncooked potatoes, onions, and fish all at once to let them cook together, we broke with tradition and added the ingredients in stages so the delicate fish didn't break down too much. Serve with soft white sandwich bread (Wonder bread is traditional) or saltines to mop up the spicy broth. Adding the fish chunks to the stew reduces the temperature of the cooking liquid so the eggs poach slowly, but be sure to watch the eggs for doneness to ensure runny yolks.

1 | Cook bacon in Dutch oven over medium heat until crispy, 9 to 11 minutes, stirring occasionally. Add onions, salt, and pepper flakes and cook until onions begin to soften, about 5 minutes.

2 | Stir in water and tomato paste, scraping up any browned bits. Add potatoes and bay leaf and bring to boil. Simmer vigorously over medium heat for 10 minutes.

3 | Reduce heat to medium-low and stir in Tabasco. Nestle fish into stew and spoon some cooking liquid over top, but do not stir. Crack eggs into stew, spacing them evenly. Cover and cook until eggs are just set, 17 to 22 minutes. Season with salt to taste. Serve, passing extra Tabasco separately.

BRAZILIAN SHRIMP AND FISH STEW (MOQUECA) | SERVES 6

SUBSTITUTIONS (for cod) BLACK SEA BASS • HADDOCK • HAKE • POLLOCK

Pepper Sauce

- 4 pickled hot cherry peppers (3 ounces)
- ½ onion, chopped coarse
- ¼ cup extra-virgin olive oil
- ⅛ teaspoon sugar

Stew

- 1 pound large shrimp (26 to 30 per pound), peeled, deveined, and tails removed
- 1 pound skinless cod fillets, ¾ to 1 inch thick, cut into 1½-inch pieces
- 3 garlic cloves, minced
- 1½ teaspoons table salt, divided
- ¼ teaspoon pepper
- 1 onion, chopped coarse
- 1 (14.5-ounce) can whole peeled tomatoes
- ¾ cup chopped fresh cilantro, divided
- 2 tablespoons extra-virgin olive oil
- 1 red bell pepper, stemmed, seeded, and cut into ½-inch pieces
- 1 green bell pepper, stemmed, seeded, and cut into ½-inch pieces
- 1 (14-ounce) can coconut milk
- 2 tablespoons lime juice

WHY THIS RECIPE WORKS

Brazilian *moqueca* stands out from other regions' fish stews in its complexity—from broth to additions. A combination of rich coconut milk, briny seafood, bright citrus, and savory vegetables produces a stew that's full-bodied, lush, and vibrant, and a garnish makes the dish fresh. Despite this complexity, moqueca is surprisingly quick to make. Cod provided firm but delicate meatiness, and shrimp plump but tender snap for varied seafood texture. To balance the richness and sweetness of the coconut milk in the broth with the bright, fresh flavor of the aromatics, we blended the onion, tomatoes, and a portion of the cilantro in the food processor until they had the texture of a slightly chunky salsa, which added body to the stew. We kept bell peppers diced for contrasting texture and bite. To ensure the seafood was properly cooked, we brought the broth to a boil, added the seafood and lime juice, covered the pot, and removed it from the heat, allowing the seafood to gently cook in the residual heat. The finisher, a home-made version of traditional Brazilian pepper sauce, truly elevated the stew with clarifying bright, vinegary tang.

1 | **For the pepper sauce** Process all ingredients in food processor until smooth, about 30 seconds, scraping down sides of bowl as needed. Season with salt to taste and transfer to bowl. Rinse out processor bowl.

2 | **For the stew** Gently toss shrimp, cod, garlic, ½ teaspoon salt, and pepper together in bowl; set aside. Process onion, tomatoes and their juice, and ¼ cup cilantro in food processor until finely chopped and mixture has texture of pureed salsa, about 30 seconds.

3 | Heat oil in Dutch oven over medium-high heat until shimmering. Add red and green bell peppers and ½ teaspoon salt and cook, stirring frequently, until softened, 5 to 7 minutes. Stir in onion-tomato mixture and remaining ½ teaspoon salt, reduce heat to medium, and cook, stirring frequently, until thickened slightly, 3 to 5 minutes (pot should not be dry).

4 | Increase heat to high, stir in coconut milk, and bring to vigorous boil. Stir in seafood mixture and lime juice, making sure all pieces are submerged in liquid. Cover pot and remove from heat. Let sit until cod flakes apart when gently prodded with paring knife and registers 135 degrees and shrimp are opaque throughout, about 5 minutes. Gently stir in 2 tablespoons pepper sauce and remaining ½ cup cilantro, being careful not to break up cod too much, and season with salt and pepper to taste. Serve, passing remaining pepper sauce separately.

KOREAN SPICY FISH STEW (MAEUNTANG)

| SERVES 6

SUBSTITUTIONS HALIBUT • MAHI-MAHI • STRIPED BASS • SWORDFISH

- 1 tablespoon vegetable oil
- 4 garlic cloves, minced
- 1 tablespoon grated fresh ginger
- 6 cups chicken or vegetable broth
- 1 cup kimchi, drained and coarsely chopped
- 1 tablespoon gochujang
- 1 tablespoon Korean chile flakes (gochugaru)
- ½ teaspoon pepper
- 1 (1½-pound) skinless red snapper fillet, 1 inch thick, cut into 2-inch pieces
- 7 ounces firm tofu, cut into 1-inch pieces
- 1 small zucchini, halved lengthwise and sliced ¼ inch thick
- 4 scallions, cut into 1-inch lengths
- ½ cup fresh cilantro leaves

WHY THIS RECIPE WORKS

If you're looking for a fiery soup to warm you up, look no further than *maeuntang*, a traditional Korean spicy fish soup that brings the heat. This soup gets its fire from both *gochujang* (a funky fermented chili, soybean, and rice paste that has sweet, spicy, and salty flavors) and *gochugaru* (red chile pepper flakes that bring bright but nuanced heat). Traditionally made with anchovy stock, we tried re-creating maeuntang using more readily available chicken broth, which gave the soup the rich body and round flavor it needed. We found that adding ginger, garlic, scallions, and a typical side accompaniment, kimchi (for acidity and fermented flavors), to the stock and simmering chunks of red snapper in it, created a rich, flavorful, and complex broth that was from the sea and nothing like chicken soup. Adding cubes of tofu and slices of zucchini—traditional mix-ins for this soup—provided mild bites to counteract the heat of our fiery broth. If you cannot find Korean chile flakes, substitute ¾ teaspoon paprika and ¼ teaspoon red pepper flakes. Serve with lime wedges, if desired.

1 | Heat oil in Dutch oven over medium heat until shimmering. Add garlic and ginger and cook until fragrant, about 30 seconds. Stir in broth, kimchi, gochujang, chile flakes, and pepper, then bring to simmer.

2 | Stir in red snapper, tofu, zucchini, and scallions. Return to gentle simmer, then reduce heat to medium-low, cover, and cook until fish flakes apart when gently prodded with paring knife, 3 to 4 minutes. Sprinkle with cilantro and serve.

MONKFISH TAGINE | SERVES 4 TO 6

SUBSTITUTIONS NONE

3 (2-inch) strips orange zest, divided

5 garlic cloves, minced, divided

2 tablespoons extra-virgin olive oil

1 large onion, halved and sliced ¼ inch thick

3 carrots, peeled, halved lengthwise, and sliced ¼ inch thick

¾ teaspoon table salt, divided

1 tablespoon tomato paste

1¼ teaspoons paprika

1 teaspoon ground cumin

½ teaspoon dried mint

¼ teaspoon saffron threads, crumbled

1 (8-ounce) bottle clam juice

1½ pounds skinless monkfish fillets, 1 inch thick, trimmed and cut into 3-inch pieces

¼ teaspoon pepper

¼ cup pitted oil-cured black olives, quartered

2 tablespoons minced fresh mint

1 teaspoon sherry vinegar

WHY THIS RECIPE WORKS

The signature sweet-and-sour flavors of a Moroccan-style tagine taste as lovely cloaking fish as they do more common chicken or lamb. Meaty monkfish fillets have a pleasantly firm texture, so they kept their shape while simmering in the pot. For sweetness, we turned to orange zest, onion, carrots, and tomato paste, which, along with fragrant paprika, cumin, dried mint, and saffron, built the base for the tagine's alluring broth. Deglazing the sautéed aromatics with a bottle of clam juice brought in a salty, briny element, bolstering the seafood flavor. For a salty, sour punch, we finished the sauce by stirring in pungent Moroccan oil-cured olives and a teaspoon of sherry vinegar. Fresh mint completed the dish with brightness. We achieved intense Moroccan flavors in just a half hour of cooking. Monkfish fillets are surrounded by a thin membrane that needs to be removed before cooking. Your fishmonger can do this for you, or you can remove it yourself (see page 13).

1 | Mince 1 strip orange zest and combine with 1 teaspoon garlic in bowl; set aside.

2 | Heat oil in Dutch oven over medium heat until shimmering. Add onion, carrots, ¼ teaspoon salt, and remaining 2 strips orange zest and cook until vegetables are softened and lightly browned, 10 to 12 minutes. Stir in tomato paste, paprika, cumin, dried mint, saffron, and remaining garlic and cook until fragrant, about 30 seconds. Stir in clam juice, scraping up any browned bits.

3 | Pat monkfish dry with paper towels and sprinkle with remaining ½ teaspoon salt and pepper. Nestle monkfish into pot, spoon some cooking liquid over top, and bring to simmer. Reduce heat to medium-low, cover, and simmer gently until monkfish is opaque in center and registers 160 degrees, 8 to 12 minutes.

4 | Discard orange zest strips. Gently stir in olives, fresh mint, vinegar, and garlic–orange zest mixture. Season with salt and pepper to taste. Serve.

CALAMARI STEW | SERVES 4 TO 6

¼ cup extra-virgin olive oil, plus extra for serving

2 onions, chopped fine

2 celery ribs, sliced thin

8 garlic cloves, minced

¼ teaspoon red pepper flakes

½ cup dry white wine

2 pounds small squid, bodies sliced crosswise into 1-inch-thick rings, tentacles halved

½ teaspoon table salt

¼ teaspoon pepper

3 (28-ounce) cans whole peeled tomatoes, drained and chopped coarse

⅓ cup pitted brine-cured green olives, chopped coarse

1 tablespoon capers, rinsed

3 tablespoons minced fresh parsley

WHY THIS RECIPE WORKS

Calamari doesn't need to be fried, and stewed calamari with tomatoes, garlic, and white wine is a classic Mediterranean dish that puts the sweet, subtle flavor of the squid front and center. Calamari needs time to become tender, but not too long—around 45 minutes of stewing is the sweet spot (longer and it becomes tough and rubbery). Canned whole tomatoes give the stew a fresh tomato flavor all year long and break down just enough to thicken the stew while remaining a distinct component. Because the tomatoes lose their fresh flavor the longer they cook, we added them to the pot after the squid had simmered for 15 minutes. Green olives and capers lent a complementary briny element, and red pepper flakes provided just the right amount of heat. Finished with fresh parsley and a drizzle of extra-virgin olive oil, the stew's a grand stage for squid. Be sure to use small squid (with bodies 3 to 4 inches in length); they cook more quickly and are more tender than larger squid.

1 | Heat oil in Dutch oven over medium-high heat until shimmering. Add onions and celery and cook until softened, about 5 minutes. Stir in garlic and pepper flakes and cook until fragrant, about 30 seconds. Stir in wine, scraping up any browned bits, and cook until nearly evaporated, about 1 minute.

2 | Pat squid dry with paper towels and sprinkle with salt and pepper. Stir squid into pot. Reduce heat to medium-low, cover, and simmer gently until squid has released its liquid, about 15 minutes. Stir in tomatoes, olives, and capers, cover, and continue to cook until squid is very tender, 30 to 35 minutes.

3 | Off heat, stir in parsley and season with salt and pepper to taste. Drizzle individual portions with extra oil and serve.

NEW ENGLAND FISH CHOWDER | SERVES 6 TO 8

SUBSTITUTIONS BLACK SEA BASS • HADDOCK • HAKE • POLLOCK

2 tablespoons unsalted butter

2 onions, chopped

4 ounces salt pork, rind removed, rinsed, and cut in half

1½ teaspoons minced fresh thyme or ½ teaspoon dried

¾ teaspoon table salt

1 bay leaf

5 cups water

2 pounds skinless cod fillets, 1 inch thick, sliced crosswise into 6 equal pieces

1½ pounds Yukon Gold potatoes, peeled and cut into ½-inch pieces

2 cups whole milk

1 tablespoon cornstarch

½ teaspoon pepper

WHY THIS RECIPE WORKS

Many modern New England fish chowders are so rich that they mask the flavor of the fish altogether, but this dish was originally cooked by sailors in water (thickened by hardtack). This version honors these simple roots by showcasing moist, tender morsels of fish in a more delicate broth. Gently poaching cod in water flavored with salt pork, onions, and herbs created a quick fish stock and eliminated any chance of overcooking the fish. After removing the cod, we cooked potatoes in the broth. Adding whole milk to this stock, as opposed to half-and-half or heavy cream, kept the chowder light and fresh-tasting and preserved the flavor of the cod. A tablespoon of cornstarch whisked into the milk before adding it to the pot coated its proteins, preventing it from curdling as the soup gently simmered with the reintroduced pieces of cod. Garnish the chowder with minced fresh chives, crisp bacon bits, or oyster crackers.

1 | Melt butter in Dutch oven over medium heat. Add onions, salt pork, thyme, salt, and bay leaf and cook until onions are softened but not browned, 3 to 5 minutes. Stir in water and bring to simmer. Off heat, gently nestle cod fillets into pot, spoon some cooking liquid over top, cover, and let fish sit until opaque and nearly cooked through, about 5 minutes. Gently transfer cod to bowl.

2 | Stir potatoes into pot and bring to simmer over medium-high heat. Cook until potatoes are tender and beginning to break apart, about 20 minutes.

3 | Meanwhile, whisk milk, cornstarch, and pepper together in bowl. Stir milk mixture into chowder and return to simmer. Return fish and any accumulated juices to pot. Remove pot from heat, cover, and let sit for 5 minutes. Discard salt pork and bay leaf. Stir gently with wooden spoon to break fish into large pieces. Season with salt and pepper to taste. Serve immediately.

LOBSTER AND CORN CHOWDER | SERVES 4 TO 6

SUBSTITUTIONS NONE

Broth

- 2 (1¼-pound) live lobsters
- 3 tablespoons vegetable oil
- 1 onion, chopped
- 1 carrot, peeled and chopped
- 1 celery rib, chopped
- 2 plum tomatoes, cored and cut into ½-inch pieces
- ⅓ cup dry white wine
- 7 cups water
- 1 bay leaf

Chowder

- 2 ears corn, husks and silk removed
- 2 slices bacon, chopped fine
- 1 onion, chopped fine
- 1 celery rib, chopped fine
- 1 teaspoon minced fresh thyme or ¼ teaspoon dried
- ¼ cup all-purpose flour
- 1 large Yukon Gold potato (10 to 12 ounces), peeled and cut into ½-inch pieces
- ¾ cup heavy cream
- 2 tablespoons minced fresh parsley
- 2 teaspoons dry sherry

WHY THIS RECIPE WORKS

This luxurious chowder is our favorite way to enjoy the summery combination of succulent lobster and sweet corn. Lobster broth gave the soup big lobster flavor. After freezing the lobsters, we sautéed them until bright red and lightly browned and then added the classic mirepoix of onion, carrot, and celery along with white wine to fortify a potent broth that we later used to poach the rest of the lobster. Bacon provided the soup with meaty backbone, while a bit of flour as well as the sweet pulp from the starchy corn cobs (kernels went in later) gave it the body of a chowder. For a final touch of complexity, we added a splash of dry sherry. Do not be tempted to substitute frozen corn for the fresh corn here; fresh corn is crucial to the flavor of this seasonal soup.

1 | **For the broth** Place lobsters in large bowl and freeze for 30 minutes. Holding lobsters firmly with dish towel, plunge tip of chef's knife into body at point where shell forms "T". Move blade straight down through head to sever. (See page 18.) Using your hands, twist tail to remove from body and repeat with claws (including arms); discard rubber bands and set lobster claws and tails aside. Flip remaining lobster bodies leg side up and cut in half lengthwise, then discard innards and feathery gills.

2 | Heat oil in Dutch oven over medium-high heat until just smoking. Add cleaned lobster bodies and cook until bright red and lightly browned, 3 to 5 minutes. Stir in onion, carrot, celery, and tomatoes and cook until softened, 5 to 7 minutes. Stir in wine and cook until nearly evaporated, about 1 minute.

3 | Stir in water and bay leaf and bring to boil. Add lobster claws and tails, reduce heat to medium-low, and simmer gently until tails register 140 degrees (insert thermometer through underside of tail into thickest part), about 4 minutes. If necessary, return claws and tails to pot for 2 minutes, until tails register 140 degrees. Remove claws and tails from pot and let cool slightly. Once cool enough to handle, remove lobster meat from shells, chop coarse, and refrigerate until ready to serve; discard shells.

4 | Meanwhile, continue to simmer lobster broth until rich and flavorful, about 45 minutes. Strain broth through fine-mesh strainer, pressing on solids to extract as much liquid as possible. Wipe out pot with paper towels.

5 | **For the chowder** Cut corn kernels off cobs; set aside. Scrape cobs clean of pulp and reserve pulp separately. Cook bacon in pot over medium heat until crisp, 5 to 7 minutes. Stir in onion and celery and cook until softened, about 5 minutes. Stir in thyme and cook until fragrant, about 30 seconds. Stir in flour and cook for 1 minute.

6 | Gradually whisk in strained lobster broth, scraping up any browned bits and smoothing out any lumps. Stir in potato and corn cob pulp and bring to boil. Reduce heat to medium-low and simmer gently until potato is nearly tender, 15 to 20 minutes.

7 | Stir in corn kernels and simmer until tender, 5 to 7 minutes. Stir in cream and return to brief simmer. Off heat, discard bay leaf, stir in parsley and sherry, and season with salt and pepper to taste. Stir in lobster meat, cover, and let sit until warmed through, about 1 minute. Serve.

sandwiches, tacos, salads, and more

CRISPY FISH SANDWICHES | SERVES 4

SUBSTITUTIONS BLACK SEA BASS • COD • HAKE • POLLOCK

Fish

- ½ cup all-purpose flour
- ½ cup cornstarch
- ½ teaspoon table salt
- ½ teaspoon baking powder
- ¾ cup plain seltzer
- 2 quarts peanut or vegetable oil for frying
- 4 (4- to 6-ounce) skinless haddock fillets, 1 inch thick

Slaw

- 1 tablespoon cider vinegar
- 1½ teaspoons sugar
- 1½ teaspoons vegetable oil
- ¼ teaspoon table salt
- ¼ teaspoon pepper
- 1½ cups shredded red or green cabbage
- 1 carrot, peeled and shredded
- 1 tablespoon minced fresh parsley or cilantro

- ⅓ cup Classic Tartar Sauce (page 70)
- 4 brioche buns, toasted

WHY THIS RECIPE WORKS

If we're not eating fried fish next to a side of fries (see page 298), we like it just as much at a picnic table on a bun. When making our own crispy fish sandwich, we were swayed by the style of sandwiches (literally) in our seaside backyard. In New England, you'll most often get your fish—usually a generous piece of haddock—topped with coleslaw and creamy tartar sauce for the perfect bite of moist, crispy fish; rich, creamy, bitey sauce; a fresh, crunchy component; and a bun to soak it all up. To enhance the freshness the slaw provided even more, we preferred a vinegar-based dressing to a traditional creamy one for extra acidity to counterbalance the fish, which we fried dunked in a seltzer-based batter. Store-bought coleslaw mix can be substituted for the cabbage, carrot, and parsley in the slaw. Use a Dutch oven that holds 6 quarts or more. We call for a slightly smaller piece of fish here to accommodate a sandwich-size bun.

1 | **For the fish** Whisk flour, cornstarch, salt, and baking powder together in large bowl. Whisk in seltzer until smooth. Cover and refrigerate for 20 minutes.

2 | Set wire rack in rimmed baking sheet. Add oil to Dutch oven until it measures about 1½ inches deep and heat over medium-high heat to 375 degrees. Pat haddock dry with paper towels and transfer to batter, tossing gently to evenly coat. Using fork, remove fish from batter, allowing excess batter to drip back into bowl, and add to hot oil, briefly dragging haddock along surface of oil to prevent sticking before gently dropping into oil. Adjust burner, if necessary, to maintain oil temperature between 350 and 375 degrees.

3 | Cook, stirring gently to prevent pieces from sticking together, until deep golden brown and crisp, about 4 minutes per side. Using spider skimmer or slotted spoon, transfer haddock to prepared rack.

4 | **For the slaw** Whisk vinegar, sugar, oil, salt, and pepper together in large bowl. Add cabbage, carrot, and parsley and toss to combine; season with salt and pepper to taste. Divide tartar sauce evenly among bun bottoms, then top with fish and slaw. Cover with bun tops. Serve immediately.

variation |
SPICY CRISPY FISH SANDWICHES

Combine ¼ cup mayonnaise, 1–2 tablespoons sriracha, ½ teaspoon grated lime zest, and 1 teaspoon lime juice in bowl. Substitute for tartar sauce.

NEW ENGLAND LOBSTER ROLLS | SERVES 6

SUBSTITUTIONS NONE

2 tablespoons mayonnaise

2 tablespoons minced celery

1½ teaspoons lemon juice

1 teaspoon minced fresh chives

⅛ teaspoon table salt

Pinch cayenne pepper

1 pound cooked lobster meat, tail meat cut into ½-inch pieces and claw meat cut into 1-inch pieces

2 tablespoons unsalted butter, softened

6 New England–style hot dog buns

6 leaves Bibb lettuce

WHY THIS RECIPE WORKS

Visitors to New England often make it a point to find themselves a lobster roll, but this luxury shouldn't be limited to vacation. To capture the best of the New England coast, we mostly adhered to tradition—lots of tender lobster coated in a light mayonnaise dressing and tucked into a buttery, perfectly toasted top-loading hotdog bun—but we added a hint of contrasting crunch in the form of small amounts of lettuce and celery (a contentious addition). For an allium note, onion and shallot were overpowering, but minced chives offered bright herb flavor. Lemon juice and a pinch of cayenne provided a nice counterpoint to the rich lobster and mayo. This recipe is best when made with lobster you've cooked yourself, and we used our Boiled Lobster (page 307), which yields 1 pound of lobster meat. Use a very small pinch of cayenne pepper, as it should not make the dressing spicy. We prefer New England–style top-loading hot dog buns, as they provide maximum surface on the sides for toasting. If using other buns, butter, salt, and toast the interior of each bun instead of the exterior.

1 | Whisk mayonnaise, celery, lemon juice, chives, salt, and cayenne together in large bowl. Add lobster and gently toss to combine.

2 | Place 12-inch nonstick skillet over low heat. Butter both sides of buns and season to taste with salt. Place buns in skillet, 1 buttered side down, increase heat to medium-low, and cook until crisp and brown, 2 to 3 minutes per side. Transfer buns to large serving platter. Line each bun with 1 lettuce leaf. Spoon lobster salad into buns and serve immediately.

SHRIMP PO' BOYS | SERVES 4

- 2 cups all-purpose flour
- ¼ cup cornmeal
- 2 tablespoons Creole seasoning
- 4 large eggs
- 1 pound large shrimp (26 to 30 per pound), peeled, deveined, and tails removed
- 2 quarts peanut or vegetable oil
- 1 cup Rémoulade (page 71)
- 4 (8-inch) sub rolls, split and toasted
- 2 cups shredded iceberg lettuce
- 2 large tomatoes, cored and sliced thin
- 1 cup dill pickle chips

WHY THIS RECIPE WORKS

This street food sandwich has been a workday favorite in Louisiana for generations, but it's really something special, delivering a full range of spicy-savory New Orleans flavors. For our shrimp sandwich salute, we turned to a three-step process for a crunchy coating on the shrimp: Toss them in a dry mixture of flour, cornmeal, and Creole seasoning; dip them in beaten eggs (with a bit of the dry mixture added to thicken the coat); then dredge them again in the flour mixture. This process allowed more batter to stick to every bend of the shrimp, maximizing crunchiness. Letting the coated shrimp rest in the refrigerator before frying them ensured that the batter didn't slough off during cooking. New Orleans–style French breads are a specialty you can't find in many places, but you can mimic the unique crunch by lightly toasting sub rolls. In addition to shredded iceberg, tomatoes, and crunchy dill pickle chips, a generous spread of sharp rémoulade sauce on each sandwich gives this street food serious street cred—and the very best flavor. Use a Dutch oven that holds 6 quarts or more. Do not refrigerate the breaded shrimp for longer than 30 minutes, or the coating will be too wet.

1 | Set wire rack in rimmed baking sheet. Whisk flour, cornmeal, and Creole seasoning together in shallow dish. Whisk eggs and ½ cup flour mixture together in second shallow dish.

2 | Place half of shrimp in flour mixture and toss to thoroughly coat. Shake off excess flour mixture, dip shrimp into egg mixture, then return to flour mixture, pressing gently to adhere. Transfer shrimp to prepared wire rack. Repeat with remaining shrimp, then refrigerate for at least 15 minutes or up to 30 minutes.

3 | Line large plate with triple layer of paper towels. Add oil to large Dutch oven until it measures about 1½ inches deep and heat over medium-high heat to 375 degrees. Carefully add half of shrimp to hot oil. Cook, stirring occasionally to prevent shrimp from sticking together, until golden brown, about 4 minutes. Using wire skimmer or slotted spoon, transfer shrimp to paper towel–lined plate. Return oil to 375 degrees and repeat with remaining shrimp.

4 | Spread rémoulade evenly on both cut sides of each roll. Divide lettuce, tomatoes, pickle chips, and shrimp evenly among rolls. Serve.

SANDWICHES, TACOS, SALADS, AND MORE

SHRIMP BURGERS | SERVES 4

SUBSTITUTIONS NONE

1 cup panko bread crumbs

1½ pounds large shrimp (26 to 30 per pound), peeled, deveined, and tails removed, divided

2 tablespoons mayonnaise

½ teaspoon table salt

¼ teaspoon pepper

⅛ teaspoon cayenne pepper

3 scallions, chopped fine

3 tablespoons vegetable oil

1 cup Classic Tartar Sauce (page 70)

4 hamburger buns, toasted if desired

4 leaves Bibb lettuce

WHY THIS RECIPE WORKS

A specialty of Southern coastal towns, shrimp burgers are all about the sweet shrimp (no bready fillers allowed), and they feature a coating that mimics the contrasting crunch of fried seafood. Forming burgers from cooked seafood is the easiest option but didn't do anything for the shrimp—the burgers turned out dry and rubbery. Starting with raw shrimp and coarsely chopping them in the food processor produced juicy burgers with better, meatier texture. Pulsing a small amount of the shrimp with mayonnaise first made an undetectable binder—the shrimp itself. Since the shrimp is meant to shine, a light hand with seasonings was best: just salt, pepper, cayenne, and some chopped scallions for freshness. To achieve the crunchy exterior of deep-fried shrimp burgers in a skillet, we ground panko to a fine powder before coating the burgers and sautéing them to a golden brown. You can use just about any size shrimp in this recipe, but avoid the tiniest shrimp as they will result in a pasty burger.

1 | Pulse panko in food processor until finely ground, about 15 pulses; transfer to shallow dish. Place one-third of shrimp (about 1 cup), mayonnaise, salt, pepper, and cayenne in now-empty processor and pulse until shrimp are finely chopped, about 8 pulses. Add remaining shrimp and pulse until coarsely chopped, about 4 pulses, scraping down sides of bowl as needed. Transfer to bowl and stir in scallions.

2 | Using your lightly moistened hands, divide shrimp mixture into 4 equal portions, then gently shape each portion into ¾-inch-thick patty. Working with 1 patty at a time, dredge in panko, pressing lightly to adhere; transfer to plate.

3 | Heat oil in 12-inch nonstick skillet over medium heat until shimmering. Cook until patties are golden brown and register 140 degrees, 3 to 5 minutes per side. Transfer burgers to paper towel–lined plate and let drain, about 30 seconds per side. Spread tartar sauce evenly among bun bottoms, then place burgers and lettuce on top. Cover with bun tops. Serve.

BEST CRAB CAKES | SERVES 4

SUBSTITUTIONS NONE

1 pound lump crabmeat, picked over for shells
1 cup milk
1½ cups panko bread crumbs, divided
¾ teaspoon table salt, divided
¼ teaspoon pepper, divided
2 celery ribs, chopped
½ cup chopped onion
1 garlic clove, smashed and peeled
1 tablespoon unsalted butter
4 ounces extra-large shrimp (21 to 25 per pound), peeled, deveined, and tails removed
¼ cup heavy cream
2 teaspoons Dijon mustard
1 teaspoon lemon juice
½ teaspoon hot sauce
½ teaspoon Old Bay seasoning
¼ cup vegetable oil, divided
Lemon wedges

WHY THIS RECIPE WORKS

It always seems like a good idea to order crab cakes when they're on the menu. But they typically arrive heavy with a flavor that isn't identifiably seafood. Crab cakes should taste like crab—sweet, plump meat held together with a binder that doesn't mask it. For convenience, these cakes work with pasteurized crabmeat found at the supermarket. (Fresh crabmeat can be hard to come by.) Jumbo lump or lump crabmeat has a satisfying texture—avoid finer, flakier backfin meat. To rid the meat of any fishiness, there's a trick: Soaking it briefly in milk washes away the compound responsible for that. To highlight the sweetness, we bound our cakes not with ingredients that muted the delicate flavor, but with shrimp mousse; pureeing shrimp released fragments of sticky muscle proteins that held the pieces of crab together. Either fresh or pasteurized crabmeat can be used (see page 15). With packaged crab, if the meat smells clean and fresh skip the soaking and straining in steps 1 and 5 and blot away any excess liquid. The crab cakes are pictured with Classic Tartar Sauce (page 70).

1 | Line rimmed baking sheet with parchment paper. Place crabmeat and milk in bowl, making sure crab is totally submerged. Cover and refrigerate for 20 minutes.

2 | Meanwhile, pulse ¾ cup panko in food processor until finely ground, about 15 pulses. Toast ground panko and remaining ¾ cup panko in 10-inch nonstick skillet over medium-high heat, stirring constantly, until golden brown, about 5 minutes. Transfer panko to shallow dish and stir in ¼ teaspoon salt and ⅛ teaspoon pepper; set aside. Wipe skillet clean with paper towels.

3 | Pulse celery, onion, and garlic in now-empty processor until finely chopped, 5 to 8 pulses, scraping down sides of bowl as needed; transfer to large bowl. Wipe processor bowl and blade clean with paper towels. Melt butter in now-empty skillet over medium heat. Add processed vegetables, remaining ½ teaspoon salt, and remaining ⅛ teaspoon pepper and cook until vegetables are softened, 4 to 6 minutes. Return vegetables to large bowl and set aside to cool. Wipe skillet clean with paper towels.

4 | Pulse shrimp in again-empty processor until finely ground, 12 to 15 pulses, scraping down sides of bowl as needed. Add cream and pulse to combine, 2 to 4 pulses; transfer to bowl with cooled vegetables.

5 | Strain soaked crabmeat through fine-mesh strainer, pressing firmly to remove milk but being careful not to break up lumps of crabmeat. Add drained crab to bowl with vegetable mixture. Fold mustard, lemon juice, hot sauce, and Old Bay into vegetable mixture, being careful not to overmix or break up lumps of

crabmeat. Using your lightly moistened hands, divide crab mixture into 8 equal portions, then firmly shape each into ½-inch-thick cake. Transfer to prepared sheet, cover with plastic wrap, and refrigerate for 30 minutes.

6 | Working with 1 cake at a time, dredge in panko, pressing lightly to adhere; return to sheet. Heat 1 tablespoon oil in now-empty skillet over medium heat until shimmering. Place 4 cakes in skillet and cook until first side is golden brown, about 3 minutes. Carefully flip cakes, add 1 tablespoon oil to skillet, and reduce heat to medium-low. Cook until second side is golden brown, 4 to 6 minutes. Transfer cakes to paper towel–lined plate and let drain, about 30 seconds per side; transfer to serving platter. Wipe skillet clean with paper towels and repeat with remaining 4 cakes and remaining 2 tablespoons oil. Serve with lemon wedges.

LEMON-BASIL COD CAKES | SERVES 4

SUBSTITUTIONS BLACK SEA BASS • HADDOCK • HAKE • POLLOCK

1½ cups panko bread crumbs, divided

1 pound skinless cod fillets, cut into 1-inch pieces

3 tablespoons mayonnaise

1 large egg, lightly beaten

2 tablespoons chopped fresh basil

2 scallions, sliced thin

1 teaspoon grated lemon zest plus 1 tablespoon juice, plus lemon wedges for serving

1 garlic clove, minced

½ teaspoon table salt

¼ teaspoon pepper

¼ cup vegetable oil

WHY THIS RECIPE WORKS

While bread crumb–topped baked cod might be a New England classic, we wanted our cod cakes to taste like cod, not bread. Processing raw fresh cod briefly in two batches avoided overworking the fish and giving the cakes a pasty texture. To hold the cakes together without a lot of bread crumbs we used an egg along with just a scant amount of crunchy panko, saving the rest of the panko for the dredge, which turned to a crisp, golden crust once cooked. For a fresh, summery flavor appropriate for a fish cake, we added a handful of bright aromatics—fresh basil, scallions, lemon zest and juice, and garlic. Be careful not to overprocess the cod in step 1. If you find that the bread crumbs are browning too quickly in step 3, reduce the heat. The cod cakes are pictured with Herb Yogurt Sauce (page 71).

1 | Spread ¾ cup panko in shallow dish. Working in 2 batches, pulse cod in food processor until coarsely chopped into ¼- to ½-inch pieces, about 3 pulses; transfer to large bowl. Gently fold in remaining ¾ cup panko, mayonnaise, egg, basil, scallions, lemon zest and juice, garlic, salt, and pepper.

2 | Using your lightly moistened hands, divide into 4 equal portions, then gently shape each portion into 3½-inch-wide cake. Working with 1 cake at a time, dredge in panko, pressing lightly to adhere; transfer to plate.

3 | Heat oil in 12-inch nonstick skillet over medium heat until shimmering. Cook cakes until well browned, 4 to 5 minutes per side. Transfer cakes to paper towel–lined plate and let drain, about 30 seconds per side. Serve with lemon wedges.

SOUTHWESTERN SALMON CAKES | SERVES 4

SUBSTITUTIONS ARCTIC CHAR • WILD SALMON

1½ cups panko bread crumbs, divided

1 pound skinless salmon fillets, cut into 1-inch pieces

3 tablespoons mayonnaise

1 (4-ounce) can whole green chiles, drained and chopped fine

2 tablespoons chopped fresh cilantro

2 scallions, sliced thin

1 teaspoon grated lime zest plus 1 tablespoon juice, plus lime wedges for serving

½ teaspoon chipotle chile powder

½ teaspoon table salt

¼ teaspoon pepper

¼ cup vegetable oil

WHY THIS RECIPE WORKS

In the seafood cake world, crisp-crusted salmon cakes aren't sea shack classics; they're a bit more refined and can serve as an elegant meal. Salmon has a distinctive flavor and moist, delicate texture, and it should stand here, not camouflaged by gluey binders. And because of that distinctive taste, salmon can handle assertive flavors. Southwestern-inspired ingredients made the cakes something different than the norm: spicy canned green chiles, fresh cilantro and scallions, lime zest and juice, and chipotle chile powder. Pulsing small pieces of salmon (raw was preferred over common canned, which turned fishy) allowed for more even chopping and resulted in small, discrete pieces of fish. Light and crisp panko also pulled double duty, binding the cakes and coating the exteriors. We like to serve a light green salad on the side. The salmon cakes are pictured with Herb Yogurt Sauce (page 71).

1 | Spread ¾ cup panko in shallow dish. Working in 2 batches, pulse salmon in food processor until coarsely chopped into ¼-inch to ½-inch pieces, about 3 pulses, transferring each batch to large bowl. Gently fold in mayonnaise, chiles, cilantro, scallions, lime zest and juice, chile powder, salt, pepper, and remaining ¾ cup panko.

2 | Using your lightly moistened hands, divide salmon mixture into 4 equal portions, then gently shape each portion into 3½-inch-wide cake. Working with 1 cake at a time, dredge in panko, pressing lightly to adhere; transfer to plate.

3 | Heat oil in 12-inch nonstick skillet over medium heat until shimmering. Cook cakes until well browned, 3 to 4 minutes per side. Transfer cakes to paper towel–lined plate and let drain, about 30 seconds per side. Serve with lime wedges.

SIZZLING SAIGON CRÊPES (BÁNH XÈO)

| SERVES 4

SUBSTITUTIONS NONE

Sauce

- 3 tablespoons sugar, divided
- 1 small Thai chile, stemmed and minced
- 1 garlic clove, minced
- ⅔ cup hot water
- 5 tablespoons fish sauce
- ¼ cup lime juice (2 limes)

- 1 head Boston lettuce (8 ounces), leaves separated and left whole
- 1 cup Thai basil leaves
- 1 cup fresh cilantro leaves and thin stems

Crêpes

- 1 cup hot water (120 to 130 degrees)
- ½ cup (3 ounces) white rice flour
- 3 tablespoons cornstarch
- ½ teaspoon ground turmeric
- ½ teaspoon table salt, divided
- 3 tablespoons vegetable oil, divided
- 4 ounces boneless country-style pork ribs, trimmed and cut into 2-inch-long matchsticks
- 1 small red onion, halved and sliced thin
- 6 ounces medium-large shrimp (31 to 40 per pound), peeled, deveined, halved lengthwise, and halved crosswise
- ⅓ cup coconut milk
- 6 ounces (3 cups) bean sprouts

WHY THIS RECIPE WORKS

Named for the sound they make when the batter hits a hot wok, sizzling Saigon crêpes are paper-thin, crispy, crackly rice flour pancakes usually stuffed with a savory but delicate pork and shrimp mixture. The crêpes are cut into pieces and folded inside lettuce leaves along with Thai basil and cilantro to form rolls. For the filling, we sautéed matchsticks of country-style ribs, which are ultraflavorful but also tender, and we stirred in pieces of delicate shrimp to cook through in the last 2 minutes and add their bursts of juicy sweetness. We used hot water in the rice flour batter to minimize the flour's gritty texture—and a generous amount of it to create a loose batter for a thin crêpe. Alongside the rolls is a bold and zesty dipping sauce of lime juice, sugar, fish sauce, garlic, and Thai chile called *nuoc cham*. To flavor every drop of sauce with garlic and chile, we used a portion of the sugar to help grind the pungent ingredients into a paste. Make sure to stir the coconut milk thoroughly to combine before measuring it. Although we prefer the richer flavor of regular coconut milk, light coconut milk can be substituted. The crêpes are fragile during the early stages of cooking, so take care not to disturb them until they loosen from the pan with nothing more than a gentle shake. If you can't find Thai basil leaves, substitute regular basil.

1 | **For the sauce** Using mortar and pestle (using flat side of chef's knife on a cutting board), mash 1 tablespoon sugar, Thai chile, and garlic to fine paste. Transfer to bowl and add hot water and remaining 2 tablespoons sugar. Stir until sugar is dissolved. Stir in fish sauce and lime juice. Divide dipping sauce among 4 individual small serving bowls, and arrange lettuce, basil, and cilantro on serving platter; set aside.

2 | **For the crêpes** Adjust oven rack to middle position and heat oven to 275 degrees. Set wire rack in rimmed baking sheet and spray with vegetable oil spray; set aside. Whisk water, rice flour, cornstarch, turmeric, and ¼ teaspoon salt in bowl until smooth.

3 | Heat 1 teaspoon oil in 12-inch nonstick skillet over medium-high heat until shimmering. Add pork and onion and cook, stirring occasionally, until pork is no longer pink and onion is softened, 5 to 7 minutes. Add shrimp and remaining ¼ teaspoon salt and continue to cook, stirring occasionally, until shrimp just begins to turn pink, about 2 minutes. Transfer mixture to second bowl. Wipe out skillet with paper towels. Add coconut milk and 2 teaspoons oil to crêpe batter and stir to combine.

4 | Heat 2 teaspoons oil in now-empty skillet over medium-high heat until just smoking. Add one-third of shrimp mixture and heat through until sizzling, about 30 seconds. Spread shrimp mixture over one half of skillet. Pour ½ cup

of batter evenly over entire skillet. (It's fine to pour batter over filling; it will drain to skillet surface. If needed, tilt pan gently to fill gaps.) Spread 1 cup bean sprouts over filling. Cook until crêpe loosens completely from bottom of pan with gentle shake, 4 to 5 minutes. Reduce heat to medium-low and continue to cook, shaking pan occasionally, until edges of crêpe are lacy and crisp and underside is golden brown, 2 to 4 minutes.

5 | Gently fold unfilled side of crêpe over sprouts. Slide crêpe onto wire rack and transfer to oven to keep warm. Repeat 2 more times with remaining oil, batter, shrimp mixture, and bean sprouts. When final crêpe is cooked, transfer all 3 crêpes to cutting board and cut each crosswise into 1¼-inch-wide strips; transfer to serving platter. To eat, wrap individual strip of crêpe and several leaves of basil and cilantro in lettuce leaf, and dip into sauce.

CALIFORNIA FISH TACOS | SERVES 6

SUBSTITUTIONS BLACK SEA BASS • HADDOCK • HAKE • POLLOCK

Pickled Onions

- 1 small red onion, halved and sliced thin
- 2 jalapeño chiles, stemmed and sliced into thin rings
- 1 cup white wine vinegar
- 2 tablespoons lime juice
- 1 tablespoon sugar
- 1 teaspoon table salt

Cabbage

- 3 cups shredded green cabbage
- ¼ cup pickling liquid from pickled onions
- ½ teaspoon table salt
- ½ teaspoon pepper

White Sauce

- ½ cup mayonnaise
- ½ cup sour cream
- 2 tablespoons lime juice
- 2 tablespoons milk

Fish

- 2 pounds skinless cod fillets, cut into 4 by 1-inch strips
- 2 teaspoons table salt, divided
- ½ teaspoon pepper
- ¾ cup all-purpose flour
- ¼ cup cornstarch
- 1 teaspoon baking powder
- 1 cup beer
- 1 quart peanut or vegetable oil
- 1 cup fresh cilantro leaves
- 24 (6-inch) corn tortillas, warmed

WHY THIS RECIPE WORKS

California-style tacos combine delicate fried white fish, crunchy cabbage, spicy pickled onions, and creamy white sauce on a corn tortilla (or two) to deliver an irresistibly dynamic combination of colors, textures, and flavors. Too often, though, the beer batter coating is thick and heavy, covering—literally and figuratively—the delicate fish. A combination of flour, cornstarch, and baking powder made our coating ethereally thin, light, and crispy. The exterior of the fried fish stayed crisp for an hour in a warm oven, making this entrée easy to prepare for company. Plus, the white sauce and pickled onions could be made two days in advance. A light-bodied American lager, such as Budweiser, works best here. Cut the fish on a slight bias if your fillets aren't quite 4 inches wide. You should end up with about 24 pieces of fish. Use a Dutch oven that holds 6 quarts or more.

1 | For the pickled onions Combine onion and jalapeños in bowl. Bring vinegar, lime juice, sugar, and salt to boil in small saucepan, then pour vinegar mixture over onion mixture and let sit for at least 30 minutes; set aside until ready to serve. (Pickled onions can be refrigerated for up to 2 days.)

2 | For the cabbage Toss all ingredients together in bowl; set aside until ready to serve.

3 | For the white sauce Whisk all ingredients together in bowl; set aside until ready to serve. (Sauce can be refrigerated for up to 2 days.)

4 | For the fish Adjust oven rack to middle position and heat oven to 200 degrees. Set wire rack in rimmed baking sheet. Pat fish dry with paper towels and sprinkle with 1 teaspoon salt and pepper. Whisk flour, cornstarch, baking powder, and remaining 1 teaspoon salt together in large bowl. Whisk in beer until smooth. Transfer cod to batter and gently toss to evenly coat.

5 | Add oil to large Dutch oven until it measures about ¾ inch deep and heat over medium-high heat to 350 degrees. Working with 5 to 6 pieces at a time, remove cod from batter, allowing excess batter to drip back into bowl, and add to hot oil, briefly dragging cod along surface of oil to prevent sticking before gently dropping into oil. Adjust burner, if necessary, to maintain oil temperature between 325 and 350 degrees. Cook, stirring gently to prevent pieces from sticking together, until golden brown and crisp, about 2 minutes per side. Using wire skimmer or slotted spoon, transfer fish to prepared rack and place in oven to keep warm. Return oil to 350 degrees and repeat with remaining fish.

6 | Divide fish, pickled onions, cabbage, white sauce, and cilantro evenly among tortillas. Serve.

SALMON TACOS | SERVES 6

Avocado Crema

- ½ avocado, chopped
- ¼ cup chopped fresh cilantro
- 3 tablespoons water
- 1 tablespoon lime juice
- 1 tablespoon plain yogurt

Tacos

- ¼ teaspoon grated lime zest plus 2 tablespoons juice
- 1 teaspoon table salt, divided
- 4 ounces collard greens, stemmed and sliced thin (2 cups)
- 4 ounces jícama, peeled and cut into 2-inch-long matchsticks
- 4 radishes, trimmed and cut into 1-inch-long matchsticks
- ½ small red onion, halved and sliced thin
- ¼ cup fresh cilantro leaves
- 1½ teaspoons chili powder
- ¼ teaspoon pepper
- 4 (6- to 8-ounce) skin-on salmon fillets, 1 inch thick
- 1 tablespoon vegetable oil
- 12 (6-inch) corn tortillas, warmed

  Hot sauce

WHY THIS RECIPE WORKS

While we love California-style fish tacos (see page 225), we're not always up for deep frying on taco Tuesday. This gave us the opportunity to branch out and make tacos with rich salmon rather than more common white fish. A flavorful spice rub gave the fillets a nice crust without the need for batter. And why not change direction on the slaw, too? Thinly sliced collard greens, radishes, cooling jícama, red onion, cilantro, and lime perfectly complemented the robust salmon. For added richness and a creamy element, we served the tacos with an avocado crema. You can substitute 2 cups thinly sliced purple cabbage for the collards if desired. If using Arctic char or wild salmon, cook the fillets until they reach 120 degrees (for medium-rare) and start checking for doneness after 2 minutes.

1 | **For the avocado crema** Process all ingredients in food processor until smooth, about 1 minute, scraping down sides of bowl as needed. Season with salt and pepper to taste; set aside until ready to serve. (Crema can be refrigerated with plastic wrap pressed flush to surface for up to 2 days.)

2 | **For the tacos** Whisk lime zest and juice and ¼ teaspoon salt together in large bowl. Add collard greens, jícama, radishes, onion, and cilantro and toss to combine; set aside.

3 | Combine chili powder, remaining ¾ teaspoon salt, and pepper in small bowl. Pat salmon dry with paper towels and sprinkle evenly with spice mixture. Heat oil in 12-inch nonstick skillet over medium-high heat until shimmering. Cook salmon, skin side up, until well browned, 3 to 5 minutes. Flip and continue to cook until salmon is still translucent when checked with tip of paring knife and registers 125 degrees (for medium-rare), 3 to 5 minutes. Transfer salmon to plate and let cool slightly, about 2 minutes. Using 2 forks, flake salmon into rough 2-inch pieces, discarding skin.

4 | Divide salmon, collard slaw, and avocado crema evenly among tortillas and drizzle with hot sauce to taste. Serve.

TUNA TOSTADAS | SERVES 6

SUBSTITUTIONS NONE

Sriracha Sauce

- ⅓ cup mayonnaise
- 1 tablespoon sriracha

Slaw

- 2 tablespoons toasted sesame oil
- 2 tablespoons rice vinegar
- 2 tablespoons soy sauce
- 2¼ teaspoons sugar
- 1½ teaspoons grated fresh ginger
- ½ head napa cabbage, shredded (about 5½ cups)

Tuna

- ¾ cup sesame seeds
- 4 (6-ounce) skinless tuna steaks, 1-inch thick
- 2 tablespoons vegetable oil, divided
- ½ teaspoon table salt
- ¼ teaspoon pepper

- 12 (6-inch) tostada shells
- 2 scallions, sliced thin on bias

WHY THIS RECIPE WORKS

We love fish tacos—from the traditional to the unique—and, as you've seen, we think they work for nearly any type of fish. But to give tuna the tortilla treatment, we turned to the taco's open-faced cousin, the tostada; we love the contrast of this fish's buttery texture with the crispy shell, and its pretty pink color provided visual appeal on top. A sesame crust added extra crunch and served as a jumping off point for a tostada with Asian-inspired ingredients. Slices of the seared tuna rest on a bed of delicate napa cabbage shreds, tossed in a soy sauce, fresh ginger, and sesame oil vinaigrette. For side slaw, we often salt our cabbage in advance but since tostadas are eaten right away, we tossed the cabbage with the dressing just before assembling the tostadas to easily avoid water-logged slaw. A spicy, creamy, tangy component comes in the form of a sriracha mayo. A sprinkling of thinly sliced scallions finishes with bright green color. We found that 1½ pounds of tuna was ideal for 12 tostadas.

1 | **For the sauce** Whisk mayonnaise and sriracha together in small bowl. Refrigerate until ready to serve.

2 | **For the slaw** Whisk sesame oil, vinegar, soy sauce, vegetable oil, sugar, and ginger together in large bowl. Set dressing aside until ready to serve.

3 | **For the tuna** Spread sesame seeds in shallow dish. Pat tuna dry with paper towels then rub steaks all over with 1 tablespoon oil and sprinkle with salt and pepper. Press both sides of each steak in sesame seeds to coat.

4 | Heat remaining 1 tablespoon oil in 12-inch nonstick skillet over medium-high heat until just smoking. Place steaks in skillet, and cook, flipping every 1 to 2 minutes, until center is translucent red when checked with tip of paring knife and registers 110 degrees (for rare), 2 to 4 minutes. Transfer steaks to cutting board and slice ¼ inch thick.

5 | Add cabbage to dressing in large bowl and toss to coat. Divide slaw, tuna, and sriracha sauce evenly among tostada shells. Sprinkle with scallions and serve.

SHRIMP TACOS | SERVES 6

SUBSTITUTIONS NONE

2 tomatoes, cored and chopped

1 small onion, chopped fine

1 jalapeño chile, stemmed, seeded, and minced

2 tablespoons ketchup

1 tablespoon lime juice, plus lime wedges for serving

2 garlic cloves, minced

Salt and pepper

1 pound large shrimp (26 to 30 per pound), peeled, deveined, and tails removed

5 tablespoons vegetable oil

12 (6-inch) corn tortillas

8 ounces Monterey Jack cheese, shredded (2 cups)

Shredded iceberg lettuce

Diced avocado

Chopped fresh cilantro

Hot sauce

WHY THIS RECIPE WORKS

These melty, crispy, shrimp-and-salsa-filled bundles might be the best tacos you've never had. (Yet.) We were inspired by a brilliant taco-shop recipe for shrimp tacos that combines the best characteristics of a taco and a quesadilla, boasting crisped corn tortillas, gooey melted cheese, and a medley of saucy shrimp, shredded lettuce, diced avocado, and chopped fresh cilantro. To achieve these results without any risky, time-consuming stovetop batch cooking, we turned to the oven. We placed six tortillas on each of two oiled rimmed baking sheets and topped them with cheese and a quick-cooked shrimp filling before baking them until the tortillas crisped and the cheese melted. Topping our "tacodillas" with shredded lettuce, fresh cilantro, and diced avocado just before serving allowed us to combine the vibrancy of a taco with the warmth and comfort of a quesadilla. We developed this recipe using Mission White Corn Tortillas, Restaurant Style, but any 100 percent corn tortillas will work here. For a spicier taco filling, reserve the jalapeño seeds and add them to the tomato mixture in step 1.

1 | Adjust oven rack to lowest position and heat oven to 450 degrees. Combine tomatoes, onion, jalapeño, ketchup, lime juice, garlic, 1 teaspoon salt, and ¼ teaspoon pepper in large bowl; set aside. Cut shrimp into ½-inch pieces.

2 | Heat 1 tablespoon oil in 12-inch skillet over medium-high heat until shimmering. Add tomato mixture and cook until liquid is slightly thickened and tomatoes begin to break down, 5 to 7 minutes. Reduce heat to medium, stir in shrimp, and cook until shrimp are just opaque, about 2 minutes.

3 | Brush 2 rimmed baking sheets with 2 tablespoons oil (1 tablespoon per sheet). Arrange tortillas in single layer on prepared sheets (6 tortillas per sheet). Brush tops of tortillas with remaining 2 tablespoons oil. Divide Monterey Jack evenly among tortillas, then top with shrimp mixture. Bake, 1 sheet at a time, until cheese melts and edges of tortillas just begin to brown and crisp, 7 to 9 minutes.

4 | Garnish with lettuce, avocado, cilantro, and hot sauce, then fold tacos in half. Transfer tacos to platter. Serve, passing lime wedges separately.

SMOKED SALMON NIÇOISE SALAD | SERVES 4

4 large eggs

1 pound small red potatoes, unpeeled, halved

¼ teaspoon table salt, plus salt for cooking potatoes and green beans

8 ounces green beans, trimmed

⅔ cup sour cream

2 tablespoons lemon juice

2 tablespoons water

1 tablespoon chopped fresh dill

⅛ teaspoon pepper

10 ounces (10 cups) mesclun

½ cup pitted kalamata olives, halved

8 ounces sliced cold-smoked salmon

WHY THIS RECIPE WORKS

French salade niçoise is an incredibly satisfying salad, with its mix of vegetables, hard-cooked eggs, olives, and canned tuna—but it could use an update. Swapping out the tuna for flavor-packed smoked salmon and pairing the more robust fish with a creamy dressing rather than the usual vinaigrette were tasteful twists on the classic. Since they're dabbed with flavorful dressing, the potatoes and green beans needed nothing more than a boil in salted water. Starting the potatoes first and adding the green beans later ensured that both vegetables finished cooking at the same time and that the green beans remained bright and vibrant. A three-ingredient (plus salt and pepper) dressing of sour cream, lemon, and dill was a fitting pairing for smoked salmon and brought this new niçoise together; we tossed a small amount with the greens to ensure even distribution and then served the rest for drizzling on top of the other components. Use red potatoes measuring 1 to 2 inches in diameter. If you don't have a steamer basket, use a spoon or tongs to gently place the eggs directly in the boiling water.

1 | Bring 1 inch water to rolling boil in large saucepan over high heat. Place eggs in steamer basket and transfer to saucepan. Cover, reduce heat to medium-low, and cook eggs for 13 minutes.

2 | When eggs are almost finished cooking, fill large bowl halfway with ice and water. Using tongs or slotted spoon, transfer eggs to ice bath and let sit for 15 minutes. Peel and halve cooled hard-cooked eggs.

3 | Bring 4 quarts water to boil in now-empty saucepan. Add potatoes and 1½ tablespoons salt, return to boil, and cook for 10 minutes. Add green beans and continue to cook until both vegetables are tender, about 4 minutes. Drain vegetables well and set aside to cool slightly.

4 | Whisk sour cream, lemon juice, water, dill, salt, and pepper in large bowl until incorporated; set aside all but ¼ cup dressing. Add mesclun to ¼ cup dressing in bowl and toss to coat, then divide mesclun among individual serving dishes. Top with potatoes, green beans, eggs, olives, and salmon and drizzle with reserved dressing. Serve.

SANDWICHES, TACOS, SALADS, AND MORE

FENNEL AND APPLE SALAD WITH SMOKED MACKEREL | SERVES 4 TO 6

SUBSTITUTIONS HOT-SMOKED SALMON • HOT-SMOKED TROUT

3 tablespoons lemon juice

1 tablespoon whole-grain mustard

1 small shallot, minced

2 teaspoons minced fresh tarragon, divided

½ teaspoon table salt

¼ teaspoon pepper

¼ cup extra-virgin olive oil

5 ounces (5 cups) watercress

2 Granny Smith apples, peeled, cored, and cut into 3-inch-long matchsticks

1 fennel bulb, stalks discarded, bulb halved, cored, and sliced thin

6 ounces hot-smoked mackerel, skin and pin bones removed, flaked

WHY THIS RECIPE WORKS

Smoked mackerel has a rich, intense flavor that goes a long way to introduce interest to salads, and hardy, flavorful fennel is a much better pairing with the rich mackerel than wimpy lettuce. Often underappreciated, raw fennel has a lively anise flavor and a wonderfully crunchy texture that make it a superb salad candidate and one that can stand up to robust ingredients. For even more green, we supplemented the thinly sliced fennel with peppery watercress, and Granny Smith apples provided sweetness and more crunch. A simple lemon and oil–based vinaigrette with fresh tarragon, shallot, and tangy whole-grain mustard enhanced every ingredient.

1 | Whisk lemon juice, mustard, shallot, 1 teaspoon tarragon, salt, and pepper together in large bowl. While whisking constantly, slowly drizzle in oil until combined. Add watercress, apples, and fennel and gently toss to coat. Season with salt and pepper to taste.

2 | Divide salad evenly among individual serving dishes, top with smoked mackerel, and sprinkle with remaining 1 teaspoon tarragon. Serve immediately.

MEDITERRANEAN COUSCOUS SALAD WITH SMOKED TROUT | SERVES 4 TO 6

SUBSTITUTIONS HOT-SMOKED MACKEREL • HOT-SMOKED SALMON

1½ cups couscous

¾ teaspoon table salt

⅓ cup extra-virgin olive oil, plus extra for drizzling

1 cup pepperoncini, stemmed and sliced into thin rings, plus 3 tablespoons brine

1 garlic clove, minced

8 ounces cherry tomatoes, halved

½ cup fresh parsley leaves

3 scallions, sliced thin

6 ounces hot-smoked trout, skin and pin bones removed, flaked

Lemon wedges

WHY THIS RECIPE WORKS

Grain and pasta salads offer a nice change from greens and a mild canvas for smoked fish. Flaking smoked trout into quick-cooking couscous brings this dinner-worthy salad to the Mediterranean. Pepperoncini and cherry tomatoes add spiciness and freshness for a simple salad with incredible complexity. A tangy vinaigrette soaks into and livens up the grains, providing a refreshing pairing to the smoky richness of the trout. The brine from the pepperoncini is an ingredient that often goes to waste—not here, as we used the brine instead of vinegar in the dressing. Tossing the cooked couscous with the dressing while it's still warm helps it absorb the dressing as it cools in the refrigerator.

1 | Bring 2 cups water to boil in medium saucepan. Remove pot from heat, then stir in couscous and salt. Cover and let sit for 10 minutes. Fluff couscous with fork.

2 | Whisk oil, brine, and garlic together in large bowl. Transfer couscous to bowl with dressing and toss to combine. Let sit until cooled completely, about 20 minutes.

3 | Add cherry tomatoes, parsley, scallions, and pepperoncini rings to cooled couscous and gently toss to combine. Season with salt, pepper, and extra olive oil to taste. Divide salad among individual serving dishes and top with smoked trout. Serve with lemon wedges.

FENNEL AND BIBB SALAD WITH SCALLOPS AND HAZELNUTS | SERVES 4

SUBSTITUTIONS NONE

- 1½ pounds large sea scallops, tendons removed
- ¾ teaspoon table salt, divided
- ½ teaspoon pepper, divided
- 7 tablespoons extra-virgin olive oil, divided
- 1 small shallot, minced
- ½ teaspoon grated lemon zest plus 1½ tablespoons juice
- 1 teaspoon Dijon mustard
- 2 heads Bibb lettuce (1 pound), torn into bite-size pieces
- 1 fennel bulb, 1 tablespoon fronds minced, stalk discarded, bulb halved, cored, and sliced thin
- 4 radishes, trimmed and sliced thin
- ¼ cup hazelnuts, toasted, skinned, and chopped
- 2 tablespoons minced fresh tarragon

WHY THIS RECIPE WORKS

Scallops come off as a little fancy: Their pristinely smooth flesh and superlative sweetness seem to call for a special occasion. But scallops don't have to be finished with a luxurious sauce at a dinner party; they're an ideal weeknight meal because they're super-quick-cooking and healthful, and just as welcome paired with greens. After quickly searing the scallops to browned perfection, we made a salad of delicate Bibb lettuce and crisp sliced fennel and radish. We tossed the vegetables with a lemon vinaigrette and topped individual portions with warm scallops, in addition to chopped toasted hazelnuts, which brought out the natural sweet nuttiness of the seared scallops, plus tarragon to emphasize the anise flavor of the fennel.

1 | Pat scallops dry with paper towels and sprinkle with ½ teaspoon salt and ¼ teaspoon pepper. Heat 1 tablespoon oil in skillet over high heat until just smoking. Add half of scallops in single layer and cook, without moving, until well browned, 1½ to 2 minutes. Flip and cook until sides are firm and centers are opaque, 30 to 90 seconds (remove scallops as they finish cooking). Transfer scallops to plate and tent with aluminum foil. Wipe out skillet with paper towels and repeat with 1 tablespoon oil and remaining scallops.

2 | Whisk shallot, lemon zest and juice, mustard, remaining ¼ teaspoon salt, and remaining ¼ teaspoon pepper together in large bowl. While whisking constantly, slowly drizzle in remaining 5 tablespoons oil until combined. Add lettuce, sliced fennel, and radishes and toss to combine. Season with salt and pepper to taste. Divide salad among individual serving dishes, then top with scallops and sprinkle with hazelnuts, tarragon, and fennel fronds. Serve.

SHRIMP AND ARUGULA SALAD WITH LEMON VINAIGRETTE | SERVES 4

3 slices hearty white sandwich bread, cut into ½-inch pieces

2 ounces Parmesan cheese, 1 ounce grated (½ cup), 1 ounce shaved with vegetable peeler

½ cup extra-virgin olive oil, divided

3 garlic cloves, minced, divided

1 pound jumbo shrimp (16 to 20 per pound), peeled, deveined, and tails removed

1½ teaspoons table salt, divided

¾ teaspoon pepper, divided

2 teaspoons balsamic vinegar

1 teaspoon Dijon mustard

½ teaspoon grated lemon zest plus 1 teaspoon juice

8 ounces (8 cups) baby arugula

WHY THIS RECIPE WORKS

Some people might follow a rule that cheese and seafood don't mix, but recipes should consider taste rather than archaic rules. Shrimp is one type of seafood that stands up quite well to cheese. They're lean and sweet and so benefit from a rich, salty counterpoint, while also being flavorful enough that they're not overshadowed by the cheese. Pairing shrimp and elegant shavings of Parmesan cheese in a refined dinner salad featuring tender but spicy baby arugula and balsamic vinaigrette proved our point. Dainty Parmesan-coated croutons give the salad crunch and more salty presence. The sautéed jumbo shrimp are an impressive topper to a salad that couldn't be easier—and couldn't look or taste better.

1 | Toss bread, grated Parmesan, 3 tablespoons oil, and two-thirds of garlic together in bowl. Cook in 12-inch nonstick skillet over medium-low heat, stirring constantly, until croutons are golden brown, about 8 minutes; transfer to plate to cool.

2 | Pat shrimp dry with paper towels, then sprinkle with ½ teaspoon salt and ¼ teaspoon pepper. Heat 2 tablespoons oil in now-empty skillet over medium-high heat until just smoking. Add shrimp and cook, stirring occasionally, until opaque throughout, 3 to 5 minutes; transfer to second plate to cool.

3 | Whisk vinegar, mustard, lemon zest and juice, remaining garlic, remaining 1 teaspoon salt, and remaining ½ teaspoon pepper together in large bowl. While whisking constantly, slowly drizzle in remaining 3 tablespoons oil until combined. Add arugula and toss to combine, then top with shrimp, croutons, and shaved Parmesan. Serve.

SHRIMP SALAD | SERVES 4

5 tablespoons lemon juice (2 lemons), spent halves reserved, divided

5 sprigs fresh parsley plus 1 teaspoon minced

3 sprigs fresh tarragon plus 1 teaspoon minced

1 tablespoon sugar

1 teaspoon black peppercorns

1 pound extra-large shrimp (21 to 25 per pound), peeled, deveined, and tails removed

Table salt for poaching shrimp

¼ cup mayonnaise

1 small shallot, minced

1 small celery rib, minced

WHY THIS RECIPE WORKS

A great deli-style shrimp salad should contain firm, tender shrimp and a creamy dressing that doesn't mask the flavor of the shrimp or drown out the other ingredients. Gently poaching the shrimp in a highly aromatic brew of water, lemon, herb sprigs, a little sugar, and peppercorns gave them flavor from the start. Flavor-infused shrimp didn't need a mask, so we kept the traditional mayonnaise in our recipe but limited the amount to ¼ cup for a pound of shrimp. This makes a light coating that gives the salad just enough moisture to bring it together so it works well on buns, in lettuce cups, or over greens. Celery adds nice crunch, and shallot, herbs, and lemon juice round out the flavors of the mayo dressing.

1 | Bring 2 cups water, ¼ cup lemon juice, reserved lemon halves, parsley sprigs, tarragon sprigs, sugar, and peppercorns to boil in medium saucepan. Stir in shrimp and 1 teaspoon salt. Cover and let sit off heat until shrimp are opaque, about 5 minutes, shaking saucepan halfway through sitting time.

2 | Meanwhile, fill large bowl halfway with ice and water. Drain shrimp and transfer to ice bath, discarding aromatics; let cool for 3 to 5 minutes. Drain shrimp and pat dry with paper towels. Cut shrimp in half lengthwise, then cut each half into thirds.

3 | Whisk mayonnaise, shallot, celery, remaining 1 tablespoon lemon juice, minced parsley, and minced tarragon together in bowl. Add shrimp and toss to combine. Season with salt and pepper to taste. Serve.

variations |

SHRIMP SALAD WITH CORN AND CHIPOTLE

Omit tarragon sprigs. Substitute 5 tablespoons lime juice and spent lime halves for lemon juice and lemon halves, ½ cup cooked corn kernels for celery, 2 tablespoons minced canned chipotle chile in adobo sauce for minced parsley, and 1 tablespoon minced fresh cilantro for minced tarragon.

SHRIMP SALAD WITH WASABI AND PICKLED GINGER

Omit tarragon sprigs and minced tarragon. Substitute 2 thinly sliced scallions for shallot and 2 tablespoons chopped pickled ginger for minced parsley. Add 1 tablespoon toasted sesame seeds and 2 teaspoons wasabi powder to mayonnaise mixture.

MEDITERRANEAN TUNA SALAD | SERVES 6

SUBSTITUTIONS NONE

3 tablespoons lemon juice, plus extra for seasoning

2 teaspoons Dijon mustard

½ teaspoon pepper

5 tablespoons extra-virgin olive oil

¼ cup minced red onion

1 garlic clove, minced

4 (5-ounce) cans solid white tuna in water, drained and flaked

2 celery ribs, minced

1 red bell pepper, stemmed, seeded, and chopped fine

¼ cup pitted kalamata olives, minced

¼ cup minced fresh parsley

WHY THIS RECIPE WORKS

A brown-bag staple, tuna salad too often turns out bland or overridden with mayonnaise so it soaks through slices of white bread (and maybe the bag, too). A staple doesn't have to be stale: This is a vibrant tuna salad recipe we'd want to bring to lunch every day. As an alternative to mayonnaise, a dressing of fruity extra-virgin olive oil, lemon juice, and Dijon mustard was a luscious base to bind our salad with bright punch. We added red onion and garlic to the mix and let them sit to temper the alliums' harsh bite in this raw application. Sweet red bell pepper, crunchy celery, and kalamata olives turned this lunchtime basic into a sophisticated meal with varied flavors and textures. Good-quality canned tuna is crucial for this recipe. Our preferred canned tuna packed in water is Wild Planet Wild Albacore Tuna. The salad is particularly great served over a bed of lettuce or as part of an open-faced sandwich.

Whisk lemon juice, mustard, and pepper together in large bowl. While whisking constantly, slowly drizzle in oil until combined. Stir in red onion and garlic and let sit for 5 minutes. Add tuna, celery, bell pepper, olives, and parsley and toss to coat. Season with extra lemon juice and pepper to taste. Serve.

variation |
MEDITERRANEAN TUNA SALAD WITH CARROTS, RADISHES, AND CILANTRO

Substitute 6 thinly sliced radishes for celery, 2 peeled and shredded carrots for bell pepper, and minced fresh cilantro for parsley.

CRAB LOUIS SALAD | SERVES 4 TO 6

SUBSTITUTIONS NONE

Dressing

- ½ cup mayonnaise
- ¼ cup sour cream
- ¼ cup finely chopped green bell pepper
- 4 scallions, sliced thin
- 2 tablespoons chopped pitted green olives
- 2 tablespoons chili sauce
- 5 teaspoons lemon juice
- 2 teaspoons chopped fresh tarragon
- ¼ teaspoon table salt
- ¼ teaspoon pepper
- ⅛ teaspoon cayenne pepper

Salad

- 3 large eggs
- 1 pound fresh crabmeat, picked over for shells and pressed dry between paper towels
- 2 heads Bibb lettuce (1 pound), leaves separated and torn into 1½-inch pieces
- 8 ounces grape tomatoes, halved
- 1 ripe avocado, halved, pitted, quartered, and sliced thin

WHY THIS RECIPE WORKS

This tangy salad of flaky crabmeat, crisp lettuce, and an array of add-ins like tomatoes and hard-cooked eggs, all mixed with a creamy Thousand Island–style dressing, was once the king of salads on the West Coast, but it seemed to have fallen out of fashion—until now. This delicious retro dish is back for contemporary tables. Here we used good-quality fresh crabmeat, as its flavor has nowhere to hide in a salad; the fresh crab has a sweet, oceany flavor and soft texture. We tossed the crab with our own version of the signature Louis dressing—bright, tangy, and creamy—and spooned it over a bed of buttery Bibb lettuce, sweet grape tomatoes, ripe avocado, and hard-cooked eggs. Chili sauce, a condiment similar to ketchup, has a sweet flavor and a subtle, spicy kick that amps up the dressing; do not substitute Asian chili-garlic sauce. If you can't find fresh crabmeat, pasteurized packaged lump crabmeat, though not as good, is a decent substitute; do not use canned crabmeat.

1 | **For the dressing** Whisk all ingredients together in bowl; set aside until ready to serve.

2 | **For the salad** Bring 1 inch water to rolling boil in medium saucepan over high heat. Place eggs in steamer basket and transfer to saucepan. Cover, reduce heat to medium-low, and cook eggs for 13 minutes. When eggs are almost finished cooking, fill large bowl halfway with ice and water. Using tongs or slotted spoon, transfer eggs to ice bath and let sit for 15 minutes. Peel and quarter cooled hard-cooked eggs.

3 | Gently toss crabmeat with ½ cup dressing in bowl. Mound lettuce in center of serving platter, then arrange tomatoes, eggs, and avocado over top. Top with dressed crab and serve, passing remaining dressing separately.

CHAPTER 5

on the grill

FLIPPING FISH FILLETS ON THE GRILL

1 Slide fish spatula between fillet and grill grate to check that fish releases easily.

2 Gently push fillet to roll it over onto the skin side.

GRILLED SALMON FILLETS | SERVES 4

SUBSTITUTIONS ARCTIC CHAR • WILD SALMON

4 (6- to 8-ounce) skin-on salmon fillets, 1 inch thick
½ teaspoon table salt
½ teaspoon pepper
2 teaspoons vegetable oil

WHY THIS RECIPE WORKS

Rich salmon tastes ultrasatisfying with grill char—when it doesn't come off mangled. Grilling delicate fish can incite fear even in confident cooks, but anyone can achieve tender flesh and crispy skin if they mind their molecules. The molecular bond between fish proteins and the grill happens in an instant, but there are two options to prevent sticking: altering the proteins on the fish's surface or placing a barrier between fish and grill. Parcooking to alter proteins seemed silly, and a physical barrier prevented grill marks. We'd need an oil barrier, but a layer wasn't enough: As oil heats, its fatty-acid chains form polymers (they stick together) in a crisscross pattern over the metal. One layer of polymers won't prevent sticking, but applying and heating oil repeatedly builds a thick layer so proteins don't come into direct contact with the metal. We use this method throughout the chapter. Finishing the salmon on the oily skin provided extra insurance. If using Arctic char or wild salmon, cook the fillets until they reach 120 degrees (for medium-rare) and start checking for doneness early. The salmon is pictured with Creamy Lemon-Garlic Sauce (page 71).

1 | Pat salmon dry with paper towels; refrigerate until ready to grill. Combine salt and pepper in bowl; set aside.

2A | For a charcoal grill Open bottom vent completely. Light large chimney starter filled with charcoal briquettes (6 quarts). When top coals are partially covered with ash, pour evenly over grill. Set cooking grate in place, cover, and open lid vent completely. Heat grill until hot, about 5 minutes.

2B | For a gas grill Turn all burners to high, cover, and heat grill until hot, about 15 minutes. Leave all burners on high.

3 | Fold paper towels into compact wad. Holding paper towels with tongs, dip in oil, then wipe grate. Dip paper towels in oil again and wipe grate for second time. Cover grill and heat for 5 minutes. Uncover and wipe grate twice more with oiled paper towels.

4 | Rub fillets evenly with oil and sprinkle flesh side with salt mixture. Place fillets on grill, flesh side down and perpendicular to grate bars. Cover grill (reduce heat to medium if using gas) and cook, without moving fillets, until flesh side is well marked and releases easily from grill, 4 to 5 minutes.

5 | Using fish spatula, gently flip salmon and continue to cook, covered, until centers of fillets are translucent when checked with tip of paring knife and register 125 degrees (for medium-rare), 4 to 5 minutes longer. (If fillets don't lift cleanly off grill, cover and continue to cook 1 minute longer, at which point they should release.) Transfer fillets to platter.

GRILLED SWORDFISH STEAKS | SERVES 4

SUBSTITUTIONS HALIBUT • MAHI-MAHI • RED SNAPPER • STRIPED BASS

4 (6- to 8-ounce) skin-on swordfish steaks, 1 inch thick

2 tablespoons extra-virgin olive oil

½ teaspoon table salt

¼ teaspoon pepper

WHY THIS RECIPE WORKS

Grilling swordfish doesn't come with as many inherent challenges as more delicate fish like salmon (see page 256), as its dense, meaty flesh generally keeps the steaks from falling apart. Ease is great, but what's even better is that thick swordfish steaks can stay on the grill for a relatively long time, picking up smoky flavor aplenty to complement the robust fish. Keeping the fish in place long enough, 6 to 9 minutes, imparted those dark grill marks that make the fish so appealing. Building a two-level fire, with two-thirds of the coals on one half of the grill and one-third on the other, allowed us to then move the fish to the cooler, less coal-heavy side to finish cooking through evenly. The swordfish is pictured with Salsa Verde (page 72).

1A | **For a charcoal grill** Open bottom vent completely. Light large chimney starter filled with charcoal briquettes (6 quarts). When top coals are partially covered with ash, pour two-thirds evenly over half of grill, then pour remaining coals over other half of grill. Set cooking grate in place, cover, and open lid vent completely. Heat grill until hot, about 5 minutes.

1B | **For a gas grill** Turn all burners to high, cover, and heat grill until hot, about 15 minutes. Leave primary burner on high and turn other burner(s) to medium-high.

2 | Brush swordfish with oil and sprinkle with salt and pepper. Fold paper towels into compact wad. Holding paper towels with tongs, dip in oil, then wipe grate. Dip paper towels in oil again and wipe grate for second time. Cover grill and heat for 5 minutes. Uncover and wipe grate twice more with oiled paper towels. Place swordfish on hotter side of grill, perpendicular to grate bars, and cook, flipping once with metal spatula, until streaked with dark grill marks, 6 to 9 minutes. Move swordfish to cooler side of grill and cook, uncovered, flipping once, until centers of swordfish are no longer translucent when checked with tip of paring knife and register 130 degrees, 3 to 6 minutes. Transfer to platter and let rest for 10 minutes. Serve.

FLIPPING WHOLE FISH ON THE GRILL

1 Slide spatula scant 1 inch under backbone edge and lift edge up.

2 Slide second spatula under, then remove first spatula, allowing fish to ease onto second spatula.

3 Place first spatula on top of fish, in same direction as second spatula; flip fish so it rests on second spatula, then ease fish onto grill.

GRILLED WHOLE RED SNAPPER | SERVES 4

SUBSTITUTIONS BLACK SEA BASS • BRANZINO

2 (1½-pound) whole red snapper, scaled, gutted, and fins snipped off with scissors

3 tablespoons extra-virgin olive oil

1 teaspoon table salt

½ teaspoon pepper

WHY THIS RECIPE WORKS

Roasting whole snapper on the grill is just as simple as oven-roasting it (see page 300) and easily delivers an impressive fish dinner in mere minutes. Coating the fish with a film of oil and just salt and pepper seasoned them and prevented sticking; we loved the clean simplicity of this preparation, as there was so much flavor imparted from the grill. To take the temperature, insert the thermometer into the fillets through the opening by the gills. If your fish are a little larger (between 1¾ and 2 pounds), grill them a minute or two longer on each side. Avoid fish weighing more than 2 pounds, as they will be hard to maneuver on the grill. If using black sea bass, cook the fish to 135 degrees.

1A| For a charcoal grill Open bottom vent completely. Light large chimney starter filled with charcoal briquettes (6 quarts). When top coals are partially covered with ash, pour evenly over grill. Set cooking grate in place, cover, and open lid vent completely. Heat grill until hot, about 5 minutes.

1B| For a gas grill Turn all burners to high, cover, and heat grill until hot, about 15 minutes. Leave all burners on high.

2| Fold paper towels into compact wad. Holding paper towels with tongs, dip in oil, then wipe grate. Dip paper towels in oil again and wipe grate for second time. Cover grill and heat for 5 minutes. Uncover and wipe grate twice more with oiled paper towels. Using sharp knife, make 3 or 4 shallow slashes, about 2 inches apart, on both sides of snapper. Rub snapper with oil and sprinkle inside and outside with salt and pepper.

3| Place snapper on grill, perpendicular to grate bars. Cook (covered if using gas) until browned and crisp, 6 to 7 minutes. Gently flip snapper and cook (covered if using gas) until flesh is no longer translucent at center, second side is blistered and crisp, and fish registers 130 degrees, 6 to 8 minutes. Carefully transfer snapper to serving dish and let rest for 10 minutes.

4| Fillet each snapper by making vertical cut just behind head from top of fish to belly. Make another cut along top of snapper from head to tail. Starting at head and working toward tail, gently slide spatula between top fillet and bones to separate; transfer fillet, skin side up, to serving platter. Gently lift tail and peel skeleton and head from bottom fillet; discard head and skeleton. Transfer second fillet, skin side up, to platter. (See page 24.) Serve.

GRILL-SMOKED SIDE OF SALMON | SERVES 6

SUBSTITUTIONS ARCTIC CHAR • WILD SALMON

5 tablespoons sugar, for brining

5 tablespoons table salt, for brining

1 (2½-pound) skin-on salmon fillet

2 tablespoons vegetable oil

1½ teaspoons paprika

1 teaspoon ground white pepper

2 cups wood chips

WHY THIS RECIPE WORKS

How many ways can you cook a fish favorite? Many, but grill-smoking offers moist, nicely crusted salmon full of smoky flavor. Traditional cold-smoking and curing salmon (cooking—but not fully cooking—salmon at 60 to 90 degrees) keeps the fish moist but requires a smoker and up to 5 days. We developed a faster "hot-smoked" option. Brining was key, and sugar in the brine improved the fish's flavor. We seasoned the salmon with paprika and white pepper and then slow-roasted it on the cooler side of a half-grill fire for more than an hour. The result was salmon that was moist but firm and flaky and just smoky enough. If the skin sticks to the grill, slide a spatula between the fillet and the skin and leave the skin behind. If using Arctic char or wild salmon, cook the fillets until they reach 130 degrees (for medium) and start checking for doneness early. The salmon is pictured with Herb Yogurt Sauce (page 71).

1 | Dissolve sugar and salt in 2 quarts cold water in large container. Submerge salmon in brine, cover, and refrigerate for 15 minutes. Remove salmon from brine, pat dry, and rub with oil. Place salmon on rimmed baking sheet; season with paprika and white pepper. Just before grilling, soak wood chips in water for 15 minutes, then drain. Using large piece of heavy-duty aluminum foil, wrap soaked chips in 8 by 4½-inch foil packet. (Make sure chips do not poke holes in sides or bottom of packet.) Cut 2 evenly spaced 2-inch slits in top of packet.

2A | **For a charcoal grill** Open bottom grill vent halfway. Light large chimney starter half filled with charcoal briquettes (3 quarts). When top coals are partially covered with ash, pour evenly over half of grill. Place wood chip packet on coals. Set cooking grate in place, cover, and open lid vent halfway. Heat grill until hot and wood chips are smoking, about 5 minutes.

2B | **For a gas grill** Remove cooking grate and place wood chip packet directly on primary burner. Set cooking grate in place, turn all burners to high, cover, and heat grill until hot and wood chips are smoking, about 15 minutes. Turn primary burner to medium and turn off other burner(s). (Adjust primary burner as needed to maintain grill temperature around 275 degrees.)

3 | Clean and oil cooking grate. Gently slide salmon from sheet onto cooler side of grill, skin-side down and perpendicular to grate bars. Cover (position lid vent over fish if using charcoal) and cook until center of salmon is translucent when checked with tip of paring knife and registers 125 degrees (for medium-rare), about 1½ hours. Using 2 spatulas, gently remove salmon from grill. Let rest for 5 minutes. Serve salmon hot or at room temperature.

GRILLED SWORDFISH SKEWERS WITH CAPONATA | SERVES 4 TO 6

SUBSTITUTIONS HALIBUT • MAHI-MAHI • RED SNAPPER • STRIPED BASS

¼ cup extra-virgin olive oil, divided

1½ tablespoons honey

1 tablespoon grated lemon zest, plus 2 lemons, halved

5 teaspoons ground coriander, divided

2 garlic cloves, minced

1¼ teaspoons table salt, divided

1 teaspoon ground cumin

½ teaspoon pepper, divided

¼ teaspoon ground cinnamon

⅛ teaspoon ground nutmeg

1½ pounds skinless swordfish steaks, 1¼ inches thick, cut into 1¼-inch pieces

12 ounces cherry tomatoes

1 small eggplant (12 ounces), cut crosswise on bias into ½-inch-thick ovals

6 scallions, trimmed

¼ cup pitted kalamata olives, chopped

2 tablespoons chopped fresh basil

WHY THIS RECIPE WORKS

Swordfish has a robust taste and calls for costarring ingredients with as much oomph. Grill flavor brings character on its own, and cubing the swordfish meant there was more surface area for char. A Sicilian-inspired grilled caponata—a saucy mix of eggplant and tomatoes with a sweet-and-sour profile—completes the supporting cast. The caponata ingredients grill alongside the swordfish. Everything comes together with a sauce made with oil, an aromatic blend of warm spices, garlic, a little honey, and juice from grilled lemons, which transform from tart and acidic to sweet and nuanced. Seasoning the swordfish with coriander, salt, and pepper adds complexity, and fresh basil freshens the dish for an all-star affair. You will need six 12-inch metal skewers for this recipe.

1 | Whisk 2 tablespoons oil, honey, lemon zest, 2 teaspoons coriander, garlic, ¾ teaspoon salt, cumin, ¼ teaspoon pepper, cinnamon, and nutmeg together in large bowl. Microwave, stirring occasionally, until fragrant, about 1 minute; set aside.

2 | Pat swordfish dry with paper towels and sprinkle with remaining 1 tablespoon coriander, remaining ½ teaspoon salt, and remaining ¼ teaspoon pepper. Thread fish onto three 12-inch metal skewers. Thread tomatoes onto remaining three 12-inch metal skewers. Brush swordfish, tomatoes, eggplant, and scallions with remaining 2 tablespoons oil.

3A | **For a charcoal grill** Open bottom vent completely. Light large chimney starter filled with charcoal briquettes (6 quarts). When top coals are partially covered with ash, pour evenly over grill. Set cooking grate in place, cover, and open lid vent completely. Heat grill until hot, about 5 minutes.

3B | **For a gas grill** Turn all burners to high, cover, and heat grill until hot, about 15 minutes. Leave all burners on high.

4 | Fold paper towels into compact wad. Holding paper towels with tongs, dip in oil, then wipe grate. Dip paper towels in oil again and wipe grate for second time. Cover grill and heat for 5 minutes. Uncover and wipe grate twice more with oiled paper towels. Place swordfish, tomatoes, eggplant, scallions, and lemon halves on grill. Cook (covered if using gas), turning as needed, until swordfish flakes apart when gently prodded with paring knife and registers 130 degrees and tomatoes, eggplant, scallions, and lemon halves are softened and lightly charred, 5 to 15 minutes. Transfer items to serving platter as they finish grilling and tent loosely with aluminum foil to keep warm. Let swordfish rest while finishing caponata.

5 | Once lemons are cool enough to handle, squeeze into fine-mesh strainer set over bowl, extracting as much juice as possible. Add juice to spiced oil-honey mixture; whisk to combine and stir in olives.

6 | Using tongs, slide tomatoes off skewers onto cutting board. Chop tomatoes, eggplant, and scallions coarse; transfer to bowl with olives and gently toss to combine. Season with salt and pepper to taste. Remove swordfish from skewers, sprinkle with basil, and serve with caponata.

GRILLED FISH TACOS | SERVES 6

SUBSTITUTIONS HALIBUT • MAHI-MAHI • RED SNAPPER • STRIPED BASS

3 tablespoons vegetable oil, divided

1 tablespoon ancho chile powder

2 teaspoons chipotle chile powder

2 garlic cloves, minced

1 teaspoon dried oregano

1 teaspoon ground coriander

1 teaspoon table salt

2 tablespoons tomato paste

½ cup orange juice

6 tablespoons lime juice (3 limes), divided, plus lime wedges for serving

2 pounds skinless swordfish steaks, 1 inch thick, cut into 1-inch-wide strips

1 pineapple, peeled, quartered, cored, and each quarter halved lengthwise

1 jalapeño chile

18 (6-inch) corn tortillas

1 red bell pepper, stemmed, seeded, and cut into ¼-inch pieces

2 tablespoons minced fresh cilantro, plus extra for serving

½ head iceberg lettuce (4½ ounces), cored and sliced thin

1 ripe avocado, halved, pitted, and sliced thin

WHY THIS RECIPE WORKS

Fish tacos from the Yucatán Peninsula are a work of art—without the batter and fry. Fish is bathed in a chile-citrus mixture and grilled wrapped in banana leaves. We wanted the same profile with a simpler approach. Although traditional recipes use whole snapper or grouper, swordfish is easier to find and strips of it stand up to flipping on the grill. We improvised the traditional chile paste with fruity ancho and smoky chipotle, along with citrusy ground coriander and oregano; we bloomed the mixture in oil with minced garlic and salt to bolster the flavors. A little tomato paste provides a layer of savory-sweet intensity, and a mix of orange and lime juices mimic Mexican sour oranges.

1 | Heat 2 tablespoons oil, ancho chile powder, and chipotle chile powder in 8-inch skillet over medium heat, stirring constantly, until fragrant, 2 to 3 minutes. Add garlic, oregano, coriander, and salt and continue to cook until fragrant, about 30 seconds longer. Add tomato paste and, using spatula, mash tomato paste with spice mixture until combined, about 20 seconds. Stir in orange juice and 2 tablespoons lime juice. Cook, stirring constantly, until thoroughly mixed and reduced slightly, about 2 minutes. Transfer chile mixture to large bowl and let cool for 15 minutes.

2 | Add swordfish to bowl with chile mixture and stir gently with rubber spatula to coat fish. Cover and refrigerate for at least 30 minutes or up to 2 hours.

3A | For a charcoal grill Open bottom vent completely. Light large chimney starter mounded with charcoal briquettes (7 quarts). When top coals are partially covered with ash, pour evenly over grill. Set cooking grate in place, cover, and open lid vent completely. Heat grill until hot, about 5 minutes.

3B | For a gas grill Turn all burners to high, cover, and heat grill until hot, about 15 minutes. Turn all burners to medium-high.

4 | Fold paper towels into compact wad. Holding paper towels with tongs, dip in oil, then wipe grate. Dip paper towels in oil again and wipe grate for second time. Cover grill and heat for 5 minutes. Uncover and wipe grate twice more with oiled paper towels. Brush both sides of pineapple with remaining 1 tablespoon oil. Place swordfish on half of grill. Place pineapple and jalapeño on other half. Cover and cook until swordfish, pineapple, and jalapeño have begun to brown, 3 to 5 minutes. Using thin spatula, flip swordfish, pineapple, and jalapeño. Cover and continue to cook until second sides of pineapple and jalapeño are browned and swordfish registers 140 degrees, 3 to 5 minutes. Transfer swordfish to large platter, flake into pieces, and tent with aluminum foil. Transfer pineapple and jalapeño to cutting board.

GRILLED COD AND SUMMER SQUASH PACKETS | SERVES 4

SUBSTITUTIONS BLACK SEA BASS • HADDOCK • HAKE • POLLOCK

½ cup extra-virgin olive oil

2 shallots, sliced thin

6 garlic cloves, sliced thin

1½ teaspoons table salt, divided

1¼ teaspoons pepper, divided

1 pound summer squash, sliced ¼ inch thick

12 ounces plum tomatoes, sliced ½ inch thick

¼ cup capers, rinsed

4 (6- to 8-ounce) skinless cod fillets, 1 inch thick

1 lemon, sliced into ¼-inch-thick rounds

2 tablespoons minced fresh parsley

WHY THIS RECIPE WORKS

Fish on the grill is quick-cooking and therefore a weeknight-friendly way to stay cool in the summer. Try to add accompaniments to the outdoor mix, however, and things get a bit more time-consuming—or your grill turns into a jigsaw puzzle. For an easy summer Wednesday night dinner on the grill, we cook fish contained in foil packets, choosing seasonal vegetables that finish at the same rate as satisfying cod fillets: summer squash and tomatoes. As the vegetables don't achieve grill char, we tossed them with some garlic oil made simply in the microwave before cooking, reserving the remainder to drizzle on before serving to make something simple extra-special. Briny capers perked up the packets, and a topping of lemon slices on the fish imparted their aroma to each component. Summer in a packet. To test for doneness without opening the foil packets, use a permanent marker to mark an "X" on the outside of the foil where the fish fillet is the thickest, then insert an instant-read thermometer through the "X" into the fish to measure its internal temperature.

1 | Spray centers of four 18 by 14-inch sheets of aluminum foil with vegetable oil spray. Microwave oil, shallots, garlic, 1 teaspoon salt, and 1 teaspoon pepper in large bowl until garlic begins to brown, about 2 minutes. Add squash, tomatoes, and capers to garlic oil and toss to coat.

2 | Pat fish dry with paper towels and sprinkle with remaining ½ teaspoon salt and remaining ¼ teaspoon pepper. Divide vegetable mixture evenly among centers of each piece of foil; reserve garlic oil in bowl. Top each vegetable pile with 1 fish fillet, then divide lemon slices evenly on top of fillets. Bring short sides of foil together and crimp to seal. Crimp remaining open ends of packets to seal.

3A | **For a charcoal grill** Open bottom vent completely. Light large chimney starter filled with charcoal briquettes (6 quarts). When top coals are partially covered with ash, pour evenly over grill. Set cooking grate in place, cover, and open lid vent completely. Heat grill until hot, about 5 minutes.

3B | **For a gas grill** Turn all burners to high, cover, and heat grill until hot, about 15 minutes. Leave all burners on high.

4 | Place packets on grill, squash side down. Cook until fish flakes apart when gently prodded with paring knife and registers 135 degrees, about 10 minutes. (To check temperature, poke thermometer through foil of 1 packet and into fish.) Carefully open packets, sprinkle with parsley, and drizzle with reserved garlic oil to taste. Serve.

ON THE GRILL

GRILLED RED CURRY MAHI-MAHI WITH PINEAPPLE SALSA | SERVES 4

SUBSTITUTIONS HALIBUT • RED SNAPPER • STRIPED BASS • SWORDFISH

2 cups ¼-inch pineapple pieces

1 scallion, sliced thin

¼ cup minced fresh cilantro

2 tablespoons vegetable oil, divided

1 tablespoon red curry paste

4 (6- to 8-ounce) skin-on mahi-mahi fillets, 1 inch thick

WHY THIS RECIPE WORKS

Mahi-mahi fillets are majestic off the grill, their sweet, delicate taste offset by rich, smoky notes. Kissed with char, the hearty, meaty fillets take well to robust flavors—here, a layer of red curry paste. Store-bought curry paste gave us nuanced, complex flavors without the intimidating ingredient list of a do-it-yourself version. With bold flavor achieved, we needed a nod to the sweet side, and a fruit salsa was just the right garnish—and it didn't take much. Pineapple pieces, plus scallion and cilantro for aroma, keep things simple and fresh so the fish is in focus.

1 | Combine pineapple, scallion, cilantro, and 1 tablespoon oil in bowl and season with salt and pepper to taste; set aside until ready to serve. Combine curry paste with remaining 1 tablespoon oil in separate bowl. Pat mahi-mahi dry with paper towels, then brush flesh side with curry paste mixture.

2A | **For a charcoal grill** Open bottom vent completely. Light large chimney starter filled with charcoal briquettes (6 quarts). When top coals are partially covered with ash, pour evenly over grill. Set cooking grate in place, cover, and open lid vent completely. Heat grill until hot, about 5 minutes.

2B | **For a gas grill** Turn all burners to high, cover, and heat grill until hot, about 15 minutes. Leave all burners on high.

3 | Fold paper towels into compact wad. Holding paper towels with tongs, dip in oil, then wipe grate. Dip paper towels in oil again and wipe grate for second time. Cover grill and heat for 5 minutes. Uncover and wipe grate twice more with oiled paper towels. Place mahi-mahi on grill, skin side up and perpendicular to grate bars. Cook (covered if using gas) until well browned on first side, about 3 minutes. Gently flip mahi-mahi and continue to cook until flesh flakes apart when gently prodded with paring knife and registers 130 degrees, 3 to 8 minutes. Transfer fillets to platter and serve with pineapple salsa.

GRILLED OYSTERS | SERVES 4 TO 6 AS AN APPETIZER

SUBSTITUTIONS CLAMS • MUSSELS

24 oysters

WHY THIS RECIPE WORKS

Shellfish is most often served steamed (either on its own or in soups and stews) or, in the case of clams and oysters, raw on the half shell, but grilling bivalves is a classy option for summer entertaining that's sure to please. These two-shelled creatures are easy to cook: When they open, they're done. The key to great oysters on the grill is not to move the shellfish around too much, and to handle them carefully. You want to preserve the juices, so when they open, transfer them with tongs to a platter, holding them steady so as not to spill any of the liquid. While oysters, clams, and mussels have different flavors and textures, all three bivalves cook for about the same time, so you can serve what you like or a medley at your next outdoor event. Adding an easy sauce or flavored butter (see our Sauces for Shellfish on page 72; the shellfish is pictured with Mignonette Sauce) will complement the natural brininess of the shellfish and liven up the party. Or simply serve with lemon wedges, hot sauce, and some salsa.

1A| For a charcoal grill Open bottom vent completely. Light large chimney starter filled with charcoal briquettes (6 quarts). When top coals are partially covered with ash, pour evenly over grill. Set cooking grate in place, cover, and open lid vent completely. Heat grill until hot, about 5 minutes.

1B| For a gas grill Turn all burners to high, cover, and heat grill until hot, about 15 minutes. Leave all burners on high.

2| Clean and oil cooking grate. Place oysters on grill and cook (covered if using gas), without turning, until oysters open, 6 to 10 minutes.

3| Using tongs, carefully transfer oysters to platter, taking care to preserve juices. Discard top shells and loosen meat in bottom shells before serving.

GRILLED LOBSTERS | SERVES 2

2 (1½- to 2-pound) live lobsters

¼ cup panko bread crumbs

1 teaspoon vegetable oil

6 tablespoons unsalted butter, melted

2 garlic cloves, minced

2 tablespoons minced fresh parsley

½ teaspoon table salt, divided

¼ teaspoon pepper, divided

Lemon wedges

WHY THIS RECIPE WORKS

If we're going to grill lobster rather than boil it, we want it to be worth it, with contrasting smoky grill flavor penetrating the sweet meat—not just coloring the shell. Splitting the lobsters in half took some care (see page 18 for information, guidance, and instruction), but was the right way to go to achieve that. Starting the lobsters cut side down and then flipping them after 2 minutes kept moisture loss to a minimum. To allow the claws to finish cooking at the same time as the tail meat, we cracked each claw before cooking so heat could better reach the meat. A buttery, herby bread-crumb topping that sizzles on the lobsters on the grill gives the lobsters dressed-up appeal. Make sure the topping is prepped before you start the grill. Don't halve the lobsters until the grill has been started. If you plan to cook more than two lobsters, you will need to cook them in batches so as not to overcrowd the grill.

1 | Place lobsters in large bowl and freeze for 30 minutes. Toss panko with oil in bowl until evenly coated. Microwave, stirring frequently, until panko is light golden brown, about 2 minutes; set aside.

2A | **For a charcoal grill** Open bottom vent completely. Light large chimney starter filled with charcoal briquettes (6 quarts). When top coals are partially covered with ash, pour evenly over grill. Set cooking grate in place, cover, and open lid vent completely. Heat grill until hot, about 5 minutes.

2B | **For a gas grill** Turn all burners to high, cover, and heat grill until hot, about 15 minutes. Leave all burners on high.

3 | Meanwhile, combine melted butter and garlic in bowl. Combine toasted panko, parsley, ¼ teaspoon salt, ⅛ teaspoon pepper, and 2 tablespoons garlic butter in second bowl; set aside. Split lobsters in half lengthwise, then clean and devein lobsters. Using meat pounder, pound each claw to crack open slightly. Sprinkle tail meat with remaining ¼ teaspoon salt and remaining ⅛ teaspoon pepper and brush lobster meat evenly with 2 tablespoons garlic butter.

4 | Clean cooking grate, then repeatedly brush grate with well-oiled paper towels until grate is black and glossy, 5 to 10 times. Place lobsters, cut side down, on grill and cook (covered if using gas) until tail meat just begins to turn opaque, about 2 minutes.

5 | Transfer lobsters, cut side up, to rimmed baking sheet. Divide panko mixture evenly among lobster halves and drizzle with remaining 2 tablespoons garlic butter. Return lobsters, shell-side down, to grill and cook (covered if using gas) until panko mixture begins to bubble and tail meat is opaque and registers 140 degrees, 4 to 6 minutes. Serve lobsters with lemon wedges.

ON THE GRILL

special occasions

ROASTED SALMON WITH ORANGE BEURRE BLANC | SERVES 4 TO 6

SUBSTITUTIONS ARCTIC CHAR • WILD SALMON

Salmon

- 15 juniper berries, toasted
- ¾ teaspoon fennel seeds, toasted
- 1 teaspoon grated orange zest
- ½ teaspoon sugar
- ½ teaspoon table salt
- ½ teaspoon pepper
- 1 (1¾- to 2-pound) center-cut skin-on salmon fillet, pin bones removed
- 1 tablespoon vegetable oil

Beurre Blanc

- 3 tablespoons dry white wine
- 2 tablespoons white wine vinegar
- 1 small shallot, minced
  Pinch table salt
- 1 tablespoon heavy cream
- 8 tablespoons unsalted butter, cut into 8 pieces and chilled
- ⅛ teaspoon sugar
- ⅛ teaspoon grated orange zest

WHY THIS RECIPE WORKS

Roasting a center-cut fillet of salmon rather than individual fillets makes serving silky fish to a crowd an impressive-looking but almost-hands-off affair. We made our salmon special with a rub of floral, pleasantly bitter juniper berries and fennel seeds. A touch of sugar balanced their bitterness and promoted browning, while orange zest added brightness. Transferring the large fillet to a preheated baking sheet was easy with a foil sling. Beurre blanc—a classic French butter sauce—offered an elegant accompaniment. We prepared it while the salmon roasted by reducing wine and vinegar, enriching them with cream and butter, and finishing with orange zest. Use heavy-duty aluminum foil measuring 18 inches wide. If using arctic char or wild salmon, cook the fillet until it reaches 120 degrees (for medium-rare) and start checking for doneness early.

1| **For the salmon** Adjust oven rack to lowest position, place rimmed baking sheet on rack, and heat oven to 500 degrees. Grind juniper berries and fennel seeds in spice grinder until coarsely ground, about 30 seconds. Transfer spices to bowl and stir in orange zest, sugar, salt, and pepper.

2| Cut piece of heavy-duty aluminum foil 12 inches longer than salmon fillet and fold lengthwise into thirds. Make 8 shallow slashes, about 3 inches long and 1 inch apart, on skin side of salmon, being careful not to cut into flesh. Pat salmon dry with paper towels and lay skin side down on foil. Rub flesh side of salmon with oil, then rub with spice mixture.

3| Reduce oven temperature to 275 degrees. Using foil sling, lay salmon on preheated sheet and roast until center is still translucent when checked with tip of paring knife and registers 125 degrees (for medium-rare), 14 to 18 minutes.

4| **For the beurre blanc** Meanwhile, bring wine, vinegar, shallot, and salt to simmer in small saucepan over medium heat and cook until about 2 scant tablespoons of liquid remain, 3 to 5 minutes. Reduce heat to medium-low and whisk in cream. Add butter, 1 piece at a time, whisking vigorously after each addition, until butter is incorporated and forms thick, pale yellow sauce, 30 to 60 seconds. Off heat, whisk in sugar. Strain sauce through fine-mesh strainer into bowl. Stir in orange zest and season with salt to taste.

5| Using foil sling, transfer salmon to cutting board or serving platter. Run thin metal spatula between salmon skin and salmon to loosen. Using spatula to hold salmon in place, gently pull foil (and skin) out from underneath salmon. Serve with beurre blanc.

MAKING THE FOIL WRAPPING

1 Working with 2 pieces of foil, fold up 1 long side of each by 3 inches.

2 Lay sheets side by side with folded sides touching, fold edges together to create secure seam, and press seam flat.

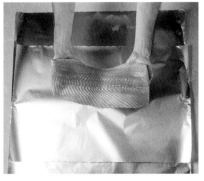

3 Center third sheet of foil over seam. Lay salmon in center of foil.

OVEN-POACHED SIDE OF SALMON

| SERVES 8 TO 10

SUBSTITUTIONS NONE

1 (4-pound) center-cut skin-on salmon fillet, pin bones removed

1 teaspoon table salt

2 tablespoons cider vinegar

6 sprigs fresh tarragon or dill, plus 2 tablespoons minced

2 lemons, sliced thin, plus lemon wedges for serving

WHY THIS RECIPE WORKS

We love the robust flavor roasting gives a side of salmon (see page 289), but poaching is an equally admirable method—for different reasons. Flavored with lemon and herbs and served cool, poached salmon is light and refreshing and looks elegant on a platter. The moist, gentle cooking method of poaching produces soft, supple salmon from end to end. It's lovely served on its own or over a salad or with a bagel or crusty bread. Cooks often poach a large fillet with a specialized fish poacher—no thanks. We moved the operation to the oven and steamed the salmon in its own moisture by wrapping the side in foil and placing it on the rack of a low oven—no special equipment needed. And no submersion in liquid meant the salmon had more concentrated flavor. We like to pair the salmon with a fresh sauce or relish; here it's pictured with Fresh Tomato Relish (page 69). Use heavy-duty aluminum foil measuring 18 inches wide. You can cook two individually wrapped sides of salmon on the upper- and lower-middle racks without altering the cooking time.

1 | Adjust oven rack to middle position and heat oven to 250 degrees. Cut 3 pieces of heavy-duty aluminum foil 12 inches longer than side of salmon. Working with 2 pieces of foil, fold up 1 long side of each by 3 inches. Lay sheets side by side with folded sides touching, fold edges together to create secure seam, and press seam flat. Center third sheet of foil over seam. Spray foil with vegetable oil spray.

2 | Pat salmon dry with paper towels and sprinkle with salt. Lay salmon, skin side down, in center of foil. Sprinkle with vinegar, then top with tarragon sprigs and lemon slices. Fold foil up over salmon to create seam on top and gently fold foil edges together to secure; do not crimp too tightly.

3 | Lay foil-wrapped salmon directly on oven rack (without baking sheet). Cook until center registers 135 to 140 degrees, 45 minutes to 1 hour. (To check temperature, poke thermometer through foil and into fish.)

4 | Remove salmon from oven and carefully open foil. Let salmon cool for 30 minutes. Pour off any accumulated liquid, then reseal salmon in foil and refrigerate until cold, at least 1 hour.

5 | Unwrap salmon and brush away lemon slices, tarragon sprigs, and any solidified poaching liquid. Transfer fish to serving platter, sprinkle with minced tarragon, and serve with lemon wedges.

PROSCIUTTO-WRAPPED COD WITH LEMON-CAPER BUTTER | SERVES 4

SUBSTITUTIONS BLACK SEA BASS • HADDOCK • HAKE • POLLOCK

4 (6- to 8-ounce) skinless cod fillets, 1 inch thick

½ teaspoon pepper

8 thin slices prosciutto (4 ounces)

1 tablespoon vegetable oil

4 tablespoons unsalted butter, softened

2 tablespoons capers, rinsed and minced

2 tablespoons minced fresh parsley

1 teaspoon grated lemon zest plus 1 tablespoon juice

1 garlic clove, minced

WHY THIS RECIPE WORKS

You might not guess it from its mild nature, but cod can become a bold dinner party centerpiece when paired with a little pork. Wrapping cod fillets in thin sheets of prosciutto before arranging the fillets in a skillet contributed meaty, salty flavor to the flaky white fish. To get good coloring and crispness on the prosciutto, we first cooked the wrapped cod on the stovetop before transferring the skillet to the oven to cook the fish through. The prosciutto infused the fish with its salty pork flavor and provided a layer of insulation for the fish during cooking, keeping it supermoist. A warm butter sauce, enlivened by capers, parsley, lemon zest and juice, and garlic, brought the dish together. Do not season the cod with salt before wrapping with the prosciutto; the briny capers and salty prosciutto add plenty of salt to the dish.

1 | Adjust oven rack to upper-middle position and heat oven to 450 degrees. Pat cod dry with paper towels and sprinkle with pepper. Wrap each fillet widthwise with 2 overlapping pieces of prosciutto.

2 | Heat oil in 12-inch ovensafe nonstick skillet over medium-high heat until just smoking. Brown prosciutto-wrapped cod lightly on both sides, 2 to 4 minutes. Transfer skillet to oven and bake until cod flakes apart when gently prodded with paring knife and registers 135 degrees, about 8 minutes.

3 | Using potholders, remove skillet from oven. Transfer cod to serving platter. Being careful of hot skillet handle, add butter, capers, parsley, lemon zest and juice, and garlic to now-empty skillet. Cook over medium heat, swirling skillet, until butter has melted. Spoon butter sauce over cod and serve.

SALT-BAKED BRANZINO | SERVES 4

SUBSTITUTIONS BLACK SEA BASS • RED SNAPPER

8 cups (3 pounds) kosher salt

2/3 cup water, plus extra as needed

4 large egg whites

2 (1½- to 2-pound) whole branzino, about 16 inches long, scaled, gutted, and fins snipped off with scissors

3 garlic cloves, minced, divided

1 lemon, sliced thin, divided, plus lemon wedges for serving

WHY THIS RECIPE WORKS

The tradition of baking whole fish in a thick salt crust goes at least as far back as fourth-century-BC Sicily. Why (beyond awe-inspiring presentation) would we do this? We found that baking branzino in a salt crust not only seasoned the fish throughout—and perfectly—but it also cooked the entire body so evenly that it produced some of the most succulent fish we've tasted. In fact, when we measured the final temperature of the salt-crusted fish, there was virtually no discrepancy between the top and bottom fillets—something impossible to achieve in fish baked directly on a baking sheet. We combined the salt with a mixture of egg whites and water to create a workable paste. Fish weighing more than 2 pounds will be hard to maneuver on the baking sheet and should be avoided. We developed this recipe using Diamond Crystal kosher salt. If using Morton kosher salt, the weight equivalence for 8 cups is 4½ pounds. To take the temperature, insert the thermometer into the fillets through the opening by the gills.

1 | Adjust oven rack to upper-middle position and heat oven to 325 degrees. Line rimmed baking sheet with parchment paper. Stir salt, water, and egg whites in large bowl until well combined. (Mixture should hold together when squeezed; if necessary, continue to stir, adding extra water, 1 tablespoon at a time, until mixture holds.)

2 | Working with 1 branzino at a time, open cavity, spread half of garlic on flesh, and stuff with half of lemon slices.

3 | Divide 3 cups of salt mixture into 2 even mounds on prepared sheet. Pat mounds into 10 by 4-inch rectangles, spaced about 1 inch apart. Lay 1 branzino lengthwise across each mound. Gently pack remaining salt mixture evenly around each branzino, leaving heads and tails exposed. Roast until branzino registers 135 degrees, 40 to 45 minutes, rotating sheet halfway through roasting. Transfer sheet to wire rack and let branzino rest for 5 minutes.

4 | Using back of serving spoon, gently tap top and sides of salt crusts to crack into large pieces and discard. Using spatula, transfer branzino to cutting board and brush away excess salt. Fillet each branzino by making vertical cut just behind head from top of fish to belly. Make another cut along top of branzino from head to tail. Starting at head and working toward tail, gently slide spatula between top fillet and bones to separate; transfer fillet, skin side up, to serving platter. Gently lift tail and peel skeleton and head from bottom fillet; discard head, skeleton, and lemon slices. Transfer second fillet, skin side up, to platter. (See page 24.) Serve with lemon wedges.

PREPARING SALT-BAKED BRANZINO

1 Divide 3 cups of salt mixture into 2 even mounds on prepared sheet. Pat mounds into 10 by 4-inch rectangles.

2 Lay 1 branzino lengthwise across each mound.

3 Gently pack remaining salt around each, leaving heads and tails exposed.

WHOLE ROAST MACKEREL | SERVES 4

3 tablespoons extra-virgin olive oil, divided

1 red bell pepper, stemmed, seeded, and chopped fine

1 red onion, chopped fine

½ preserved lemon, pulp and white pith removed, rind rinsed and minced (2 tablespoons)

⅓ cup pitted brine-cured green olives, chopped

1 tablespoon minced fresh parsley

4 (8- to 10-ounce) whole mackerel, scaled, gutted, and fins snipped off with scissors

1 teaspoon table salt, divided

1 teaspoon pepper, divided

Lemon wedges

WHY THIS RECIPE WORKS

Mackerel is rich and pungent and maintains its tender, moist texture best when roasted whole—and it's sure to impress because each slender fish is enough to serve one person and is presented as such. Because mackerel can stand up to anything, we decided to double down on flavor by pairing the fish with a robust stuffing. Inspired by the aromatic ingredients in Moroccan cuisine, we tucked a combination of sweet red bell pepper, fragrant preserved lemon, and briny green olives into each fish. With our stuffed fish lined up on a rimmed baking sheet for optimum air circulation, we roasted them in a hot oven. After just 10 minutes or so, we had four perfectly cooked, superflavorful fish. If you can't find preserved lemons, you can substitute 2 tablespoons of finely grated lemon zest. To take the temperature, insert the thermometer into the fillets through the opening by the gills. The mackerel heads can be removed before serving, if desired.

1 | Adjust oven rack to middle position and heat oven to 500 degrees. Heat 2 tablespoons oil in 12-inch skillet over medium-high heat until shimmering. Add bell pepper and onion and cook until vegetables are softened and well browned, 8 to 10 minutes. Stir in preserved lemon and cook until fragrant, about 30 seconds. Off heat, stir in olives and parsley and season with salt and pepper to taste.

2 | Grease rimmed baking sheet with remaining 1 tablespoon oil. Open cavity of each mackerel, sprinkle flesh with ¼ teaspoon salt and ¼ teaspoon pepper, and spoon one-quarter of filling into opening. Place mackerel on prepared sheet, spaced at least 2 inches apart. Roast until mackerel registers 135 degrees, 10 to 12 minutes. Carefully transfer mackerel to serving platter and let rest for 5 minutes. Serve with lemon wedges.

BOILED LOBSTER | MAKES 1 POUND MEAT; SERVES 4

SUBSTITUTIONS NONE

4 (1¼-pound) live lobsters
⅓ cup table salt

WHY THIS RECIPE WORKS

If you have seafood crackers, melted butter, and lots of napkins, a lobster boil is an instant summer party. But cooking lobster at home can be a daunting process: How do you deal with that thrashing tail, and how do you know when it's done? Most cooks find putting live lobsters into a pot unpleasant. To sedate the lobster before cooking and minimize the time it spent moving in the pot, we went with a simple process: a 30-minute stay in the freezer, which rendered the lobster motionless before it went into the pot. After a few flutters, all motion stopped. To determine doneness (who wants chewy lobster?), we poked the thermometer in the underside of the meaty tail. At 135 degrees, the target temperature for white fish, the meat was still translucent and a bit floppy. Five degrees higher guaranteed tender claws and knuckles and a pleasantly resilient tail. To cook four lobsters at once, you will need a pot with a capacity of at least 3 gallons. If your pot is smaller, boil the lobsters in batches. Start timing the lobsters from the moment they go into the pot. Serve with melted butter and lemon wedges.

1 | Place lobsters in large bowl and freeze for 30 minutes. Meanwhile, bring 2 gallons water to boil in large pot.

2 | Add lobsters and salt to pot, arranging with tongs so that all lobsters are submerged. Cover pot, leaving lid slightly ajar, and adjust heat to maintain gentle boil. Cook for 8 minutes; then, holding lobster with tongs, insert thermometer through underside of tail into thickest part; meat should register 140 degrees. If necessary, return lobster to pot for 2 minutes, until tail registers 140 degrees.

3 | Serve immediately or transfer lobsters to rimmed baking sheet and set aside until cool enough to remove meat (see page 19), about 10 minutes. (Lobster meat can be refrigerated in airtight container for up to 24 hours.)

ROASTED STUFFED LOBSTER TAILS | SERVES 4

SUBSTITUTIONS NONE

6 tablespoons unsalted butter, divided

½ cup panko bread crumbs

2 celery ribs, chopped fine

1 shallot, minced

¼ teaspoon table salt

3 tablespoons dry sherry

8 ounces extra-large shrimp (21 to 25 per pound), peeled, deveined, tails removed, and chopped

¼ cup chopped fresh parsley

1½ teaspoons grated lemon zest, plus lemon wedges for serving

4 (5- to 6-ounce) lobster tails

WHY THIS RECIPE WORKS

Classic as it may be, boiling fresh lobster (see page 307) isn't the only way to cook it. Roasting heightens and concentrates lobster's delicate flavor so it's as rich as its notoriety implies. We chose to stuff readily available tails (often sold frozen) before roasting for extra richness and an upscale presentation. Tails turn chewy when overcooked, so after splitting the shell's underside and loosening the meat to make room for the stuffing, we kept the rest of the protective shell intact. A filling of chopped shrimp and buttery panko heightened the sweet, rich lobster taste; chopped parsley, grated lemon zest, and dry sherry offered a fresh, well-rounded profile. We mounded the luxurious stuffing into the tails and roasted them in a baking dish; the panko became more gorgeously browned as the meat gently cooked through. These tails were full-flavored and totally indulgent; plus, this approach made it possible to tuck into a lobster feast any day of the year. To thaw frozen lobster tails, let them sit either in the refrigerator for 24 hours or submerged in cold water for 30 minutes to 1 hour.

1 | Adjust oven rack to middle position and heat oven to 350 degrees. Melt 4 tablespoons butter in 10-inch skillet over medium heat. Add panko and cook, stirring often, until crumbs are dark golden brown, about 2 minutes. Transfer panko to large bowl and let cool slightly. Wipe skillet clean with paper towels.

2 | Melt remaining 2 tablespoons butter in now-empty skillet over medium heat. Add celery, shallot, and salt and cook until softened, 3 to 5 minutes. Stir in sherry and cook until reduced slightly, about 30 seconds. Transfer vegetable mixture to bowl with panko. Stir in shrimp, parsley, and lemon zest until well combined.

3 | Using kitchen shears, cut lengthwise through soft shell on underside of each lobster tail. Cut meat in half using paring knife, taking care not to cut through outer shell. With lobster tail cut side up, grasp each side with your hands and crack outer shell, opening cut side to expose meat. Lift meat from shell to loosen, then tuck back into shell.

4 | Arrange lobster tails cut side up in 13 by 9-inch baking dish, alternating tails front to back. Spoon stuffing evenly into tails, mounding stuffing slightly. Roast until stuffing is golden brown and lobster registers 140 degrees, 20 to 25 minutes. Serve with lemon wedges.

variation |
ROASTED STUFFED LOBSTER TAILS WITH FENNEL AND PERNOD
Substitute 1 finely chopped fennel bulb (about 1 cup) for celery. Substitute ¼ cup minced fennel fronds, if available, for parsley and 3 tablespoons Pernod for sherry.

BUTTERFLYING A LOBSTER TAIL

1 Using kitchen shears, cut lengthwise through soft shell on underside of lobster tail. Cut meat in half using paring knife; do not cut through outer shell.

2 With lobster tail cut side up, grasp each side with your hands and crack outer shell, opening cut side to expose meat.

SPECIAL OCCASIONS

309

LOBSTER FETTUCCINE WITH FENNEL AND TARRAGON | SERVES 4 TO 6

SUBSTITUTIONS NONE

2 tablespoons extra-virgin olive oil

1 small onion, chopped fine

½ fennel bulb, stalks discarded, bulb cored and chopped fine

¼ teaspoon table salt, plus salt for cooking pasta

2 garlic cloves, minced

1½ teaspoons minced fresh thyme

⅛ teaspoon cayenne pepper

⅓ cup dry sherry

1 cup heavy cream

1 pound cooked lobster meat, cut into ⅓-inch pieces

1 pound fettuccine

2 tablespoons minced fresh tarragon

2 teaspoons lemon juice

Grated Parmesan cheese

WHY THIS RECIPE WORKS

Dotted with tender bites of lobster and infused with the sweet anise notes of fennel and tarragon, this luxuriously creamy pasta dish sets the tone for an elegant dinner. We began by softening onion and fennel in olive oil before blooming thyme, garlic, and cayenne for a base that was complex in flavor but didn't overwhelm the star: sweet lobster. We built the sauce from there, adding a hit of dry sherry and cream, plus some of the pasta cooking water to thicken it while keeping it from turning overly rich. After simmering the sauce, we added generous chunks of cooked lobster, allowing them to warm through before serving. After combining the lobster, sauce, and pasta, we stirred in tarragon at the end to keep the herb's flavor fresh, and lemon juice offered a bright finish. You can purchase cooked lobster meat or boil your own (see page 307).

1 | Heat oil in 12-inch skillet over medium heat until shimmering. Add onion, fennel, and salt and cook until softened, about 5 minutes. Stir in garlic, thyme, and cayenne and cook until fragrant, about 30 seconds. Stir in sherry and simmer until it has nearly evaporated, about 4 minutes. Stir in cream and cook until slightly thickened, about 2 minutes. Off heat, stir in lobster.

2 | Meanwhile, bring 4 quarts water to boil in large pot. Add pasta and 1 tablespoon salt and cook, stirring often, until al dente. Reserve 1 cup cooking water, then drain pasta and return it to pot. Add ½ cup cooking water, lobster with sauce, tarragon, and lemon juice and toss to combine. Season with salt and pepper to taste and adjust consistency with reserved cooking water as needed. Serve immediately in warm bowls, passing Parmesan separately.

LINGUINE WITH SEAFOOD | SERVES 6

6 tablespoons extra-virgin olive oil, divided

12 garlic cloves, minced

¼ teaspoon red pepper flakes

1 pound littleneck or cherrystone clams, scrubbed

1 pound mussels, scrubbed and debearded

1¼ pounds cherry tomatoes (half of tomatoes halved, remaining tomatoes left whole), divided

1 (8-ounce) bottle clam juice

1 cup dry white wine

1 cup minced fresh parsley, divided

1 tablespoon tomato paste

4 anchovy fillets, rinsed, patted dry, and minced

1 teaspoon minced fresh thyme

½ teaspoon table salt, plus salt for cooking pasta

1 pound linguine

1 pound extra-large shrimp (21 to 25 per pound), peeled and deveined

8 ounces squid, sliced crosswise into ½-inch-thick rings

2 teaspoons grated lemon zest, plus lemon wedges for serving

WHY THIS RECIPE WORKS

Italian seafood pastas such as *linguine allo scoglio* promise noodles teeming with shellfish and saturated with clean, briny-sweet flavor. And while many versions are chock-full of shrimp, clams, mussels, lobster, scallops, squid, or any combination thereof, the pasta rarely tastes much like the sea. To create a pasta dish with rich, savory seafood flavor in every bite, we made a sauce with clam juice and four minced anchovies, which fortified the juices shed by the shellfish. Cooking the shellfish in a careful sequence ensured that every piece was plump and tender. We parboiled the linguine and then finished cooking it directly in the sauce; the noodles soaked up flavor while shedding starches that thickened the sauce. Fresh cherry tomatoes, lots of garlic, fresh herbs, and lemon made for a bright, complex-tasting sauce. For a simpler version, you can omit the clams and squid and increase the amounts of mussels and shrimp to 1½ pounds each; increase the amount of salt in step 2 to ¾ teaspoon. If you can't find fresh squid, it's available frozen at many supermarkets and typically has the benefit of being precleaned; thaw it before cutting and cooking.

1 | Heat ¼ cup oil in large Dutch oven over medium-high heat until shimmering. Add garlic and pepper flakes and cook until fragrant, about 1 minute. Add clams, cover, and cook, shaking pot occasionally, for 4 minutes. Add mussels, cover, and continue to cook, shaking pot occasionally, until clams and mussels have opened, 3 to 4 minutes. Transfer clams and mussels to bowl, discarding any that haven't opened, and cover to keep warm; leave any broth in pot.

2 | Add whole tomatoes, clam juice, wine, ½ cup parsley, tomato paste, anchovies, thyme, and salt to pot and bring to simmer over medium-high heat. Reduce heat to medium and cook, stirring occasionally, until tomatoes have started to break down and sauce is reduced by one-third, about 10 minutes.

3 | Meanwhile, bring 4 quarts water to boil in large pot. Add pasta and 1 tablespoon salt and cook, stirring often, for 7 minutes. Reserve ½ cup cooking water, then drain pasta.

4 | Add pasta to sauce in Dutch oven and cook over medium heat, stirring gently, for 2 minutes. Reduce heat to medium-low, stir in shrimp, cover, and cook for 4 minutes. Stir in squid, lemon zest, halved tomatoes, and remaining ½ cup parsley; cover and continue to cook until shrimp and squid are just cooked through, about 2 minutes. Gently stir in clams and mussels. Remove pot from heat, cover, and let stand until clams and mussels are warmed through, about 2 minutes. Season with salt and pepper to taste and adjust consistency with reserved cooking water as needed. Transfer to large serving dish, drizzle with remaining 2 tablespoons oil, and serve, passing lemon wedges separately.

GRILLED PAELLA | SERVES 8

1½ pounds boneless, skinless chicken thighs, trimmed and halved crosswise

1¾ teaspoons table salt, divided

1 teaspoon pepper

12 ounces jumbo shrimp (16 to 20 per pound), peeled and deveined

5 tablespoons extra-virgin olive oil, divided

6 garlic cloves, minced, divided

1¾ teaspoons hot smoked paprika, divided

3 tablespoons tomato paste

4 cups chicken broth

⅔ cup dry sherry

1 (8-ounce) bottle clam juice

Pinch saffron threads, crumbled (optional)

1 onion, chopped fine

½ cup jarred roasted red peppers, rinsed, patted dry, and chopped fine

3 cups Arborio rice

1 pound littleneck or cherrystone clams, scrubbed

8 ounces Spanish-style chorizo sausage, cut into ½-inch pieces

1 cup frozen peas, thawed

Lemon wedges

WHY THIS RECIPE WORKS

This flavor-packed Spanish rice dish is a one-pan showpiece that's made for entertaining. The rice absorbs liquid, and the grains in contact with the pan form a caramelized crust known as *socarrat*. While many modern recipes are cooked indoors, paella was originally made on the grill. A roasting pan was easy to maneuver and had plentiful surface area to maximize the amount of rice crust. Building a large fire and fueling it with fresh coals ensured that the heat would last through cooking. Nestling the shellfish into the center allowed it to release its flavorful juices into the rice without overcooking. You will need a heavy-duty roasting pan that measures at least 14 by 11 inches. If the exterior of your pan is dark, the cooking times will be on the lower side of the ranges.

1 | Pat chicken dry with paper towels and season both sides with 1 teaspoon salt and pepper. Toss shrimp with 1½ teaspoons oil, ½ teaspoon garlic, ¼ teaspoon paprika, and ¼ teaspoon salt in bowl until evenly coated; set aside.

2 | Heat 1½ teaspoons oil in medium saucepan over medium heat until shimmering. Add remaining garlic and cook, stirring constantly, until garlic sticks to bottom of saucepan and begins to brown, about 1 minute. Add tomato paste and remaining 1½ teaspoons paprika and continue to cook, stirring constantly, until dark brown bits form on bottom of saucepan, about 1 minute. Stir in broth, sherry, clam juice, and saffron, if using. Increase heat to high and bring to boil. Remove saucepan from heat and set aside.

3A | **For a charcoal grill** Open bottom vent completely. Light large chimney starter mounded with charcoal briquettes (7 quarts). When top coals are partially covered with ash, pour evenly over grill. Using tongs, arrange 20 unlit briquettes evenly over coals. Set cooking grate in place, cover, and open lid vent completely. Heat grill until hot, about 5 minutes.

3B | **For a gas grill** Turn all burners to high, cover, and heat grill until hot, about 15 minutes. Leave all burners on high.

4 | Clean and oil cooking grate. Place chicken on grill and cook until both sides are lightly browned, 5 to 7 minutes; transfer chicken to plate and clean cooking grate.

5 | Place roasting pan on grill (turning burners to medium-high if using gas) and add remaining ¼ cup oil. When oil begins to shimmer, add onion, red peppers, and remaining ½ teaspoon salt. Cook, stirring frequently, until onion begins to brown, 4 to 7 minutes. Stir in rice (turning burners to medium if using gas) until grains are well coated with oil.

6 | Arrange chicken around perimeter of pan. Pour chicken broth mixture and any accumulated chicken juices over rice. Smooth rice into even layer, making sure no rice sticks to sides of pan or rests atop chicken. When liquid reaches gentle simmer, place shrimp in center of pan in single layer. Arrange clams in center of pan, evenly dispersing with shrimp and pushing hinge side of clams into rice slightly so they stand up. Distribute chorizo evenly over surface of rice. Cook, moving and rotating pan to maintain gentle simmer across entire surface of pan, until rice is almost cooked through, 12 to 18 minutes. (If using gas, heat can also be adjusted to maintain simmer.)

7 | Sprinkle peas over paella, cover grill, and cook until liquid is absorbed and rice on bottom of pan sizzles, 5 to 8 minutes. Uncover and continue to cook, checking frequently, until uniform golden-brown crust forms on bottom of pan, 8 to 15 minutes. (Slide pan around grill as needed for even crust formation.) Remove from grill, cover, and let sit for 10 minutes. Serve with lemon wedges.

RED WINE–BRAISED OCTOPUS | SERVES 4

SUBSTITUTIONS NONE

1 (4-pound) octopus, rinsed

1 tablespoon extra-virgin olive oil

2 tablespoons tomato paste

4 garlic cloves, peeled and smashed

1 sprig fresh rosemary

2 bay leaves

½ teaspoon pepper

Pinch ground cinnamon

Pinch ground nutmeg

1 cup dry red wine

2 tablespoons red wine vinegar

2 tablespoons unflavored gelatin

2 teaspoons chopped fresh parsley

WHY THIS RECIPE WORKS

Working with octopus may seem intimidating, but braising it in an intense, silky red wine sauce is a common Mediterranean technique with large rewards. Octopus flesh is a dense array of thin muscle fibers reinforced by a network of collagen and connective tissue, so it can be tough and chewy. Most of the octopus in the United States is frozen, and we found that simply defrosting it helped lead to tender octopus; the ice crystals tore through the tough muscle fibers and helped them break down during cooking. Octopus is made up of almost half salt water by weight and releases its salty juices into the braising liquid, making it unpalatable, so we cook the octopus in water first. However, since octopus contains a lot of collagen, which transforms into gelatin as it cooks, we also lost the viscosity and velvety texture. To counteract this, we added powdered gelatin to our robust wine sauce. For information on octopus, see page 20.

1 | Using sharp knife, separate octopus mantle (large sac) and body (lower section with tentacles) from head (midsection containing eyes); discard head. Place octopus in large pot, cover with water by 2 inches, and bring to simmer over high heat. Reduce heat to low, cover, and simmer gently, flipping octopus occasionally, until skin between tentacle joints tears easily when pulled, 45 minutes to 1¼ hours.

2 | Transfer octopus to cutting board and let cool slightly. Measure out and reserve 3 cups octopus cooking liquid; discard remaining liquid and wipe pot dry with paper towels. While octopus is warm, use paring knife to cut mantle into quarters, then trim and scrape away skin and interior fibers; transfer to bowl. Using your fingers, remove skin from body, being careful not to remove suction cups. Cut tentacles from around core of body in three sections; discard core. Separate tentacles and cut into 2-inch lengths; transfer to bowl.

3 | Heat oil in now-empty pot over medium-high heat until shimmering. Add tomato paste and cook, stirring constantly, until beginning to darken, about 1 minute. Stir in garlic, rosemary sprig, bay leaves, pepper, cinnamon, and nutmeg and cook until fragrant, about 30 seconds. Stir in reserved octopus cooking liquid, wine, vinegar, and gelatin, scraping up any browned bits. Bring to boil and cook, stirring occasionally, for 20 minutes.

4 | Stir in octopus and any accumulated juices and bring to simmer. Cook, stirring occasionally, until octopus is tender and sauce has thickened slightly and coats back of spoon, 20 to 25 minutes. Off heat, discard rosemary sprig and bay leaves. Stir in parsley and season with pepper to taste. Serve.

small plates

SIZZLING GARLIC SHRIMP | SERVES 8

1 pound large shrimp (26 to 30 per pound), peeled, deveined, and tails removed

½ cup extra-virgin olive oil, divided

14 garlic cloves, peeled (2 minced, 12 whole), divided

¼ teaspoon table salt

1 bay leaf

1 (2-inch) piece mild dried chile, such as New Mexico, roughly torn, with seeds

1 tablespoon minced fresh parsley

1½ teaspoons sherry vinegar

WHY THIS RECIPE WORKS

This classic tapas restaurant dish is known for its dramatic entrances: The potent aroma of garlic and the sound of the sizzling shrimp precede its arrival. For an equally impressive and flavorful version that we could make at home, we began by briefly marinating the shrimp in garlic, olive oil, and salt. Soaking the shrimp for at least half an hour allowed the flavors to permeate completely. Next, we focused on the cooking oil. We infused the oil with more garlic flavor by heating smashed cloves in the oil. Think the garlic stopped there? We also fried up slices of garlic for a crunchy contrast to the shrimp. A bay leaf contributed a savory boost, and dried chile added mild heat. With the flavor down, we introduced the shrimp, cooking them gently in their marinade before ramping up the heat to achieve a lively sizzle. A splash of sherry vinegar and minced parsley added before the skillet left the stove offered a fresh, tangy finish. You can substitute ¼ teaspoon paprika for the dried chile if necessary. For a true sizzling effect, just before serving, transfer the cooked shrimp mixture to an 8-inch cast-iron skillet that has been heated for 2 minutes over medium-high heat. Serve with crusty bread for dipping in the richly flavored olive oil.

1 | Toss shrimp with 2 tablespoons oil, minced garlic, and salt in bowl and let sit at room temperature for at least 30 minutes or up to 1 hour.

2 | Meanwhile, using flat side of chef's knife, smash 4 whole garlic cloves. Heat smashed garlic and remaining 6 tablespoons oil in 12-inch skillet over medium-low heat, stirring occasionally, until garlic is light golden brown, 4 to 7 minutes; let oil cool completely. Using slotted spoon, discard smashed garlic.

3 | Thinly slice remaining 8 garlic cloves. Return skillet with cooled oil to low heat and add sliced garlic, bay leaf, and chile. Cook, stirring occasionally, until garlic is tender but not browned, 4 to 7 minutes. (If garlic has not begun to sizzle after 3 minutes, increase heat to medium-low.)

4 | Increase heat to medium-low and add shrimp with marinade. Cook, without stirring, until oil starts to bubble gently, about 2 minutes. Using tongs, flip shrimp and continue to cook until almost cooked through, about 2 minutes. Increase heat to high and add parsley and vinegar. Cook, stirring constantly, until shrimp are cooked through and oil is bubbling vigorously, 15 to 20 seconds. Discard bay leaf. Serve immediately.

BAKED CRAB DIP | SERVES 8 TO 10

SUBSTITUTIONS NONE

2 (12-inch) baguettes, sliced ¼ inch thick on bias

¼ cup extra-virgin olive oil, divided

1 onion, chopped fine

1 teaspoon Old Bay seasoning

1 teaspoon ground coriander

8 ounces cream cheese, cut into 8 pieces and softened

½ cup mayonnaise

4 teaspoons minced fresh parsley, divided

¼ teaspoon table salt

¼ teaspoon pepper

12 ounces lump crabmeat, picked over for shells and pressed dry between paper towels

WHY THIS RECIPE WORKS

In its ideal form, crab dip is a decadent party appetizer that's served warm and is full of creamy, meaty seafood and savory spices. A cast-iron skillet is the perfect oven-to-table vessel; it retains heat beautifully, so it ensures that your guests will enjoy the dip while it's hot. To keep this party-starter fun, we made a quick batch of crostini to scoop the rich dip with no need for a spoon. Prebaking the bread before adding it to the skillet ensured that the toasts stayed crisp when loaded up with dip. To make a savory base for the crab dip, we first cooked onion in the skillet, adding a bit of Old Bay seasoning and coriander—common friends of crab. We then removed the sautéed onions from the skillet and combined them with cream cheese, mayonnaise, and parsley. After gently folding the crabmeat into the mixture (we used a much higher ratio of sweet crab to cream cheese than in other recipes), we put the whole thing back in the skillet and baked it until warmed and bubbly, with crostini fanned around the perimeter. To soften the cream cheese quickly, microwave it for 20 to 30 seconds.

1 | Adjust oven racks to upper-middle and lower-middle positions and heat oven to 400 degrees. Arrange bread slices in even layer on 2 rimmed baking sheets and bake until dry and crisp, about 10 minutes, rotating sheets and flipping slices halfway through baking. Brush crostini with 2 tablespoons oil and season with salt and pepper; set aside.

2 | Heat 10-inch ovensafe skillet over medium heat for 3 minutes. Add remaining 2 tablespoons oil and heat until shimmering. Add onion and cook until softened, about 5 minutes. Stir in Old Bay and coriander and cook until fragrant, about 30 seconds; transfer to large bowl. Stir cream cheese, mayonnaise, 1 tablespoon parsley, salt, and pepper into onion mixture until thoroughly combined. Gently fold in crabmeat.

3 | Spread dip evenly in now-empty skillet, then shingle crostini around edge, submerging narrow ends in crab mixture. Transfer skillet to oven and bake until dip is heated through and crostini are golden brown, about 10 minutes. Sprinkle with remaining 1 teaspoon parsley. Serve.

SHRIMP COCKTAIL | SERVES 6

SUBSTITUTIONS NONE

Cocktail Sauce

 1 cup ketchup

 2 tablespoons lemon juice

 2 tablespoons prepared horseradish, drained, plus extra for seasoning

 2 teaspoons hot sauce, plus extra for seasoning

 ⅛ teaspoon table salt

 ⅛ teaspoon pepper

Shrimp

 2 teaspoons lemon juice

 2 bay leaves

 1 teaspoon black peppercorns

 1 teaspoon Old Bay seasoning

 1 pound extra-large shrimp (21 to 25 per pound), peeled and deveined

   Table salt for cooking shrimp

WHY THIS RECIPE WORKS

Shrimp cocktail is a classic starter for surf or turf dishes—but bland, rubbery shrimp often hide behind the zippy cocktail sauce dip. We wanted to make shrimp cocktail that boasted tender, sweet shrimp. To infuse the shrimp with as much flavor as possible, we poached them in a simple mixture of water and seasonings, including Old Bay, which delivered a perceptible depth of flavor to the shrimp. We brought the water and aromatics to a boil, took the pot off the heat, and added the shrimp, leaving them to poach for 5 minutes—a method that delivers perfectly tender, not rubbery, shrimp every time. Buy refrigerated prepared horseradish, not the shelf-stable kind, which contains preservatives and additives.

1 | For the cocktail sauce Whisk all ingredients together in bowl and season with extra horseradish and hot sauce to taste. (Sauce can be refrigerated for up to 4 days; bring to room temperature before serving.)

2 | For the shrimp Bring 3 cups water, lemon juice, bay leaves, peppercorns, and Old Bay to boil in large saucepan. Stir in shrimp and 1 tablespoon salt. Cover and let sit off heat until shrimp are opaque, about 5 minutes, shaking saucepan halfway through sitting time.

3 | Meanwhile, fill large bowl halfway with ice and water. Drain shrimp and transfer to ice bath, discarding aromatics; let cool for 3 to 5 minutes. Drain shrimp and transfer to separate bowl. Cover and refrigerate until thoroughly chilled, at least 1 hour or up to 24 hours. Serve with cocktail sauce.

POPCORN SHRIMP | SERVES 4

1½ pounds large shrimp (26 to 30 per pound), peeled, deveined, and tails removed

3 quarts peanut or vegetable oil, divided

1½ tablespoons Old Bay seasoning, divided

1 teaspoon grated lemon zest, plus lemon wedges for serving

1 garlic clove, minced

1½ cups all-purpose flour

½ cup cornstarch

2 teaspoons pepper

1 teaspoon baking powder

1½ cups bottled clam juice

WHY THIS RECIPE WORKS

When properly fried, popcorn shrimp are just as crunchy, salty, and irresistible as their namesake snack. Sadly, most recipes produce greasy, gummy shrimp, often coated in too much bland batter. We wanted shrimp coated in a light, flavorful batter and fried until just golden brown. For a crisp coating, we replaced some of the flour with cornstarch. A little baking powder increased browning and provided a bit of lift to the batter. Old Bay seasoning added flavor to the batter, giving these popcorn shrimp a serious upgrade. To impart a brininess that complemented the shrimp, we replaced the water in the batter with clam juice but reduced the liquid amount so that the coating clung to the shrimp. We also wanted to boost the flavor of the shrimp themselves, so we marinated them in a little oil, lemon zest, garlic, and more Old Bay before coating. Be sure to leave plenty of space between the frying shrimp to prevent them from sticking together. You will need a Dutch oven that holds 6 quarts or more.

1 | Toss shrimp, 1 tablespoon oil, ½ teaspoon Old Bay, lemon zest, and garlic in large bowl. Refrigerate, covered, for at least 30 minutes or up to 1 hour.

2 | Adjust oven rack to middle position and heat oven to 200 degrees. Combine flour, cornstarch, pepper, baking powder, and remaining 4 teaspoons Old Bay in large bowl. Stir clam juice into flour mixture until smooth. Fold marinated shrimp into batter until evenly coated.

3 | Heat remaining oil in large Dutch oven over medium-high heat to 375 degrees. Set wire rack in rimmed baking sheet and line plate with triple layer of paper towels. Working quickly, add one-quarter of shrimp, one at a time, to oil. Fry, stirring frequently, until golden brown, about 2 minutes. Let shrimp drain on prepared plate, then transfer shrimp to prepared wire rack and place in oven to keep warm. Return oil to 375 degrees and repeat with remaining shrimp. Serve with lemon wedges.

BROILED BACON-WRAPPED SEA SCALLOPS | SERVES 6 TO 8

SUBSTITUTIONS NONE

4 slices bacon

24 large sea scallops, tendons removed

¼ teaspoon table salt

⅛ teaspoon pepper

Pinch cayenne pepper

2 tablespoons minced fresh chives

WHY THIS RECIPE WORKS

Bacon-wrapped *anything* is always a party hit, but bacon's smoky flavor pairs especially well with sweet scallops for a simple appetizer that's impressive enough to be a passed hors d'oeuvre. The challenges are making sure that the bacon is crisp but still pliable enough to wrap around the scallops, and that the balance between bacon and scallop is right. We found that a whole slice of bacon was much too much for one scallop—the smokiness was overwhelming and it also turned the appetizer greasy. Smaller strips of bacon worked better. Wrapping bacon from the package around the scallops was easy because of its pliability, but the scallops finished cooking before the bacon had time to brown and crisp. To even out the timing, we parcooked the bacon in the microwave, which had the added benefit of rendering some of the bacon fat ahead of time to get rid of grease. We could still wrap the bacon around the scallops—and the broiler finished the job. The result was a plump, succulent scallop dressed in crisp bacon, ready to be picked up with a toothpick.

1 | Adjust oven rack 6 inches from broiler element and heat broiler. Set wire rack in rimmed baking sheet.

2 | Slice each piece of bacon lengthwise into 2 long, thin strips, then cut each strip into 3 short pieces (total of 24 bacon pieces). Spread bacon pieces out over 4 layers of paper towels on plate, then cover with 2 more layers of paper towels. Microwave until bacon fat begins to render but bacon is still pliable, 1 to 2 minutes.

3 | Meanwhile, place scallops in bowl. Sprinkle salt, pepper, and cayenne over scallops and toss to coat.

4 | Wrap 1 piece of microwaved bacon around center of each scallop and place, seam side down, on prepared wire rack. Broil until sides of scallops are firm and edges of bacon are brown, rotating sheet halfway through cooking, 3 to 4 minutes. Skewer scallops with toothpicks, transfer to serving platter, and sprinkle with chives. Serve immediately.

variation |
BROILED BACON-WRAPPED SHRIMP
Substitute 1 pound extra-large shrimp (21 to 25 per pound), peeled and deveined, for scallops.

BUCKWHEAT BLINI WITH SMOKED SALMON | MAKES ABOUT 60 BLINI; SERVES 12 TO 14

SUBSTITUTIONS NONE

½ cup all-purpose flour

½ cup buckwheat flour

1 tablespoon sugar

½ teaspoon table salt

½ teaspoon baking powder

¼ teaspoon baking soda

¾ cup buttermilk

½ cup whole milk

1 large egg

2 tablespoons unsalted butter, melted and cooled, plus extra for cooking blini

1 cup sour cream

1 pound sliced smoked salmon, cut into 2-inch lengths

½ cup capers, drained and rinsed

2 large shallots, minced

½ cup minced fresh chives

WHY THIS RECIPE WORKS

Blini, sometimes called *oladi*, are silver dollar–size buckwheat pancakes with an earthy, tangy flavor that make an excellent and refined cocktail hors d'oeuvre when served with a briny smoked salmon topping. While many blini are yeasted, we wanted a less time-consuming version, so we looked to recipes leavened with baking powder and baking soda. These versions, however, were less tangy. To make up for that, we added some buttermilk. Since buckwheat flour lacks gluten, we cut it with some all-purpose flour for pancakes that had enough structure so they wouldn't fall apart. The pancakes stand up to a dollop of cooling sour cream; some bright, salty capers; delicious smoked salmon; and a sprinkling of fresh chives. They're a platform to show how seafood can be the most stellar of fancy-party starters. Buckwheat flour can be found in natural foods stores and well-stocked supermarkets.

1 | Whisk all-purpose flour, buckwheat flour, sugar, salt, baking powder, and baking soda together in large bowl. Whisk buttermilk, milk, egg, and melted butter together in second bowl. Whisk buttermilk mixture into flour mixture until just combined (do not overmix).

2 | Brush bottom and sides of 12-inch nonstick skillet very lightly with extra melted butter; heat skillet over medium heat until butter stops sizzling. Using scant 1 tablespoon batter each, scoop 6 to 8 blini into skillet. Cook until large bubbles begin to form on tops of blini, 1½ to 2 minutes. Flip blini and cook until second side is golden, about 1½ minutes.

3 | Transfer blini to wire rack. Repeat with additional butter and remaining batter. Let blini cool slightly. (Blini can be stacked between individual sheets of parchment paper, wrapped in plastic wrap, and frozen for up to 1 week. Thaw in refrigerator for 24 hours, then spread out on baking sheet and warm in 350-degree oven for about 5 minutes.) To serve, arrange blini on serving platter and top with sour cream, salmon, capers, shallots, and chives.

GRAVLAX | MAKES ABOUT 1 POUND; SERVES 6

SUBSTITUTIONS NONE

⅓ cup packed light brown sugar

¼ cup kosher salt

1 (1-pound) center-cut skin-on salmon fillet

3 tablespoons brandy

1 cup coarsely chopped fresh dill

WHY THIS RECIPE WORKS

Compared with its cousins smoked salmon and nova, which are usually brined and then smoked, gravlax relies on a one-step process, so it's a great way to cure fish at home—and impress all your friends. The name, derived from *gravad lax* (Swedish for "buried salmon"), alludes to covering the fish with a salt-and-sugar cure (and typically aromatic dill). We call for skin-on salmon because it makes cutting clean slices of the cured fish easier. A splash of brandy assisted in the preserving process while also providing moisture to help the cure adhere and adding some of its sweet, round flavor. Most recipes for gravlax use granulated sugar, but we opted for brown sugar; its deeper flavor better complemented the salmon. Pressing the rubbed salmon under a few cans helped it release moisture and gave the fillet a firmer, more sliceable texture. We basted the salmon with the released liquid once a day to help speed up the curing process and to keep it from drying out. Serve gravlax sliced thin on its own or on blini (see page 333) or rye bread with cream cheese and accoutrements. For easier slicing, freeze the gravlax for 30 minutes.

1 | Combine sugar and salt in bowl. Place salmon, skin side down, in 13 by 9-inch glass baking dish. Drizzle with brandy, making sure to cover entire surface. Rub salmon evenly with sugar-salt mixture, pressing firmly to adhere. Cover with dill, pressing firmly to adhere.

2 | Cover salmon loosely with plastic wrap, top with square baking dish or pie plate, and weight with several large, heavy cans. Refrigerate until salmon feels firm, about 3 days, basting salmon with liquid released into dish once a day.

3 | Scrape dill off salmon. Remove salmon from dish and pat dry with paper towels before slicing. (Unsliced gravlax can be wrapped tightly in plastic and refrigerated for up to 1 week; slice just before serving.)

BAKED STUFFED SHRIMP | SERVES 4 TO 6

SUBSTITUTIONS NONE

¾ cup panko bread crumbs

⅓ cup mayonnaise

2 tablespoons water

2 tablespoons minced fresh parsley

2 scallions, chopped fine

1 tablespoon Dijon mustard

2 garlic cloves, minced

2 teaspoons grated lemon zest, divided, plus 1 tablespoon juice, plus lemon wedges for serving

¼ teaspoon table salt, divided
   Pinch cayenne pepper

12 extra-jumbo shrimp (U15), peeled and deveined

1 tablespoon extra-virgin olive oil

WHY THIS RECIPE WORKS

Shrimp, whether poached or roasted, are a natural appetizer. Beyond being a crowd-pleaser, they're perfectly portioned and fun, and they feature a natural tail for picking up and eating at a party. To double the fun, we wanted a version with a rich, buttery stuffing. Panko bread crumbs, fresh herbs, some zesty Dijon mustard, aromatic garlic, and bright lemon bound with mayonnaise made a spoonable mixture to fill the shrimp. But how? The stuffing wouldn't just stay put along the shrimp's curve, making this a fork-and-knife dish—no fun. To prepare the shrimp for the stuffing—and not the other way around—we butter-flied each shrimp to open it up and cut a slit down the shrimp so it would lie flat. We placed the stuffing right on the slit so it would sit tight. After broiling, the shrimp was tender and the stuffing became browned and crisp. It's amazing how much richness you can fit into a shrimp.

1 | Adjust oven rack to upper-middle position and heat oven to 375 degrees. Spread panko in even layer on rimmed baking sheet and bake until golden, 3 to 5 minutes, stirring halfway through baking. Transfer panko to large bowl to cool. Line now-empty sheet with aluminum foil.

2 | Once panko has cooled, stir in mayonnaise, water, parsley, scallions, mustard, garlic, 1 teaspoon lemon zest and juice, ⅛ teaspoon salt, and cayenne; set aside.

3 | Pat shrimp dry with paper towels. Using paring knife and holding shrimp with curve facing you, cut along back of shrimp to butterfly. Cut 1-inch long slit through center of each butterflied shrimp so they lie flat.

4 | Toss shrimp, oil, remaining 1 teaspoon lemon zest, and remaining ⅛ teaspoon salt together in bowl to coat then lay shrimp butterflied side down on prepared sheet. Measure out 1 tablespoon filling and place over slit on shrimp, pressing gently to adhere. Repeat with remaining filling and shrimp. Bake until shrimp are opaque throughout, 12 to 15 minutes, rotating sheet halfway through baking.

5 | Remove shrimp from oven and heat broiler. Broil shrimp until crumbs are deep golden brown and crisp, 1 to 3 minutes. Serve with lemon wedges.

MUSSELS ESCABÈCHE | SERVES 6 TO 8

SUBSTITUTIONS NONE

⅔ cup dry white wine

2 pounds mussels, scrubbed and debearded

⅓ cup extra-virgin olive oil

½ small red onion, sliced ¼ inch thick

4 garlic cloves, sliced thin

2 bay leaves

2 sprigs fresh thyme

2 tablespoons minced fresh parsley, divided

¾ teaspoon smoked paprika

¼ cup sherry vinegar

¼ teaspoon table salt

⅛ teaspoon pepper

WHY THIS RECIPE WORKS

Mussels escabèche calls for pickling briny mussels in an aromatic mixture of vinegar, olive oil, and fragrant spices; we thought this sounded like a unique addition to any appetizer spread. The first step in creating our recipe was figuring out how to cook the mussels so they'd be plump and tender. We found that steaming them in a mixture of white wine and water infused them with flavor from the start; bringing the cooking liquid to a boil before adding the mussels ensured that they cooked quickly, reducing the risk of overcooking. After removing the mussels from their shells, we made the marinade by blooming our aromatics in oil; a bay leaf offered depth, and smoked paprika provided earthy nuance. A healthy dose of sherry vinegar was necessary to pickle the mussels; its bright, bold flavor gave each small bite big impact. We suggest serving these mussels with toothpicks for grabbing and extra bread for dipping in the flavorful marinade. We prefer the bright flavor of these mussels after a quick pickling period of just 15 minutes, but the mussels can be refrigerated for up to 2 days in their vinegar brine. Let the mussels come to room temperature before serving.

1 | Bring wine and ⅔ cup water to boil in Dutch oven over high heat. Add mussels, cover, and cook, stirring occasionally, until mussels open, 3 to 6 minutes. Strain mussels and discard cooking liquid and any mussels that have not opened. Let mussels cool slightly, then remove mussels from shells and place in large bowl; discard shells.

2 | Heat oil in now-empty pot over medium heat until shimmering. Add onion, garlic, bay leaves, thyme, 1 tablespoon parsley, and paprika. Cook, stirring often, until garlic is fragrant and onion is slightly wilted, about 1 minute.

3 | Off heat, stir in vinegar, salt, and pepper. Pour mixture over mussels and let sit for 15 minutes. (Mussels can be refrigerated for up to 2 days; bring to room temperature before serving.) Season with salt and pepper to taste and sprinkle with remaining 1 tablespoon parsley before serving.

SHRIMP AND CABBAGE POTSTICKERS

| MAKES 24 POTSTICKERS; SERVES 6

SUBSTITUTIONS NONE

Scallion Dipping Sauce

- ¼ cup soy sauce
- 2 tablespoons rice vinegar
- 2 tablespoons mirin
- 2 tablespoons water
- 1 scallion, minced
- 1 teaspoon chili oil (optional)
- ½ teaspoon toasted sesame oil

Potstickers

- 3 cups minced napa cabbage
- ¾ teaspoon table salt
- 12 ounces large shrimp (26 to 30 per pound), peeled, deveined, and tails removed
- 4 scallions, minced
- 4 teaspoons soy sauce
- 1½ teaspoons grated fresh ginger
- 1 garlic clove, minced
- 1 large egg, lightly beaten
- ⅛ teaspoon pepper
- 24 round gyoza wrappers
- 4 teaspoons vegetable oil, divided

WHY THIS RECIPE WORKS

Shrimp potstickers should be one of the most comforting appetizers—soft, savory pillows filled with tender shrimp. But too often a flavorless, heavy filling is wrapped in a doughy blanket, saved only by the sauce. To lighten the filling, we used a more-generous-than-normal amount of crunchy cabbage and incorporated a lightly beaten egg. Garlic, ginger, scallions, and soy flavored the filling. A sequence of browning, steaming, and cranking up the heat produced potstickers with a pleasing balance of ultra-appealing soft and crispy textures. Serve the first batch immediately and then cook the second batch.

1 | **For the scallion dipping sauce** Combine all ingredients in bowl; set aside for serving.

2 | **For the potstickers** Toss cabbage and salt in colander set over bowl. Let sit until cabbage begins to wilt, about 20 minutes; press cabbage gently with rubber spatula to squeeze out excess moisture. Meanwhile, pulse shrimp in food processor until finely chopped, about 10 pulses. Combine shrimp, cabbage, scallions, soy sauce, ginger, garlic, egg, and pepper in bowl. Cover and refrigerate until mixture is well chilled, at least 30 minutes and up to 24 hours.

3 | Working with 4 wrappers at a time (cover others with damp paper towel), place 1 tablespoon filling in center of each wrapper, brush edges with water, fold wrapper in half, and pinch dumpling closed, pressing out any air pockets. Place dumpling on 1 side and gently flatten bottom. Transfer to baking sheet and cover with clean, damp dish towel. Repeat with remaining wrappers and filling. (Potstickers can be frozen in single layer until firm; transfer chilled potstickers to zipper-lock bag and store for up to 1 month. Do not thaw.)

4 | Line large plate with double layer of paper towels. Brush 2 teaspoons oil over bottom of 12-inch nonstick skillet and arrange half of dumplings in skillet, flat side down (overlapping just slightly if necessary). Place skillet over medium-high heat and cook dumplings, without moving, until golden brown on bottom, about 5 minutes.

5 | Reduce heat to low, add ½ cup water, and cover immediately. Continue to cook until most of water is absorbed and wrappers are slightly translucent, about 10 minutes. Uncover skillet, increase heat to medium-high, and continue to cook, without stirring, until dumpling bottoms are well browned and crisp, 3 to 4 minutes. Slide dumplings onto prepared plate, browned side down, and let drain briefly. Transfer dumplings to serving platter. Let skillet cool until just warm, then wipe clean with paper towels and repeat steps 4 and 5 with remaining dumplings, remaining 2 tablespoons oil, and another ½ cup water. Serve with dipping sauce.

FILLING AND WRAPPING THE POTSTICKERS

1 Place 1 tablespoon filling in center of wrapper. Brush edges with water and fold wrapper in half.

2 Pinch dumpling closed, pressing out any air pockets.

3 Place dumpling on 1 side and gently flatten bottom.

SMALL PLATES

341

SALT COD FRITTERS | MAKES 24 FRITTERS; SERVES 6 TO 8

SUBSTITUTIONS NONE

1 pound salt cod, checked for bones and rinsed thoroughly

12 ounces russet potatoes, peeled and cut into 1-inch pieces

6 garlic cloves, smashed and peeled

½ cup heavy cream

2 tablespoons minced fresh chives

1 large egg, lightly beaten

2 teaspoons grated lemon zest, plus lemon wedges for serving

¼ teaspoon table salt

⅛ teaspoon pepper

⅛ teaspoon baking powder

1 quart peanut or vegetable oil

WHY THIS RECIPE WORKS

Drying and salting cod was once done as a preservation method but is now just plain desirable—cod becomes tender, buttery, and meaty with a firm, steak-like texture. Fritters using it are a popular bar snack in Portugal and Spain. They're small, deep-fried bites with a supercrisp exterior and creamy, briny filling—there's not much to dislike. Unlike *croquetas*, which are bound by a béchamel sauce, fritters are typically made from a simple base of potato and egg, along with aromatics and a bit of liquid (water, milk, or cream). We loved the simplicity and decided to keep things authentic, forgoing additions we've seen like bread crumbs to bind. Russet potatoes provide the perfect texture and their mild flavor doesn't interfere with the filling; an egg gives body and structure; and heavy cream adds just the right amount of richness for creamy contrast to the brininess. A touch of baking powder keeps this mixture light through frying. Look for salt cod in fish markets and some well-stocked supermarkets. It is shelf stable and typically packaged in a wooden box or plastic bag. Be sure to change the water when soaking the salt cod as directed in step 1, or the fritters will taste unpalatably salty.

1 | Submerge salt cod in large bowl of cold water and refrigerate until cod is soft enough to break apart easily with your fingers, about 24 hours, changing water twice during soaking.

2 | Drain cod, transfer to large saucepan along with potatoes and garlic, and cover with water by 2 inches. Bring to boil, then reduce to medium heat and simmer until potatoes are tender, 15 to 20 minutes.

3 | Drain cod mixture in colander, then transfer to large bowl. Using potato masher, mash until mixture is mostly smooth. Stir in heavy cream, chives, egg, lemon zest, salt, pepper, and baking powder until well incorporated. (Mixture can be refrigerated in airtight container for up to 2 days. Let sit at room temperature for 30 minutes before frying.)

4 | Line serving platter with triple layer of paper towels. Pinch off and roll cod mixture into 24 balls (about 2 tablespoons each) and arrange on large plate. Add oil to large Dutch oven until it measures about ¾ inch deep and heat over medium-high heat to 375 degrees. Add half of fritters to oil and cook until golden all over, about 6 minutes, stirring to prevent sticking. Adjust burner, if necessary, to maintain oil temperature between 350 and 375 degrees. Using wire skimmer or slotted spoon, transfer fritters to prepared platter. Return oil to 375 degrees and repeat with remaining balls. Season with salt to taste. Serve immediately with lemon wedges.

FLUKE CRUDO WITH FURIKAKE | SERVES 4 TO 6

SUBSTITUTIONS SUSHI-GRADE STRIPED BASS • SUSHI-GRADE TUNA

12 ounces skinless sushi-grade fluke fillets
1½ tablespoons extra-virgin olive oil
1 tablespoon lemon juice
1 tablespoon soy sauce
2 teaspoons Furikake (recipe follows)

WHY THIS RECIPE WORKS

At its simplest, fish crudo is nothing more than raw seafood dressed with olive oil, salt, and acid (such as lemon juice or good-quality vinegar), which allows you to really appreciate the fresh fish's clean taste. We love fluke served raw: It's thin and delicate and a little sweet. Once you have the freshest fish, it's just about contrasting it with the right garnish; we added flavor and texture to our recipe by finishing the dish with the Japanese seaweed–sesame seed spice blend known as furikake, which is at once briny, earthy, and nutty. The sprinkled furikake created a beautiful presentation, ensured that each bite packed an umami-rich punch, and added nice crunch against the fish. You can purchase furikake or make your own. For information on purchasing fish for raw applications, see page 29. Inspect the fillets for bones and remove before slicing.

1 | Using sharp knife, cut fluke lengthwise into 2- to 3-inch-wide strips. Slice each strip crosswise on bias into ⅛-inch-thick slices. Arrange fluke attractively on individual chilled plates.

2 | Whisk oil, lemon juice, and soy sauce together in small bowl. Drizzle sauce over fluke and sprinkle with furikake. Serve immediately.

FURIKAKE
MAKES ABOUT ½ CUP

You can find nori sheets and bonito flakes in most well-stocked supermarkets.

2 nori sheets, torn into 1-inch pieces
3 tablespoons sesame seeds, toasted
1½ tablespoons bonito flakes
1½ teaspoons sugar
1½ teaspoons flake sea salt

Process nori in spice grinder until coarsely ground and pieces are no larger than ½ inch, about 15 seconds. Add sesame seeds, bonito flakes, and sugar and pulse until coarsely ground and pieces of nori are no larger than ¼ inch, about 2 pulses. Transfer to small bowl and stir in salt. (Furikake can be stored in airtight container at room temperature for up to 3 weeks.)

PERUVIAN CEVICHE WITH RADISHES AND ORANGE | SERVES 6 TO 8

SUBSTITUTIONS HALIBUT • BLACK SEA BASS

1 pound skinless red snapper fillets, ½ inch thick

3½ teaspoons kosher salt, divided

¾ cup lime juice (6 limes)

3 tablespoons extra-virgin olive oil, divided

1 tablespoon ají amarillo chile paste

2 garlic cloves, peeled

3 oranges

8 ounces radishes, trimmed, halved, and sliced thin

¼ cup coarsely chopped fresh cilantro

1 cup corn nuts

1 cup lightly salted popcorn

WHY THIS RECIPE WORKS

Ceviche, the Latin American dish in which pieces of raw fish are "cooked" in an acidic marinade until the flesh firms and turns opaque, is a lively summer go-to that both allows fresh seafood to shine and awakens the palate for the meal to come. To create a flavorful yet balanced liquid and sauce, we made what's known as a *leche de tigre* ("tiger's milk") by blending lime juice, ají amarillo chile paste, garlic, extra-virgin olive oil, and a small amount of fish for body. Once strained, the liquid was an intensely flavorful and silky-textured emulsion. We then soaked thinly sliced and briefly salted red snapper in the *leche* for 30 to 40 minutes until it was just opaque and slightly firm. To complete the dish, we added sweet oranges; crisp, peppery radishes; and chopped cilantro. We served the ceviche with corn nuts and popcorn, both traditional in Latin America, which provided salty crunch. For information on purchasing fish for raw applications, see page 29. Ají amarillo chile paste can be found in the Latin section of grocery stores; if you can't find it, you can substitute one stemmed and seeded habanero chile. Serving the popcorn and corn nuts separately allows diners to customize their ceviche to suit their taste.

1 | Using sharp knife, cut snapper lengthwise into ½-inch-wide strips. Slice each strip crosswise ⅛ inch thick. Set aside ⅓ cup (2½ ounces) fish pieces. Toss remaining fish with 1 teaspoon salt and refrigerate for at least 10 minutes or up to 30 minutes.

2 | Meanwhile, process reserved fish pieces, remaining 2½ teaspoons salt, lime juice, 2 tablespoons oil, chile paste, and garlic in blender until smooth, 30 to 60 seconds. Strain mixture through fine-mesh strainer set over large bowl, pressing on solids to extract as much liquid as possible; discard solids. (Sauce can be refrigerated for up to 24 hours. It will separate slightly; whisk to recombine before proceeding with recipe.)

3 | Cut away peel and pith from oranges. Holding fruit over bowl, use paring knife to slice between membranes to release segments. Cut orange segments into ¼-inch pieces. Add oranges, salted fish, and radishes to bowl with sauce and toss to combine. Refrigerate for 30 to 40 minutes (for more-opaque fish, refrigerate for 45 minutes to 1 hour).

4 | Add cilantro to ceviche and toss to combine. Portion ceviche into individual bowls and drizzle with remaining 1 tablespoon oil. Serve, passing corn nuts and popcorn separately.

CÓCTEL DE CAMARÓN | SERVES 6

SUBSTITUTIONS NONE

1¼ pounds large shrimp (26 to 30 per pound), peeled, deveined, and tails removed

¼ teaspoon table salt, plus salt for cooking shrimp

1 cup V8 juice, chilled

½ cup ketchup

3 tablespoons lime juice (2 limes), plus lime wedges for serving

2 teaspoons hot sauce, plus extra for serving

½ English cucumber, cut into ½-inch pieces

1 cup finely chopped red onion

1 avocado, halved, pitted, and cut into ½-inch pieces

¼ cup chopped fresh cilantro
Saltines

WHY THIS RECIPE WORKS

Mexican shrimp cocktail combines tender shrimp with crunchy cucumber and onion and creamy avocado in a gently spicy tomato-based sauce. It has a livelier personality than the American dish: Eaten ice-cold with a spoon and saltines, it's like a festive, shrimp-packed Bloody Mary or gazpacho. Our poaching method for Shrimp Cocktail (page 327) produces reliably plump, tender shrimp, so there was no need to abandon it. We cut the shrimp into bite-size pieces that were easy to eat. For a sauce that wasn't too sweet, we used a combination of savory V8 and ketchup plus lime juice and hot sauce. V8's slightly viscous consistency, along with the ketchup, gave the sauce body to coat the shrimp. The balanced flavor of Valentina, Cholula, or Tapatío hot sauce works best. If using a spicier, vinegary hot sauce such as Tabasco, start with half the amount called for and adjust to your taste. Saltines are a traditional accompaniment, but tortilla chips or thick-cut potato chips are also good.

1 | Bring 3 cups water to boil in large saucepan over high heat. Stir in shrimp and 1 tablespoon salt. Cover and let sit off heat until shrimp are opaque, about 5 minutes, shaking saucepan halfway through sitting time.

2 | Meanwhile, fill large bowl halfway with ice and water. Drain shrimp and transfer to ice bath; let cool for 3 to 5 minutes. Drain and cut each shrimp crosswise into 3 pieces.

3 | Combine V8 juice, ketchup, lime juice, hot sauce, and salt in bowl. Add cucumber, onion, and shrimp and stir until evenly coated. Stir in avocado and cilantro. Portion cocktail into individual bowls or glasses and serve immediately, passing saltines, lime wedges, and extra hot sauce separately.

SPRING ROLLS WITH SHRIMP

| **MAKES** 8 SPRING ROLLS; SERVES 4 TO 6

SUBSTITUTIONS NONE

Peanut Dipping Sauce

- ¼ cup creamy peanut butter
- ¼ cup hoisin sauce
- ¼ cup water
- 2 tablespoons tomato paste
- 1 teaspoon Asian chili-garlic sauce (optional)
- 2 teaspoons peanut or vegetable oil
- 2 garlic cloves, minced
- 1 teaspoon red pepper flakes

Spring Rolls

- 2½ tablespoons lime juice (2 limes)
- 1½ tablespoons fish sauce
- 1 teaspoon sugar
- 8 ounces extra-large shrimp (21 to 25 per pound), peeled, deveined, and tails removed
- Table salt for cooking shrimp
- 3 ounces rice vermicelli
- 1 large carrot, peeled and shredded
- ⅓ cup chopped dry-roasted peanuts
- 2 Thai chiles or 1 jalapeño chile, stemmed, seeded, and minced
- 1 large cucumber, peeled, halved lengthwise, seeded, and cut into 2-inch matchsticks
- 4 leaves red leaf lettuce or Boston lettuce, halved lengthwise
- 8 (8-inch) round rice paper wrappers
- ½ cup fresh Thai basil leaves or mint leaves, small leaves left whole, medium and large leaves torn into ½-inch pieces
- ½ cup fresh cilantro leaves

WHY THIS RECIPE WORKS

Spring rolls are the most refreshing of dishes—refreshing to eat and refreshing to make because there's very little cooking. A platter of them, accompanied by rich peanut dipping sauce, is an unexpected and impressive starter to a party. In addition to the shrimp, they're packed with fresh, crunchy, colorful vegetables, and they've got a crave-worthy salty, sweet, sour, and spicy profile. Marinating the noodles and vegetable filling ingredients gave our spring rolls better, more cohesive flavor than others. You can substitute ½ teaspoon red pepper flakes for the fresh chiles. If you can't find Thai basil, do not substitute regular basil; mint makes a better substitute. The spring rolls are best eaten immediately, but they can be covered with a clean, damp dish towel and refrigerated for up to 4 hours.

1 | **For the peanut dipping sauce** Whisk peanut butter, hoisin, water, tomato paste, and chili-garlic sauce, if using, together in small bowl. Heat oil, garlic, and pepper flakes in small saucepan over medium heat until fragrant, 1 to 2 minutes. Stir in peanut butter mixture; bring to simmer, then reduce heat to medium-low and cook, stirring occasionally, for 3 minutes. (Sauce should have ketchup-like consistency; if too thick, add water, 1 teaspoon at a time, until sauce reaches proper consistency.) Transfer sauce to bowl and let cool completely.

2 | **For the spring rolls** Combine lime juice, fish sauce, and sugar in small bowl; set aside.

3 | Bring 3 cups water to boil in large saucepan. Stir in shrimp and 1 tablespoon salt. Cover and let sit off heat until shrimp are opaque, about 5 minutes, shaking saucepan halfway through sitting time.

4 | Meanwhile, fill large bowl halfway with ice and water. Drain shrimp and transfer to ice bath; let cool for 3 to 5 minutes. Drain shrimp, coarsely chop, and transfer to separate bowl.

5 | Bring 2 quarts water to boil in now-empty saucepan. Stir in rice vermicelli. Cook until noodles are tender but not mushy, 3 to 4 minutes. Drain noodles and rinse under cold running water until cool. Drain again and transfer to bowl. Toss 2 tablespoons fish sauce mixture with noodles; set aside.

6 | Combine carrot, peanuts, and Thai chiles in small bowl. Add 1 tablespoon fish sauce mixture; toss to combine. Toss cucumber in remaining 1 tablespoon fish sauce mixture.

7 | Arrange lettuce on platter. Spread clean, damp kitchen towel on counter. Fill 9-inch pie plate with 1 inch room-temperature water. Working with 1 wrapper at a time, immerse each in water until just pliable, about 2 minutes; lay softened

wrapper on towel. Scatter about 6 basil leaves and 6 cilantro leaves over wrapper. Arrange 5 cucumber sticks horizontally on wrapper, leaving 2-inch border at bottom. Top with 1 tablespoon carrot mixture, then arrange about 2½ tablespoons noodles on top of carrot mixture. Place about 2 tablespoons shrimp on top of noodles. Fold bottom of wrapper up over filling, then roll wrapper up into tight spring roll. Set roll on 1 lettuce piece on platter. Cover with second damp dish towel until all rolls are formed. Serve with peanut dipping sauce, wrapping lettuce around exterior of each roll.

FRIED CALAMARI | SERVES 4

SUBSTITUTIONS NONE

½ cup milk
1 teaspoon table salt
1½ cups all-purpose flour
1 tablespoon baking powder
½ teaspoon pepper
1 pound squid, bodies sliced crosswise ¾ inch thick, extra-long tentacles trimmed to match length of shorter ones
2 quarts vegetable oil
Lemon wedges

WHY THIS RECIPE WORKS

Almost every red-sauce Italian joint has a perfunctory fried calamari appetizer option, and that ubiquity detracts from what the dish really should be: tender, lightly springy squid encased in a crispy, lacy, golden-brown crust. Slicing the squid bodies into generous ¾-inch-thick rings (rather than the usual skinny rings) maintained their tenderness throughout frying. To keep the coating on the squid, we dipped the squid in milk before dredging; as a bonus, the proteins in the milk encouraged further browning of the flour. Salting the milk bath, rather than the flour or the fried pieces, seasoned the squid evenly. And adding baking powder to the dredge lightened the texture of the coating. We rested the dredged pieces while the oil heated to give the coating time to hydrate, preventing a dusty film from forming on the exterior. If desired, omit the lemon wedges and serve with marinara sauce or a creamy sauce (see page 70). Use a Dutch oven that holds 6 quarts or more for this recipe. You can double this recipe and fry the calamari in four batches; the amount of oil remains the same.

1 | Set wire rack in rimmed baking sheet. Set second wire rack in second sheet and line with triple layer of paper towels. Heat oven to 200 degrees.

2 | Whisk milk and salt together in bowl. Combine flour, baking powder, and pepper in second bowl. Add squid to milk mixture and toss to coat. Using your hands or slotted spoon, remove half of squid, allowing excess milk mixture to drip back into bowl, and add to bowl with flour mixture. Using your hands, toss squid to coat evenly. Gently shake off excess flour mixture and place coated squid in single layer on unlined rack. Repeat with remaining squid. Let sit for 10 minutes.

3 | While squid rests, heat oil in Dutch oven over high heat to 350 degrees. Carefully add half of squid and fry for exactly 3 minutes (squid will be golden brown). Using slotted spoon or spider skimmer, transfer calamari to paper towel–lined rack; transfer to oven to keep warm. Return oil to 350 degrees and repeat with remaining squid. Transfer calamari to platter and serve immediately with lemon wedges.

CHILI-MARINATED CALAMARI WITH ORANGES | SERVES 6 TO 8

SUBSTITUTIONS NONE

2 tablespoons baking soda

1½ teaspoons table salt, plus salt for brining and cooking squid

2 pounds squid, bodies sliced crosswise into ¼-inch-thick rings, tentacles halved

¼ cup extra-virgin olive oil

3 tablespoons red wine vinegar

2½ tablespoons harissa

2 garlic cloves, minced

1 teaspoon Dijon mustard

½ teaspoon pepper

2 oranges

1 red bell pepper, stemmed, seeded, and cut into 2-inch-long matchsticks

2 celery ribs, sliced thin on bias

1 shallot, sliced thin

⅓ cup hazelnuts, toasted, skinned, and chopped

3 tablespoons chopped fresh mint

WHY THIS RECIPE WORKS

Calamari aren't only meant to be fried. They're well suited to small plates because their mild flavor and pleasing chew are the perfect vehicle for a host of bold flavors. We sought to show the fresher side of calamari in an aromatic, Spanish-inspired salad. After grilling, broiling, and sautéing the squid, all of which resulted in overcooked, chewy squid, we settled on blanching it in boiling water. Soaking the raw squid in a brine of baking soda and salt first tenderized the squid so that it was less likely to become rubbery when cooked. To ensure that both the bodies and tentacles were done at the same time, we added the thicker tentacles to the pot 30 seconds before adding the bodies. After blanching, we transferred the squid to an ice water bath to halt the cooking. We dressed the squid with a piquant mixture of tangy red wine vinegar and—looking to Spain's North African neighbors—spicy harissa chile paste, then stirred in pieces of orange, bell pepper, and celery for contrasting flavors and textures. Hazelnuts, stirred in just before serving, gave the salad some richness and crunch. Be sure to use small squid (with bodies 3 to 4 inches in length) because they cook more quickly and are more tender than larger squid. For the best flavor and texture, we recommend allowing the salad to marinate for the full 24 hours.

1 | Dissolve baking soda and 1 tablespoon salt in 3 cups cold water in large container. Submerge squid in brine, cover, and refrigerate for 15 minutes. Remove squid from brine and separate bodies from tentacles.

2 | Bring 8 cups water to boil in large saucepan over medium-high heat. Fill large bowl halfway with ice and water. Add 2 tablespoons salt and tentacles to boiling water and cook for 30 seconds. Add bodies and cook until bodies are firm and opaque throughout, about 90 seconds. Drain squid, transfer to ice bath, and let sit until chilled, about 5 minutes.

3 | Whisk oil, vinegar, harissa, garlic, mustard, salt, and pepper together in large bowl. Drain squid well and add to bowl with dressing.

4 | Cut away peel and pith from oranges. Quarter oranges, then slice crosswise into ½-inch-thick pieces. Add oranges, bell pepper, celery, and shallot to squid and toss to coat. Cover and refrigerate for at least 1 hour or up to 24 hours. Stir in hazelnuts and mint and season with salt and pepper to taste before serving.

NUTRITIONAL INFORMATION FOR OUR RECIPES

To calculate the nutritional values of our recipes per serving, we used The Food Processor SQL by ESHA research. When using this program, we entered all the ingredients, using weights for important ingredients such as most vegetables. We also used our preferred brands in these analyses. Any ingredient listed as "optional" was excluded from the analyses. We did not include salt or pepper for food that's "seasoned to taste." If there is a range in the serving size, we used the highest number of servings to calculate the nutritional values.

	Calories	Total Fat (g)	Sat Fat (g)	Chol (mg)	Sodium (mg)	Total Carb (g)	Dietary Fiber (g)	Total Sugars (g)	Protein (g)
EVERYDAY ESSENTIALS									
Roasted Salmon Fillets	370	25	5	95	390	0	0	0	35
Miso-Marinated Salmon	510	24	5	95	1040	28	0	22	38
Sesame-Crusted Salmon	550	40	8	95	470	9	4	0	41
Pan-Seared Salmon Steaks	626	41	8	140	634	8	0	0	52
Pan-Roasted Cod	146	5	1	58	284	1	0	1	23
Butter-Basted Fish Fillets with Garlic and Thyme	350	25	11	120	370	0	0	0	30
Oven-Steamed Fish with Scallions and Ginger	314	10	1	99	792	8	1	3	43
Crunchy Oven-Fried Fish Fillets	452	19	6	173	595	34	3	3	35
Crunchy Oven-Fried Fish Sticks	*701*	*36*	*6*	*232*	*909*	*43*	*3*	*2*	*49*
Nut-Crusted Cod Fillets	350	17	2	120	550	15	2	3	36
Perfect Poached Fish	380	23	5	95	390	1	0	0	35
Crispy Pan-Seared Black Sea Bass	230	10	1.5	70	620	1	0	1	31
Sautéed Tilapia	212	10	1	78	383	0	0	0	31
Pan-Fried Sole	348	23	7	99	505	13	1	0	23
Sole Meunière	*262*	*18*	*8*	*79*	*354*	*9*	*1*	*0*	*15*
Fried Catfish	755	51	5	76	725	47	2	5	27
Pecan-Crusted Trout	800	67	9	171	650	7	3	1	43
Pan-Roasted Monkfish	256	17	3	35	431	5	2	1	21
Pan-Seared Tuna Steaks	220	4.5	0.5	65	370	1	0	1	42
Sesame-Crusted Pan-Seared Tuna Steaks	*403*	*21*	*3*	*66*	*476*	*7*	*3*	*0*	*46*
Pan-Seared Swordfish Steaks	310	16	3.5	130	450	0	0	0	39
Halibut en Cocotte with Roasted Garlic and Cherry Tomatoes	326	16	3	100	721	5	1	2	39
Salmon en Cocotte	*372*	*26*	*8*	*70*	*440*	*8*	*1*	*2*	*21*
Broiled Bluefish	320	20	3.5	105	480	1	0	0	34
Pan-Seared Scallops	232	14	4	56	668	6	0	0	21
Pan-Seared Shrimp	184	9	1	214	963	2	0	0	23
Garlicky Roasted Shrimp with Parsley and Anise	265	19	6	211	858	3	0	0	21
Garlicky Roasted Shrimp with Cilantro and Lime	*282*	*20*	*2*	*191*	*857*	*3*	*1*	*0*	*21*

	Calories	Total Fat (g)	Sat Fat (g)	Chol (mg)	Sodium (mg)	Total Carb (g)	Dietary Fiber (g)	Total Sugars (g)	Protein (g)
EVERYDAY ESSENTIALS, *continued*									
Roasted Mussels	520	19	6	140	1450	19	0	1	54
Roasted Mussels with Leeks and Pernod	*650*	*27*	*7*	*140*	*1480*	*35*	*2*	*6*	*56*
Clams Steamed in White Wine	574	13	6	159	2738	27	2	4	68
Clams Steamed in Beer	*360*	*10*	*1.5*	*90*	*1820*	*15*	*1*	*1*	*45*
Caper-Currant Relish	110	11	1.5	0	105	5	1	3	0
Fresh Tomato Relish	30	2.5	0	0	0	2	1	1	1
Grapefruit-Basil Relish	90	2.5	0	0	0	2	1	1	1
Tangerine-Ginger Relish	*70*	*2.5*	*0*	*0*	*0*	*12*	*2*	*9*	*1*
Orange-Avocado Relish	*120*	*10*	*1.5*	*0*	*0*	*10*	*4*	*4*	*2*
Mango-Mint Chutney	90	3	0	0	0	15	2	13	1
Oregano–Black Olive Relish	60	6	1	0	45	1	0	0	0
Spicy Cucumber Relish	15	0	0	0	0	3	1	1	1
Green Olive, Almond, and Orange Relish	50	4.5	0	0	120	3	1	1	2
Classic Tartar Sauce	321	33	5	17	381	6	0	5	0
Comeback Sauce	70	7	1	0	140	1	0	1	0
Lemon-Garlic Sauce	90	10	1.5	5	90	0	0	0	0
Herb Yogurt Sauce	10	.5	0	0	5	1	0	1	1
Old Bay Dipping Sauce	50	4.5	1.5	5	85	1	0	0	1
Rémoulade	204	22	3	11	227	1	0	1	0
Almond Vinaigrette	120	11	1.5	0	15	3	1	2	1
Cilantro Chimichurri	10	0	0	0	5	1	0	0	0
Salsa Verde	369	37	5	2	305	8	2	1	3
Green Zhoug	100	11	1.5	0	75	1	0	0	0
Orange-Lime Dressing	70	7	1	0	0	1	0	1	0
Mignonette Sauce	10	0	0	0	0	2	0	1	0
Spicy Lemon Butter	100	111	7	30	240	0	0	0	0
Tangy Soy-Citrus Sauce	5	0	0	0	270	1	0	0	0
Chipotle-Cilantro Compound Butter	110	11	7	30	0	2	0	1	0
Chive-Lemon Miso Compound Butter	120	11	7	30	240	3	0	2	1
Parsley-Caper Compound Butter	100	11	7	30	35	0	0	0	0
Parsley-Lemon Compound Butter	100	11	7	30	0	1	0	0	0
Tarragon-Lime Compound Butter	100	11	7	30	0	1	0	0	0
Tapenade Compound Butter	120	12	7	30	95	1	0	0	0
EASY WEEKNIGHT DINNERS									
Roasted Salmon and Broccoli Rabe with Pistachio Gremolata	547	38	7	109	770	6	4	1	46
Pomegranate Roasted Salmon with Lentils and Chard	650	33	6	95	1000	42	10	10	47
Sweet-and-Sour Salmon with Bok Choy	600	40	7	95	640	24	2	19	37
Black Rice Bowls with Salmon	540	18	2.5	60	410	64	9	7	31
Farfalle with Salmon, Leeks, and Asparagus	570	22	10	70	180	64	2	5	24

	Calories	Total Fat (g)	Sat Fat (g)	Chol (mg)	Sodium (mg)	Total Carb (g)	Dietary Fiber (g)	Total Sugars (g)	Protein (g)
EASY WEEKNIGHT DINNERS, *continued*									
Lemon-Herb Roasted Cod with Crispy Garlic Potatoes	450	20	7	95	540	32	2	1	34
Roasted Cod with Artichokes, Olives, and Sun-Dried Tomatoes	360	19	2.5	75	940	13	1	1	34
Hake in Saffron Broth with Chorizo and Potatoes	330	13	4	95	780	10	1	2	37
Seared Breaded Haddock with Broccoli and Vinaigrette	480	33	4.5	95	1020	14	3	2	32
Cod Baked in Foil with Leeks and Carrots	300	12	7	105	710	12	2	4	32
Thai-Style Halibut and Creamy Coconut Couscous Packets	500	13	11	90	730	54	3	0	38
Roasted Snapper and Vegetables with Mustard Sauce	530	26	4	65	960	29	5	7	41
Thai Curry Rice with Mahi-Mahi	550	14	9	125	1180	63	1	3	41
Sautéed Tilapia with Blistered Green Beans and Pepper Relish	390	22	3.5	85	990	12	4	6	38
Moroccan Fish and Couscous Packets	530	17	3	70	960	54	5	1	38
Cornmeal Catfish and Southwestern Corn	750	41	13	165	1360	47	2	6	48
Pan-Seared Trout with Brussels Sprouts and Bacon	500	32	6	95	820	17	4	3	36
Roasted Trout with White Bean and Tomato Salad	700	41	6	115	870	30	9	6	51
Roasted Halibut with Potatoes, Corn, and Andouille	892	54	18	177	1369	50	5	9	54
Lemon-Poached Halibut with Roasted Fingerling Potatoes	370	9	1.5	85	710	33	1	2	36
Baked Halibut with Cherry Tomatoes and Chickpeas	540	24	3.5	85	1480	37	12	4	44
Tuna Steaks with Cucumber-Peanut Salad	380	17	2	65	910	8	2	2	47
Seared Tuna Steaks with Wilted Frisée and Mushroom Salad	450	22	3.5	65	770	12	2	7	46
Shrimp Risotto	370	13	6	120	1250	42	3	3	18
Tuscan Shrimp and Beans	260	10	1.5	95	1100	24	6	4	19
One-Pan Shrimp Pad Thai	510	14	1.5	145	890	75	2	21	25
Baked Shrimp and Orzo with Feta and Tomatoes	560	11	4.5	160	1140	79	4	11	36
Lemony Linguine with Shrimp and Spinach	560	19	5	85	470	60	1	2	20
Shrimp Fra Diavolo with Linguine	539	16	2	95	820	65	5	6	22
Stir-Fried Shrimp and Broccoli	190	5	0.5	145	1300	13	3	3	20
Fried Brown Rice with Pork and Shrimp	460	12	2.5	175	1700	59	1	4	26
Baked Scallops with Couscous, Leeks, and Orange Vinaigrette	500	19	2.5	40	960	51	1	3	28
Spanish-Style Brothy Rice with Clams and Salsa Verde	560	32	4.5	15	430	45	3	2	13

	Calories	Total Fat (g)	Sat Fat (g)	Chol (mg)	Sodium (mg)	Total Carb (g)	Dietary Fiber (g)	Total Sugars (g)	Protein (g)
EASY WEEKNIGHT DINNERS, continued									
Israeli Couscous with Clams, Leeks, and Tomatoes	720	9	3.5	60	1180	106	3	8	41
Garlicky Spaghetti with Clams	600	20	3.5	20	610	84	4	3	43
Mussels Marinara with Spaghetti	542	12	2	43	1492	75	8	10	33
SOUPS, STEWS, AND CHOWDERS									
Rich and Velvety Shrimp Bisque	521	27	13	255	1973	17	2	5	34
Clam and White Bean Stew with Linguiça	400	12	4	50	820	42	20	3	28
Bouillabaisse	260	9	1.5	80	880	11	1	4	27
New England Clam Chowder	370	22	12	75	640	29	1	3	15
Manhattan Clam Chowder	230	4	1	50	1180	23	3	4	21
Provençal Fish Soup	230	9	2.5	65	1060	5	2	2	26
Miso Dashi Soup with Halibut	280	8	1	85	1120	13	4	3	39
Cioppino	420	20	6	105	990	15	2	5	35
Cod in Coconut Broth with Lemon Grass and Ginger	270	11	4.5	75	800	10	2	3	33
Thai-Style Hot-and-Sour Soup with Shrimp and Rice Vermicelli	230	2	0	145	1470	32	1	5	20
Gumbo	560	37	8	232	1714	21	3	3	37
Seafood and Chorizo Stew	447	22	7	217	1614	15	6	7	47
Eastern North Carolina Fish Stew	350	17	6	255	940	16	1	5	32
Brazilian Shrimp and Fish Stew (Moqueca)	380	27	14	105	910	12	2	5	24
Korean Spicy Fish Stew (Maeuntang)	200	6	0.5	40	830	7	1	3	28
Monkfish Tagine	190	7	1	30	490	13	3	5	18
Calamari Stew	330	13	2	350	1030	23	3	9	27
New England Fish Chowder	347	17	7	75	1068	23	3	5	25
Lobster and Corn Chowder	469	24	9	287	1593	25	4	6	36
SANDWICHES, TACOS, SALADS, AND MORE									
Crispy Fish Sandwiches	760	47	8	115	1100	58	1	9	26
Spicy Crispy Fish Sandwiches	*760*	*47*	*8*	*115*	*1120*	*58*	*1*	*9*	*26*
New England Lobster Rolls	244	10	4	108	561	21	1	3	17
Shrimp Po' Boys	1050	72	10	265	1400	76	2	12	28
Shrimp Burgers	727	53	7	198	1438	36	2	4	26
Best Crab Cakes	448	26	8	180	924	23	2	5	29
Lemon-Basil Cod Cakes	380	20	3	100	490	25	0	1	25
Southwestern Salmon Cakes	800	66	10	80	700	25	1	1	27
Sizzling Saigon Crêpes (Bánh Xèo)	400	17	5	75	1430	45	3	13	18
California Fish Tacos	850	40	5	80	1750	84	4	15	37
Salmon Tacos	310	14	1.5	40	450	29	6	1	18
Tuna Tostadas	500	30	4.5	50	880	22	2	4	33
Shrimp Tacos	390	26	8	35	720	32	1	6	12

	Calories	Total Fat (g)	Sat Fat (g)	Chol (mg)	Sodium (mg)	Total Carb (g)	Dietary Fiber (g)	Total Sugars (g)	Protein (g)
SANDWICHES, TACOS, SALADS, AND MORE, *continued*									
Spicy Shrimp Lettuce Wraps	216	12	2	143	685	12	2	7	17
Caesar Salad	421	32	5	70	650	20	2	1	10
Salmon, Avocado, Grapefruit, and Watercress Salad	340	22	3	30	510	23	11	11	15
Smoked Salmon Niçoise Salad	450	19	6	295	480	25	4	5	45
Fennel and Apple Salad with Smoked Mackerel	200	14	2.5	20	310	12	3	7	7
Mediterranean Couscous Salad with Smoked Trout	360	16	2.5	30	950	37	3	1	17
Fennel and Bibb Salad with Scallops and Hazelnuts	430	31	4	40	1180	15	4	4	24
Shrimp and Arugula Salad with Lemon Vinaigrette	455	33	7	153	978	16	2	3	25
Shrimp Salad	210	12	2	149	732	8	1	4	16
Shrimp Salad with Corn and Chipotle	*237*	*13*	*2*	*149*	*1157*	*14*	*2*	*6*	*17*
Shrimp Salad with Wasabi and Pickled Ginger	*218*	*14*	*2*	*149*	*732*	*8*	*1*	*4*	*16*
Mediterranean Tuna Salad	250	15	2.5	40	430	3	1	1	23
Mediterranean Tuna Salad with Carrots, Radishes, and Cilantro	*250*	*15*	*2.5*	*40*	*430*	*4*	*1*	*2*	*23*
Crab Louis Salad	330	24	4.5	160	740	10	4	4	22
ON THE GRILL									
Grilled Salmon Fillets	485	44	7	66	329	1	0	0	20
Grilled Swordfish Steaks	168	12	2	45	181	0	0	0	13
Grilled Tuna Steaks with Vinaigrette	510	29	4.5	90	220	2	0	2	55
Grilled Blackened Red Snapper	344	15	6	104	555	4	2	0	46
Grilled Whole Trout with Orange and Fennel	470	24	4	165	750	1	0	1	59
Grilled Whole Trout with Marjoram and Lemon	*470*	*24*	*4*	*165*	*750*	*1*	*0*	*1*	*59*
Grilled Whole Red Snapper	440	15	2.5	12	125	1090	0	0	70
Grill-Smoked Side of Salmon	440	30	6	105	350	1	0	0	39
Grilled Swordfish Skewers with Caponata	310	18	3	75	600	12	4	8	24
Grilled Fish Tacos	610	25	3.5	100	630	63	6	19	35
Smoked Fish Tacos	630	34	7	70	1420	51	1	17	30
Grilled Cod and Summer Squash Packets	430	29	4	75	1170	8	2	3	32
Grilled Red Curry Mahi-Mahi with Pineapple Salsa	260	8	1	125	410	12	1	9	32
Grilled Oysters	15	0	0	15	120	1	0	0	3
Grilled Jalapeño and Lime Shrimp Skewers	222	12	2	214	965	4	0	1	24
Caribbean Shrimp Skewers	*206*	*9*	*1*	*214*	*966*	*7*	*0*	*4*	*24*
Red Chile and Ginger Shrimp Skewers	*178*	*5*	*1*	*214*	*1405*	*7*	*0*	*4*	*24*
Grilled Lobsters	520	37	22	345	1450	9	0	0	35

	Calories	Total Fat (g)	Sat Fat (g)	Chol (mg)	Sodium (mg)	Total Carb (g)	Dietary Fiber (g)	Total Sugars (g)	Protein (g)
SPECIAL OCCASIONS									
Roasted Salmon with Orange Beurre Blanc	450	36	14	115	300	2	0	1	27
Oven-Poached Side of Salmon	260	12	2	100	250	0	0	0	36
Prosciutto-Wrapped Cod with Lemon-Caper Butter	340	19	9	125	950	2	0	0	39
Oil-Poached Snapper with Tomato Vinaigrette	530	44	6	40	610	8	1	2	25
Roasted Crab-Stuffed Flounder	380	21	12	160	1140	13	1	2	32
Fish and Chips	1070	46	6	115	1990	102	0	0	51
Whole Roast Snapper with Citrus Vinaigrette	560	30	5	175	1020	3	1	1	65
Salt-Baked Branzino	460	8	2.5	225	570	1	0	0	95
Whole Roast Mackerel	370	28	5	80	850	6	2	2	22
Boiled Lobster	116	1	0	191	635	0	0	0	25
Roasted Stuffed Lobster Tails	370	18	11	320	1600	10	1	1	36
Roasted Stuffed Lobster Tails with Fennel and Pernod	*380*	*18*	*11*	*320*	*1600*	*12*	*1*	*2*	*36*
Lobster Fettuccine with Fennel and Tarragon	653	24	12	180	1095	76	4	5	31
Linguine with Seafood	702	19	3	229	1505	73	5	5	51
Grilled Paella	680	26	6	175	1960	63	3	3	47
Red Wine–Braised Octopus	480	8	1.5	220	1120	14	0	1	71
SMALL PLATES									
Sizzling Garlic Shrimp	170	15	2	70	390	2	0	0	8
Provencal-Style Anchovy Dip	160	15	1.5	5	210	5	2		5
Baked Crab Dip	300	22	7	55	410	14	0	1	11
Shrimp Cocktail	128	1	0	143	963	14	2	8	16
Popcorn Shrimp	440	16	1.5	175	580	49	0	0	22
Broiled Bacon-Wrapped Sea Scallops	90	6	2	20	340	2	0	0	7
Broiled Bacon-Wrapped Shrimp	*100*	*6*	*2*	*80*	*490*	*1*	*0*	*0*	*10*
Buckwheat Blini with Smoked Salmon	130	7	3	35	480	10	1	3	9
Gravlax	110	6	1.5	25	700	4	0	4	9
Baked Stuffed Shrimp	262	17	3	127	838	12	1	1	16
Mussels Escabèche	160	9	1.5	30	400	6	0	0	14
Shrimp and Cabbage Potstickers	460	6	1	110	1281	76	3	1	22
Salt Cod Fritters	170	10	4	65	1290	9	1	1	12
Fluke Crudo with Furikake	80	5	1	25	240	0	0	0	7
Peruvian Fish Ceviche with Radishes and Orange	324	20	3	27	568	19	5	7	21
Cóctel de Camarón	166	6	1	119	832	15	3	8	15
Spring Rolls with Shrimp	191	5	1	48	626	29	2	3	9
Fried Calamari	400	17	2	265	970	37	0	1	23
Chili-Marinated Calamari with Oranges	260	15	2	265	580	11	2	4	19

CONVERSIONS AND EQUIVALENTS

Some say cooking is a science and an art. We would say geography has a hand in it, too. Flours and sugars manufactured in the United Kingdom and elsewhere will feel and taste different from those manufactured in the United States. So we cannot promise that a loaf of bread you bake in Canada or England will taste the same as a loaf baked in the States, but we can offer guidelines for converting weights and measures. We also recommend that you rely on your instincts when making our recipes. Refer to the visual cues provided. If the dough hasn't come together as described, you may need to add more flour—even if the recipe doesn't tell you to. You be the judge.

The recipes in this book were developed using -standard U.S. measures following U.S. government guidelines. The charts below offer equivalents for U.S. and metric measures. All conversions are approximate and have been rounded up or down to the nearest whole number.

Example

1 teaspoon	=	4.9292 milliliters, rounded up to 5 milliliters
1 ounce	=	28.3495 grams, rounded down to 28 grams

Volume Conversions

U.S.	METRIC
1 teaspoon	5 milliliters
2 teaspoons	10 milliliters
1 tablespoon	15 milliliters
2 tablespoons	30 milliliters
¼ cup	59 milliliters
⅓ cup	79 milliliters
½ cup	118 milliliters
¾ cup	177 milliliters
1 cup	237 milliliters
1¼ cups	296 milliliters
1½ cups	355 milliliters
2 cups (1 pint)	473 milliliters
2½ cups	591 milliliters
3 cups	710 milliliters
4 cups (1 quart)	0.946 liter
1.06 quarts	1 liter
4 quarts (1 gallon)	3.8 liters

Weight Conversions

OUNCES	GRAMS
½	14
¾	21
1	28
1½	43
2	57
2½	71
3	85
3½	99
4	113
4½	128
5	142
6	170
7	198
8	227
9	255
10	283
12	340
16 (1 pound)	454

Conversions For Common Baking Ingredients

Because measuring by weight is far more accurate than measuring by volume, and thus more likely to produce reliable results, in our recipes we provide ounce measures in addition to cup measures for many ingredients. Refer to the chart below to convert these measures into grams.

INGREDIENT	OUNCES	GRAMS
Flour		
1 cup all-purpose flour*	5	142
1 cup cake flour	4	113
1 cup whole-wheat flour	5½	156
Sugar		
1 cup granulated (white) sugar	7	198
1 cup packed brown sugar (light or dark)	7	198
1 cup confectioners' sugar	4	113
Butter†		
4 tablespoons (½ stick or ¼ cup)	2	57
8 tablespoons (1 stick or ½ cup)	4	113
16 tablespoons (2 sticks or 1 cup)	8	227

* U.S. all-purpose flour, the most frequently used flour in this book, does not contain leaveners, as some European flours do. These leavened flours are called self-rising or self-raising. If you are using self-rising flour, take this into consideration before adding leaveners to a recipe.

† In the United States, butter is sold both salted and unsalted. We recommend unsalted butter. If you are using salted butter, take this into consideration before adding salt to a recipe.

Oven Temperature

FAHRENHEIT	CELSIUS	GAS MARK
225	105	¼
250	120	½
275	135	1
300	150	2
325	165	3
350	180	4
375	190	5
400	200	6
425	220	7
450	230	8
475	245	9

Converting Temperatures From an Instant-Read Thermometer

We include doneness temperatures in many of the recipes in this book. We recommend an instant-read thermometer for the job. Refer to the table above to convert Fahrenheit degrees to Celsius. Or, for temperatures not represented in the chart, use this simple formula:

Subtract 32 degrees from the Fahrenheit reading, then divide the result by 1.8 to find the Celsius reading.

Example

"Flip chicken, brush with remaining glaze, and cook until breast registers 160 degrees, 1 to 3 minutes."

To convert

160°F − 32 = 128°

128° ÷ 1.8 = 71.11°C, rounded down to 71°C

INDEX

Note: Page references in *italics* indicate photographs.

10/20-4

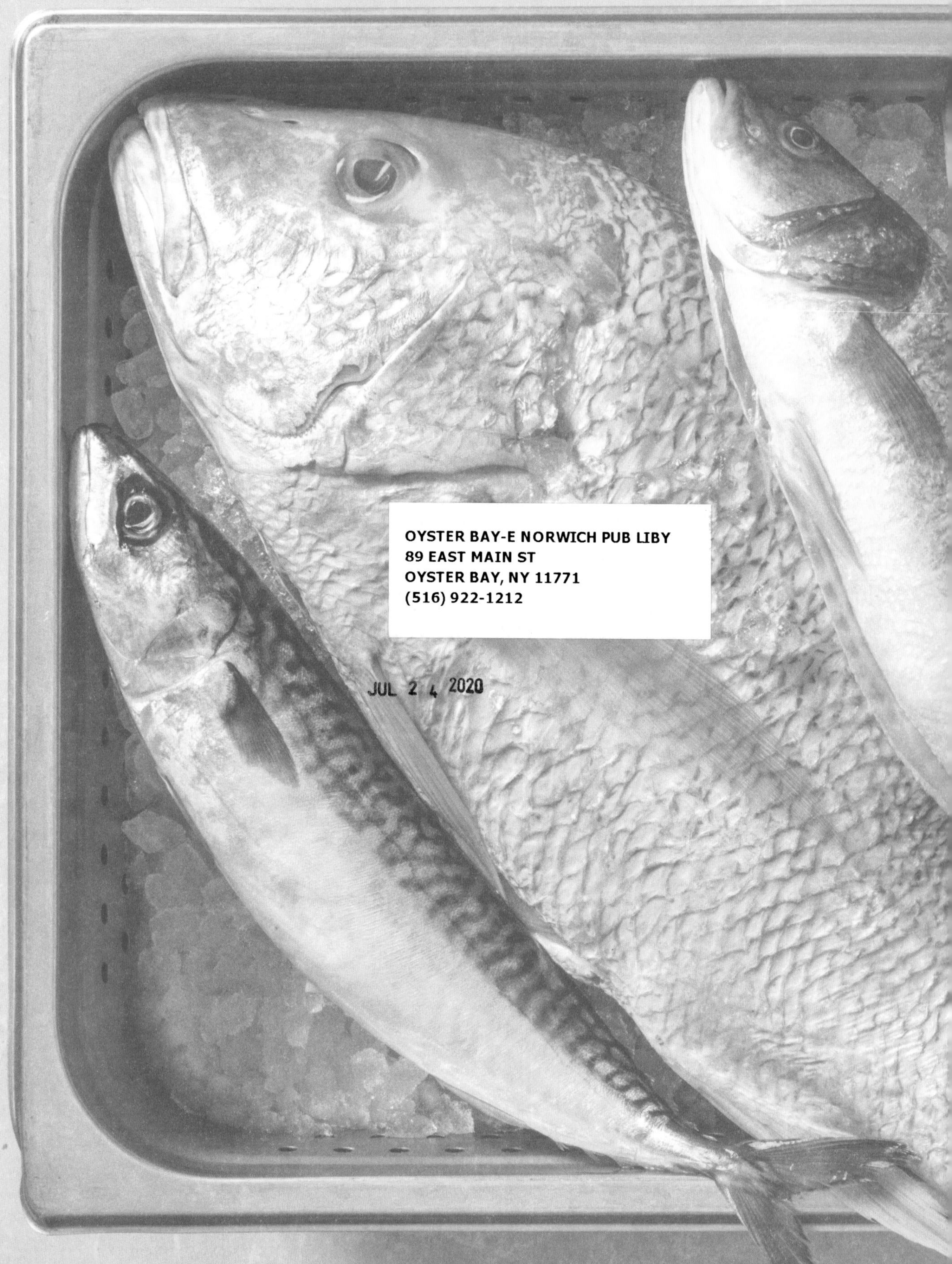